KT-195-384

Praise for *Leading Organizational Learning*

"If the great challenge of an information-age economy is to make ideas, knowledge, and learning more and more productive, then this book makes an invaluable contribution. It is a textbook on knowledge management—at once rich in theory and rich in down-to-earth examples."
   —Nathaniel Branden, author of *The Six Pillars of Self-Esteem* and *Self-Esteem at Work*

"*Leading Organizational Learning* provides a fair and comprehensive look at the field that some consider the key to tomorrow's organizational success— and others call a fad. You'll come out of reading the book with an opinion much closer to the key-to-success end of the spectrum, but you will also be informed and educated by the honesty of the authors, who go out of their way to acknowledge the faddishness that has sometimes characterized the field of knowledge management. An interesting and a useful book by some very thoughtful people."
   —William Bridges, author of *Transitions, Managing Transition,* and *Creating You & Co.*

"Marshall Goldsmith and his coauthors have assembled a who's who of experts in organizations and leadership to summarize their latest thoughts in this book. This is an essential book for today's managers and leaders."
   —Subir Chowdhury, chairman and CEO, ASI Consulting Group, and author, *The Power of Six Sigma, Design For Six Sigma,* and *Organization 21C*

"*Leading Organizational Learning* is one of those rare books that combines deep wisdom with practical ideas to use on Monday morning!"
   —Richard J. Leider, founder of The Inventure Group and best-selling author of *Repacking Your Bags* and *Whistle While You Work*

"We all need to share information, learning, and knowledge to be successful, and this book is a must-read for us. People whose organizations have an established knowledge inventory or database but need to create a more efficient and/or more realistic process for accessing learning will find this book very helpful as well. This is also a great book for people who are at the forefront of learning—including consultants, CLOs, and HR heads."

—Quinn Mills, professor of business administration,
   Harvard Business School

"Knowledge, people, and relationships are the critical assets of our time. Leaders who leverage this human side of business will stand above the rest. *Leading Organizational Learning* will help foster the learning necessary to lead change. This book is just the tool for you."

—Bob Rosen, CEO, Healthy Companies International, and best-selling
   author of *Global Literacies*, *Leading People*, and *The Healthy Company*

"I found this to be a fascinating and illuminating compilation of points of view and techniques for these mysterious concepts of organizational learning and knowledge management."

—Edgar H. Schein, Sloan Fellows Professor of Management Emeritus,
   MIT Sloan School of Management

"*Leading Organizational Learning* reflects the reality that effective organizational learning does not just happen—that leaders have to work at making learning an integral value and practice of their culture. This practical handbook offers frameworks and guidelines for making organizational learning a competitive advantage. Leaders positioning their enterprises for the future definitely will find this book helpful."

—R. Roosevelt Thomas Jr., CEO, Roosevelt Thomas Consulting
   & Training

"Your ability to learn and apply new ideas and information determines the success or failure of your organization. This book equips you with the critical insights and strategies you need to master the twenty-first century!"

—Brian Tracy, author, *TurboStrategy*

Other Publications from The Leader to Leader Institute

Organizational Leadership Resource

The Drucker Foundation Self-Assessment Tool

The Drucker Foundation Future Series

The Leader of the Future, *Frances Hesselbein, Marshall Goldsmith, Richard Beckhard, Editors*

The Organization of the Future, *Frances Hesselbein, Marshall Goldsmith, Richard Beckhard, Editors*

The Community of the Future, *Frances Hesselbein, Marshall Goldsmith, Richard Beckhard, Richard F. Schubert, Editors*

Wisdom to Action Series

Leading for Innovation, *Frances Hesselbein, Marshall Goldsmith, Iain Somerville, Editors*

Leading Beyond the Walls, *Frances Hesselbein, Marshall Goldsmith, Iain Somerville, Editors*

Leaderbooks

The Collaboration Challenge: How Nonprofits and Businesses Succeed Through Strategic Alliances, *James E. Austin*

Meeting the Collaboration Challenge (workbook and video)

Journal and Related Books

Leader to Leader Journal

Leader to Leader: Enduring Insights on Leadership from the Drucker Foundation's Award-Winning Journal, *Frances Hesselbein, Paul Cohen, Editors*

On Creativity, Innovation, and Renewal, *Frances Hesselbein, Rob Johnston, Editors*

On High-Performance Organizations, *Frances Hesselbein, Rob Johnston, Editors*

On Leading Change, *Frances Hesselbein, Rob Johnston, Editors*

On Mission and Leadership, *Frances Hesselbein, Rob Johnston, Editors*

Video Training Resources

Excellence in Nonprofit Leadership Video, *featuring Peter F. Drucker, Max De Pree, Frances Hesselbein, and Michele Hunt. Moderated by Richard F. Schubert*

Leading in a Time of Change: What It Will Take to Lead Tomorrow, *a conversation with Peter F. Drucker and Peter M. Senge, introduction by Frances Hesselbein*

Lessons in Leadership Video, *with Peter F. Drucker*

Peter Drucker: An Intellectual Journey, *interviews with Peter Drucker*

Online Resources

www.leadertoleader.org

About The Leader to Leader Institute

The Leader to Leader Institute has its roots in the social sector and its predecessor, the Peter F. Drucker Foundation for Nonprofit Management, which in January 2003 transferred its ongoing activities to the new identity. The Institute furthers its mission "to strengthen the leadership of the social sector" by providing educational opportunities and resources to leaders.

The Institute serves as a broker of intellectual capital, bringing together the finest thought leaders, consultants, and authors in the world with the leaders of social sector voluntary organizations. By providing intellectual resources to leaders in the business, government, and social sectors, and by fostering partnerships across these sectors, the Leader to Leader Institute works to strengthen social sector leaders of the United States and of nations around the globe.

The Leader to Leader Institute believes that a healthy society requires three vital sectors: a public sector of effective governments; a private sector of effective businesses; and a social sector of effective community organizations. The mission of the social sector is changing lives. It accomplishes this mission by addressing the needs of the spirit, the mind, and the body—of individuals, the community, and society. The social sector also provides a significant sphere for individuals and corporations to practice effective and responsible citizenship.

The Leader to Leader Institute is a 501(c)3 charitable organization. It does not make financial grants. Its offerings fall in three areas:

- Supporting social sector leaders of character and competence
- Forging cross-sector partnerships that deliver social sector results
- Providing leadership resources that engage and inform social sector leaders

For more information, see leadertoleader.org.

Leading
Organizational
Learning

Harnessing the Power of Knowledge

Marshall Goldsmith
Howard Morgan
Alexander J. Ogg
Editors

Forewords by
Niall FitzGerald and Frances Hesselbein

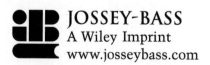

JOSSEY-BASS
A Wiley Imprint
www.josseybass.com

leader to leader
INSTITUTE

Copyright © 2004 by John Wiley & Sons, Inc. All rights reserved.
Published by Jossey-Bass
A Wiley Imprint
989 Market Street, San Francisco, CA 94103-1741   www.josseybass.com

No part of this publication may be reproduced, stored in a retrieval system, or transmitted in
any form or by any means, electronic, mechanical, photocopying, recording, scanning, or
otherwise, except as permitted under Section 107 or 108 of the 1976 United States Copyright
Act, without either the prior written permission of the Publisher, or authorization through
payment of the appropriate per-copy fee to the Copyright Clearance Center, Inc., 222
Rosewood Drive, Danvers, MA 01923, 978-750-8400, fax 978-646-8600, or on the web at
www.copyright.com. Requests to the Publisher for permission should be addressed to the
Permissions Department, John Wiley & Sons, Inc., 111 River Street, Hoboken, NJ 07030,
201-748-6011, fax 201-748-6008, e-mail: permcoordinator@wiley.com.

Jossey-Bass books and products are available through most bookstores. To contact Jossey-Bass
directly call our Customer Care Department within the U.S. at 800-956-7739, outside the
U.S. at 317-572-3986, or fax 317-572-4002.

Jossey-Bass also publishes its books in a variety of electronic formats. Some content that
appears in print may not be available in electronic books.

Library of Congress Cataloging-in-Publication Data

Leading organizational learning : harnessing the power of knowledge / by
Marshall Goldsmith, Howard Morgan, and Alexander J. Ogg, editors.
    p. cm.
Includes bibliographical references and index.
  ISBN 0-7879-7218-5 (alk. paper)
  1. Organizational learning. 2. Knowledge management. I. Goldsmith,
Marshall. II. Morgan, Howard J. III. Ogg, Alexander J., 1954-
  HD58.82.L37 2004
  658.4'038—dc22
                 2003024738

Printed in the United States of America
FIRST EDITION
HB Printing   10 9 8 7 6 5 4 3 2 1

Contents

Figures and Exhibits

Foreword

Any organization that does not continuously seek new sources of competitive advantage will fade and die. When competitive advantage is found, it must be nurtured and sustained, but perversely, as with all living organisms, it begins to die at birth. The Holy Grail is unique competitive advantage.

Yet any organization has only one truly unique competitive advantage: its knowledge. Knowledge that is built up over the history of the organization and that exists at a point in time across its geography. So it is the source of life for any company. How strange, then, that we cannot define knowledge accurately, catalogue it effectively, or use it efficiently.

Best practice is probably 20 percent utilization. For what other asset would we accept such low productivity, let alone the one that is ours uniquely and is essential to sustaining competitive advantage?

Knowledge resides in people—and there's the rub. People travel; they leave or retire, taking their knowledge with them. Corporate memory can be developed and sustained, but it must be a conscious and continuous process.

Knowledge must be accessible and shared to have value. People need the means and the motivation to share generously. They need the skill to identify and spread the ideas of value and to avoid being sucked into a swamp of useless information. One of my predecessors once remarked wistfully, "If only Unilever knew what Unilever knows." I would update that remark by adding, "and then did something with it!"

The series of articles brought together in this book is an Aladdin's cave, and the editors have laid it out so that the most valuable jewels are instantly accessible. If this helps us understand better how knowledge and learning move through people and organizations, how we as leaders can create a path for knowledge, and how we best apply that knowledge for organizational effectiveness, we will probably improve utilization to a modest 40 percent, which is a mere 100 percent improvement!

Unique and sustained competitive advantage, here I come.

London, England   Niall FitzGerald
December 2003   Chairman, Unilever

Foreword

Ideas on the move do not wait for the reluctant, resistant, would-be leader. They move on the winds of change; sometimes they are just straws in the wind that we try to grasp. The leaders of change, the leaders of tomorrow, have invested in the future of their people, the future of the organization, through powerful learning opportunities—continuous, continuing learning opportunities for every member, every leader of the enterprise—from the leader on the loading dock to the CEO. The organization is a learning organization—deliberately and exuberantly celebrated as such. Learning as a value has permeated the culture and has moved into the lives of the people and throughout the organization until there is no question *if*, only *how, when,* and *where*. The way has long been accepted and celebrated as part of the vision of the future of the organization.

Leading change is an integral part of organizational learning. Learning that is focused on the future, on the changing organization in a rapidly changing environment—a future few can describe in a world that has changed forever.

When the roll is called in 2010, the organizations responding will be those that saw organizational learning as the key investment in building the viable, relevant, effective organization of the future—highly effective, highly competitive, highly successful. Without the investment in organizational learning, the other investments will not matter. The organization of the future will be defined by its ability to provide learning at every level. This is an indispensable part of the planning, the strategy, and the blueprint for the organization of tomorrow.

This book, *Leading Organizational Learning,* is a handbook for the future—a handbook for leaders of the future, leading a band of learners focused on tomorrow. Every chapter, by great thought leaders, delivers messages that inspire, illuminate, and help chart the way into an uncertain future that we have yet to define. *Leading Organizational Learning* is a great compendium of future-focused thinking and experience that can be a treasured companion on our journey to new significance, new effectiveness, new relevance.

New York, New York   Frances Hesselbein
December 2003

Preface

Today, with the added pressures of the electronic revolution, we are inundated with information. What is important? What needs attention? We know that the answers to these questions probably already exist within our organizations, but we have yet to map the easiest and most accessible routes to them. In addition, because of the rapid pace of change in organizations today, it is often the case that knowledge and learning are lost when an individual moves on, meaning that those new to an organization or a position must reinvent the wheel. This book is a response to the fact that on the whole, organizations and leaders have grappled with, but not yet mastered, learning and knowledge sharing. Thus a strong market exists for those who can efficiently fill or help others fill the ever-growing need for information and knowledge.

Leading Organizational Learning will help you, as leaders, understand how to locate, share, and use information more efficiently. Our book will help you identify sources of learning inefficiency as well as how to close the gap between knowledge and people and thus create success for your organizations. The articles in this book, written by some of the world's leading thought leaders, include the latest and most up-to-date ideas, concepts, and practices on the subject of organizational learning. The prestigious group of contributors to this volume includes global and industry leaders who run major corporations and advise the CEOs, managing directors, and presidents of leading countries and organizations worldwide.

Opening *Leading Organizational Learning*, feel free to begin with any topic, contribution, or author that seems familiar or interesting. Progress through the book in any order, or proceed chapter by chapter if you prefer.

For your convenience, our book is divided into five parts: "Challenges and Dilemmas," "Processes That Work," "Leaders Who Make a Difference," "Changes for the Future," and "Case Studies and Examples." Part One, "Challenges and Dilemmas," opens with "Why Aren't Those Specials Selling Today?" in which Elliott Masie gives a real-life business example of how a problem is solved by moving ideas. Fons Trompenaars and Charles Hampden-Turner discuss five organizational cultures and how each reconciles knowledge management dilemmas in "Five Dilemmas of Knowledge Management." In "Effectively Influencing Up: Ensuring That Your Knowledge Makes a Difference," Marshall Goldsmith offers ten guidelines intended to help key employees and knowledge workers do a better job of influencing upper management. Niko Canner and Jon Katzenbach explain the upside and downside of knowledge management in "Where 'Managing Knowledge' Goes Wrong and What to Do Instead." Marc Effron concludes this part with "Knowledge Management Involves Neither Knowledge nor Management," in which he touts the benefits of person-to-person contact as the best way to move ideas through an organization.

Part Two, "Processes That Work," begins with "The Real Work of Knowledge Management," in which Margaret Wheatley discusses the Information Age and the definition of knowledge, the beliefs that prevent knowledge management, and the principles that facilitate it. Dave Ulrich and Norm Smallwood introduce us to the three building blocks of learning organizations in "Tangling with Learning Intangibles." Larraine Segil explores knowledge sharing, organization to organization, through outsourcing, alliances, and profit-centered activities in "When Transferring Trapped Corporate Knowledge to Suppliers Is a Winning Strategy." In "Informal Learning: Developing a Value for Discovery,"

Marcia Conner explores informal learning—how people learn on the job. Sandy Ogg and Tom Cummings discuss how larger organizations can leverage their "bigness" and benefit from "early information" to compete with smaller competitors in "The Company as a Marketplace for Ideas: Simple but Not Easy." In "Knowledge Mapping: An Application Model for Organizations," Spencer Clark and Richard Mirabile propose a method of knowledge mapping to effectively organize and use knowledge in decision making. This part concludes with "Just-in-Time Guidance" by Calhoun Wick and Roy Pollock. The authors outline opportunities and principles for applying information technology to leadership development guidance.

Part Three, "Leaders Who Make a Difference," opens with "What Leading Executives Know—and You Need to Learn," Howard Morgan's examination of the knowledge and attributes that are integral to the success of today's executives. Gary Heil and Linda Alepin, in "Rethinking Our Leadership Thinking: Choosing a More Authentic Path," advocate the development of authenticity as a way for leaders to keep ideas moving and people stimulated. In "Learning at the Top: How CEOs Set the Tone for the Knowledge Organization," James Bolt and Charles Brassard investigate how CEOs do and do not learn and why they should. James Belasco discusses the development and promotion of "learner-leaders" in organizations in "Unleash the Learning Epidemic." Alexander Horniman's "Leading: A Performing Learning Art" defines leader-learners as creative innovative learners who base learning on knowledge (facts), thinking, and understanding. In the last chapter in Part Three, "What's the Big Idea? The 'Little Things' That Build Great Leadership in Organizations," Lauren Cantlon and Robert Gandossy explore five nuances of great companies.

Part Four, "Changes for the Future," begins with a chapter by Betsy Jacobson and Beverly Kaye, "Learning Stored Forward: A Priceless Legacy," which defines explicit and tacit knowledge and discusses the passing of knowledge from person to person. In

"Developing New Ideas for Your Clients—and Convincing Them to Act," Andrew Sobel explains how consultants can help organizations to develop ideas. Jon Powell reviews knowledge management over the past decade, highlighting its successes and failures and providing tips for future learning, in "Making Knowledge Move." In "The Role of Change Management in Knowledge Management," Marc Rosenberg adds the human element, change management, to knowledge management, giving us an equation that just may work. In the final chapter in this part, "Building Social Connections to Gain the Knowledge Advantage," Susan Jackson and Niclas Erhardt lay out the myths and realities of knowledge management and discuss how organizations can get knowledge moving.

Part Five, "Case Studies and Examples," opens with "Some Key Examples of Knowledge Management," in which W. Warner Burke explores key examples and lessons for leaders in the domain of knowledge management. Allan Cohen's "Leadership and Access to Ideas" delves into the concept of interaction in the form of leaders asking for employees for new business ideas. In "Capturing Ideas, Creating Information, and Liberating Knowledge," Peter Drummond-Hay and Barbara Saidel use their experiences at Russell Reynolds to define a new role, "the connector," whose purpose is to join people to information and people to people. Fred Harburg discusses Motorola's Leadership Supply Initiative as a best practice case example in "Learning at the Speed of Flight." In "The Audacity of Imagination: How Lilly Is Creating 'Research Without Walls,'" Sharon Sullivan, Bryan Dunnivant, and Laurie Sachtleben reveal Eli Lilly Company's strategy for learning, gathering ideas, and researching new products. Using Goldman-Sachs as an example, Steffen Landauer and Steve Kerr bring Part Five to a close with "Developing a Learning Culture on Wall Street: One Firm's Experience," which discusses obstacles that financial firms face in creating a learning culture.

Leading Organizational Learning is our attempt to bring you the newest and most innovative ideas on the subjects of leadership and learning. We hope you will enjoy our book and will glean much knowledge from its chapters, written by many of the top minds in their fields. Last but not least, we hope that you and your organizations will be inspired to continually strive for a learning future!

December 2003

Marshall Goldsmith
Rancho Santa Fe, California

Howard J. Morgan
Rancho Santa Fe, California

Alexander J. Ogg
Rotterdam, The Netherlands

Acknowledgments

The thoughts, insights, and visions expressed in *Leading Organizational Learning* represent the thinking of some of the world's most knowledgeable minds. We thank them for unselfishly sharing their ideas with you. The value of an edited book depends on individuals like them and their willingness to share with readers.

Capturing those thoughts and creating a valuable book is more challenging. The credit for taking the individual masterpieces and making them a true collection of art is solely credited to our managing editor, Sarah McArthur. Sarah's patience and thoroughness with the editing process continues to amaze us, and the quality of her work is equal to the quality of the contributors.

We would also like to thank Dorothy Hearst and all of the staff of Jossey-Bass for their commitment to this project and their supporting our vision. Their commitment to the distribution of quality business resources is appreciated and recognized.

Any labor of love requires the patience of spouses. Ours were no exception. Special thanks go to Lyda, Patrice, Maria, Heather, Michael, Alexander, and Kathryn.

—M.G., H.J.M., A.J.O.

Part One

Challenges and Dilemmas

Chapter One

Why Aren't Those Specials Selling Today?

Elliott Masie

It was the day after Thanksgiving and all the boxes were stacked. You know that Friday, the huge shopping day after the turkey is digested, when citizens flock to stores and malls to start their search for a great holiday gift. Throughout the United States, at Wal-Mart stores, there was a "killer" combination special—a computer, monitor, and printer at an extremely awesome price. Boxes of this combo product were stacked, bar-coded, and ready to be taken away by eager shoppers. Wal-Mart, an aggressive user of real-time inventory control and predictive shopping models, had full confidence that thousands of these high-tech bargains would leave their stores across the country in the shopping basket of shoppers that Friday.

We cut to Wal-Mart headquarters on Friday morning and look over the shoulder of a merchandising manager. Something is wrong! Very few of this product have been purchased throughout the country, and stores have already been open for five hours, with shoppers in every aisle. What could be wrong? He drills down to the store-by-store sales data and finds a single store where people have started to purchase this product after a few hours of no sales. Perhaps there is a clue to this dilemma at that location. He picks up the phone, calls the store, and hears this from the electronics department manager:

> For the first few hours, we had people looking at the boxes of computers, but no one was buying. A couple of shoppers asked me if there really was a computer, color monitor, and a printer in

this small box. They figured that you could not fit all that equipment in that box, so they probably would just get a coupon that
would have to be mailed in for the printer at a later date. In other
words, they could not visually see and perceive the value of this
special. I took one of the boxes, sliced open the side panel so that
shoppers could see the contents, and placed it next to the stack of
boxes. Almost instantly, customers started to purchase the computer
specials.

Back at headquarters, the merchandising manager knew what
he had to do. He had to create an instant learning, knowledge, and
action moment for electronics departments around the country. He
put together a quick note detailing how to display the product, and
within a few hours, the marketing display was modified. Sure
enough, all around the country, hour-by-hour sales of the product
reached their original planned levels.

What do we call this process? Knowledge management? Supply
chain management? E-learning? Customer relationship monitor-
ing? Best practice harvesting? Collaborative real-time innovation?
Actually, it's a blend of all of those things. It combines all of these
corporate processes, but even more important, it demonstrates how
an organization committed to being smart, in real time, can leverage an active learning network to learn and teach. My use of the
word *network* should not take you to a hardware or even software
image. What Wal-Mart used that day was a combination of information, analysis, investigation, communication, and digitally based
learning.

Factors at Work

In this particular case, the factors at work that are critical to moving learning around the organization rapidly include predictive
modeling, real-time information and real-time learning, people,
encouragement of initiative and innovation, rapid authoring of
learning, and the second wave of learning implementation.

Predictive Modeling

Wal-Mart had a clear model for how this product would perform on a daily, if not hourly, basis. The model was aligned with the assumptions behind the decision to offer this computer at its "special" price. The manager and even the stores could have their models to check both assumptions and implementation quickly. It also allowed headquarters to look at patterns between stores to unveil any anomalies or innovations in implementation that might reveal real-time learning.

Predictive models give us a way to "bet" on a probable outcome and to alert us to the need to check our assumptions and even implementation at every point along the way. In widely dispersed organizations, these predictive models are even more critical, as they can serve as early-warning systems for other stores. In the case at hand, the stores on the West Coast were alerted earlier in the day about this problem and were able to make on-the-fly changes. The key is to not get overly invested in the predictions. Build a model that can not only point out flaws in the plan but also validate how good the planning was.

Real-Time Information for Real-Time Learning

Corporations must create new learning at the speed of change to stay competitive. In the case of Wal-Mart, if headquarters had to wait until the end of the week or the end of month to make changes, corrective action would have been delayed beyond salvation. Any enterprise has to assume that a percentage of its plans are flawed; how rapidly flaws are discovered is directly related to how rapidly we can learn, correct, test, and disseminate. Real-time information can also lead to multiple attempts at correction. One food store chain tries multiple approaches when a problem in stores is noted. Several simultaneous corrections are made by different stores, with the ability to rapidly track which approach has the greatest impact on sales.

People: Adding Texture to Data

I am not pleading for "air traffic controllers" to watch radar screens of sales and to issue edicts for change. All the data do is to highlight a point of investigation. It was critical for the manager at Wal-Mart's headquarters to be able to talk to the person in the store who had decided to cut open the box. Small changes often make big differences. That store would rarely regard what one of its employee's did as being significant. From the store's perspective, it was just a matter of opening the box. However, in the interview process, headquarters can start to see a "best or better" practice that might be sharable across the enterprise. The headquarters staff members have to view themselves as football coaches sitting in the bleachers. They can use information and dialogue to reveal the texture and details, which is where knowledge is most often located.

Encouraging Local Initiative and Innovation

If the local store did not feel that it had "permission" to slice open one box and put it on display, since it was not ordered to do so by headquarters, a solution would not have been found as rapidly. For innovation to come from all points on the learning network, there needs to be a culture that encourages a degree of innovation and also that creates opportunities to share these small changes openly as part of a "let's find ways of improving things" attitude.

Learning Authored Rapidly

My colleagues in the e-learning world often think that learning has to be polished and highly produced to be acceptable in a corporate culture. Bluntly, the accuracy of the content and the speed of dissemination are the top two qualities. A quick fax would work if it were received and read immediately by someone in every store. However, learning networks are being built that will allow richer and more rapid dissemination than the fax solution.

The Second Wave, Where Learning Is Better

That day the only learning that had to be disseminated to the associates in the store was "Open the box so that customers can see that it contains a computer, monitor, and printer." These small, incremental bursts of knowledge, skills, or procedures are often the most crucial interventions. We can't just focus on large best practices or on formal e-learning courses and training programs. Operational lessons will often be found in the tweaks and improvements, in the smaller chunks. These must be delivered electronically and as part of an ongoing connection between the worker and multiple sources of knowledge. We also can't overwhelm the workforce with too many bursts of knowledge. There are only so many blasts from headquarters that the workforce will accept with gratitude. After that point, employee reception weakens and passivity grows.

Increasing Speed to Learning

There are key innovations that organizations are making in building learning networks that increase the speed to learning. They come in two arenas: knowledge and learning authoring and knowledge and learning connections.

Fast to Author

In the old days (five or ten years ago), the authoring of content often took weeks or months. One manufacturing company planned on fourteen months from the point of determining what learning was to be authored and when it actually reached learners. The company had fifty-seven quality control steps in the authoring process, and often thirty or forty people would touch the learning content along the way. That just won't do when the speed of business is marked by quarters and when the speed of change is often measured in days or hours.

Organizations are creating faster and more informal ways of authoring content. The challenge is to bring content to workers rapidly and also to create it in a format that will be compelling enough and engaging enough to capture their attention. Organizations are building content templates that have a richness of design and allow a subject matter expert, such as the merchandising manager at headquarters, to drag and drop content into a design framework that is familiar and acceptable to the learner. This means we are putting a learning-authoring dimension into the knowledge management model. As key managers determine what knowledge should be disseminated, they want to rapidly author it in a way that has instructional integrity, efficiency of use for the learner, and speed of delivery. Watch for more learning templates to be deployed between content or knowledge management systems that will increase the speed to learning.

Imagine the Wal-Mart scenario, just a few years hence:

- The change in how the computer box was opened and displayed would be authored as a change in an existing module on displaying that item. The merchandising manager would just highlight changes in the existing content.
- The store that made the change would have access to a digital still or video camera to take a quick shot of how it is displaying the item.
- This content would be made available in a text format that could be easily translated into multiple languages for the diverse workforce and would share text of the video content for the hearing-challenged workforce.
- This authoring would be done with a simple drag-and-drop approach that embodies good instructional design, and the output would be rapidly disseminated by store associates.

Fast to Connect

The speed of learning is also determined by how rapidly knowledge can reach the working associates in an enterprise. Although there are formal learning experiences that are best delivered in a class-room or a longer-duration e-learning model, there are many instances when we want to deliver knowledge right to the worker.

Over the next few years, we will see an evolution of the electronics of learning. This means that learning and knowledge will flow to a wider range of non-PC devices. Here are just a few examples:

Point-of-sale knowledge. Manufacturers of cash registers are starting to build in the capacity to deliver e-learning to the worker, in between customer interactions. In this example, imagine if Wal-Mart could send that video alert to the cash registers in the electronics department. A light might come on when a critical piece of learning was available, and an associate who was not serving a customer could display it right on the point-of-sale register screen.

Mobile device convergence. Mobile telephones are rapidly converging with other devices, including digital cameras, video displays, and pocket PCs. Add wireless connectivity within the store, and you can imagine the ability to reach employees right on their belt-based phone device. These devices might even indicate the location of the associate who is nearest to the boxes that need to be altered.

Smart displays. Currently, we think of a computer display as linked to a specific computer. However, soon the displays will be seen as wireless and wired aspects of the network. This means that we can deliver knowledge to a wide range of monitors and displays located in a store or other work setting. A store associate might be notified about the need to open that box and might select a gas plasma screen in the electronics department to display a quick tutorial on how to alter the box.

In-ear coaching. This might make some readers uneasy, but I can imagine providing each worker with a small wireless earpiece that combines microphone and headset speaker. A coach at headquarters would have the ability to use verbal knowledge dissemination to the appropriate employee in every store.

Personalization. The learning provided to workers will be personalized to reflect their experience, their context, and their comfort. By building learning in small, deployable chunks, often called *learning objects*, the organization will start to customize what is disseminated. For example, for some workers, the only information that is needed in our example is "Cut open the box to show the three components." Others might need to see a video step-by-step procedure. Personalization is of key importance to increased acceptance of knowledge management and e-learning.

Feedback, compliance, and cycles. Learning dissemination requires a loop back from the learner to the source. In our example, headquarters would ask other stores to send in any innovations and changes they made with this item, as well as to indicate that they had adjusted the display according to the updated suggestions. (This allows headquarters to confirm the relationship between this change and any increase in sales.)

Deploying a learning network, in terms of technology and learning methodology, can result in a dramatic change in the speed to learning. Of course, the process has to be managed for potential overload. If new instructions descend on employees every hour, they will quickly be ignored, and local initiative will decrease dramatically. Too much conversation in the world of learning has been about learning management systems and knowledge management systems, with a focus on server-like technology. I am much more interested in the learning network that is built by headquarters and distributed to employees. The network should be the gossamer thread that carries knowledge and learning in a bilateral fashion from and to the frontline employee!

Conclusion

Let's borrow a phrase from the Department of Defense. The DoD uses the word *readiness* to talk about training. What is the state of readiness in your organization's learning network? Could you have discovered the problem like Wal-Mart did? Would you have had the real-time analysis and intervention to rapidly discover a "better practice"? And how rapidly could you have spun this improvement around to all of your associates throughout the enterprise? Readiness to deploy learning and knowledge is a key metric as we face the future in our businesses.

Speed to learning is a provocative metric of how well organizations have evolved their cultures and targeted their technology to accelerate the movement of knowledge and how receptive their workforce is to learning in real time.

> **Elliott Masie** is an internationally recognized speaker, futurist, humorist, author, and consultant on the critical topics of technology, business, learning, and workplace productivity. He is editor of *TechLearnTrends*, an Internet newsletter read by more than forty thousand business executives worldwide, and *Learning Decisions*, a subscription newsletter. He heads the Masie Center, a think tank focused on how organizations can absorb technology and create continuous learning and knowledge within the workforce. He leads a consortium of Fortune 500 companies that explores the future of technology in the workplace. He has developed models for disseminating technology throughout organizations, providing workforce development with technology and making sense of the buzz and hype of the *e-* and *dotcom* world. He is considered one of the leading experts in the emerging field of digital collaboration. Contact: emasie@masie.com; http://www.masie.com

Chapter Two

Five Dilemmas of Knowledge Management

Fons Trompenaars

Charles Hampden-Turner

Over the past decade, knowledge management has gained an important place in management thinking and it is a crucial process within the learning organization. Obviously, the development from an industrial to a knowledge economy has been the major rationale for its popularity. Yet similar to the latest management fads around management by objectives and teamwork, it is also a reaction to the absence of certain values in our Western society.

To process knowledge effectively has perhaps become today's most important competitive advantage. It determines innovative competence—the way you can apply and retain the core competencies within an organization—and the way the organization learns. Effective knowledge management is dependent on the type of organizational culture in which it reconciles dilemmas. I have identified five types of dilemmas:

1. Universal versus particular knowledge
2. Individual versus team knowledge
3. Specific and codified versus diffuse and implicit knowledge
4. Top-down versus bottom-up knowledge
5. Inside-out to outside-in knowledge

Universal Versus Particular Knowledge

A process controller at Motorola once told me that in an attempt to improve the cleaning process of electronic circuits of global systems for mobile telecommunication, he came up with the idea of using sharper brushes. Not only did they clean more effectively, it turned out, but they also cut through many of the essential circuits, resulting in more than $100,000 in damage.

Bob Galvin, CEO of Motorola at the time, asked the process controller to come to his room. Galvin didn't fire the employee but instead asked him to write a report on how these types of errors could be avoided in the future. After reading the report, Galvin thanked him because the new ideas in the employee's report would save the company more than a million dollars. Knowledge management is effective only when you create an "error-correcting" system that learns continuously from its mistakes. In the long run, there is nothing more dangerous than an errorless system.

Individual Versus Team Knowledge

Perhaps it is the individualism inherent in American society that drives our need for knowledge management. Our educational systems are based on accumulating knowledge individually. Students are thrown into a competitive game in which only the fittest survive. However, the organizations in which the graduates come to work pay a price. More communitarian cultures, such as France and Japan, face the opposite problem. A Canadian student once appealed forcefully to our intercultural knowledge and experience. In his university in Montreal, French students were not playing on a level field with their American colleagues. Almost all French students were cheating during their exams by sharing information among themselves. Can you justify this by attributing it to cultural differences in a nonjudgmental way? "Yes, through knowledge management," we told him. French people, like the Japanese, have a much greater talent for joint preparation and the sharing of knowledge among colleagues.

Americans have the opposite challenge, which is how to share individually gained knowledge with a group. For instance, during a stay at Wharton, a student colleague solved this challenge creatively: he removed all the chapters that we needed to read for the next exam from the book. Nobody could get to that source. Thus, it became clear that if one student is set against the other in competition for grades, knowledge remains a relative concept.

Specific and Codified Versus Diffuse and Implicit Knowledge

Many organizations have a treasure trove of implicit or "tacit" knowledge, in the words of Nonaka and Takeuchi.[1] Their success will depend on how this can be transferred into something concrete, such as an explicit product. Nonaka and Takeuchi use Matsushita's development of the world's first fully automated home bakery machine as an example. When the inventors couldn't fully understand the mechanism for kneading the dough, one of their software programmers was apprenticed to the top baker at the Osaka International Hotel. Only after he had mastered the implicit knowledge of dough kneading was he able to transfer this information to his colleague engineers.

Americans have the mirror image of this experience. When guiding the integration of the Japanese Isuzu truck division with General Motors' truck division, we noticed that the Americans were quite upset by the Japanese. The Americans used about 30 percent of their time to codify and write up their knowledge in handbooks and procedures. However, the knowledge of the Japanese is stored in their network of relationships. Do you need any written documents in your family to understand each other? The Americans reacted to this situation by asking, "How can you ever learn from each other and transfer that knowledge and experience if you don't write it up?" We suggested explaining to the Japanese how to write effective handbooks. Much shorter and efficient manuals of explicit knowledge were the result. This is a very different approach from "Shut up and listen." The Americans had chosen a type of reasoning in which the interaction with the Japanese created a bond that enabled knowledge to be stored on the network.

Top-Down Versus Bottom-Up Knowledge

Specifics about clients and products are stored in the heads of individual staff members. Middle management translates these into information that is in turn organized as knowledge by top management. For effective knowledge management, the reconciliation of this dilemma can be found in "middle-up-down," in which middle management is the bridge between the standards of top management and the chaotic reality of those on the front lines. The other way around is the knowledge of top management, which is often just as crucial in organizing and defining the information coming from within the organization.

Inside-Out to Outside-In Knowledge

Effective knowledge management is not constrained by the walls of the organization. Inner-oriented cultures prefer to start from enhancing the internal processes. Externally oriented cultures prefer to start with the insights and needs of the client. The internal and external environments need to be amalgamated to attain not a "balanced" but an "integrated" organization, in which the client has a direct influence on internal processes, which in turn serves to increase the knowledge of the client.

Conclusion

In all of these dilemmas, the context of organizational culture dictates the preference or the starting point of reconciliation, but effective knowledge management is dictated by the integration of rules and exceptions, group and individual, explicit and implicit, top and bottom, and inner and outer worlds.

Fons Trompenaars is founder of Trompenaars Hampden-Turner Intercultural Management Consulting. He is interested in the differences in conceptions of organizational structure in various cultures. He is the author of *Riding the Waves of Culture: Understanding Cultural Diversity in Business,* which has sold more than 180,000 copies, and *Did the Pedestrian Die?* He cowrote, with Charles Hampden-Turner, *Seven Cultures of Capitalism, Building Cross-Cultural Competence, Mastering the Infinite Game,* and *21 Leaders for the 21st Century.* He was awarded the International Professional Practice Area Research Award by the American Society for Training and Development (ASTD) and has been named one of the top five management consultants by a leading business magazine. Contact: fons@thtconsulting.com; http://www.thtconsulting.com

Charles Hampden-Turner is director of research and development for Trompenaars-Hampden Turner. He is also a senior research associate at the Judge Institute of Management Studies at Cambridge University and a fellow of the Cybernetics Society. He has taught at Harvard University, Brandeis University, and the University of Toronto. A recipient of Guggenheim, Rockefeller, and Ford Foundation fellowships, he is also a past winner of the Douglas McGregor Memorial Award. He is the author of seventeen books, including *Riding the Waves of Culture* with Fons Trompenaars, which has been translated into nine languages, including Chinese and Japanese. His most recent books include *Twenty-One Leaders for the Twenty-First, Building Cross-Cultural Competence, Mastering the Infinite Game,* and *The Seven Cultures of Capitalism.* He has published in the *Harvard Business Review* and the *Financial Times* and has been featured in several television documentaries. Contact: charles@thtconsulting.com; http://www.7d-culture.nl

Chapter Three

Effectively Influencing Up

Ensuring That Your Knowledge Makes a Difference

Marshall Goldsmith

"The great majority of people tend to focus downward," writes Peter Drucker. "They are occupied with efforts rather than results. They worry over what the organization and their superiors 'owe' them and should do for them. And they are conscious above all of the authority they 'should have.' As a result they render themselves ineffectual."[1]

Peter Drucker has written extensively about the impact of the knowledge worker on modern organizations. Knowledge workers can be defined as people who know more about what they are doing than their managers do. While many knowledge workers have years of education and experience in training for their positions, they often have little training in how to effectively influence upper management.

In Chapter Twenty-Four in this book, Warner Burke pointed out that "Knows how to influence up in a constructive way" scored in last place in managerial effectiveness ratings on all items when people evaluated their managers at NASA—immediately before the *Columbia* space shuttle exploded. Although lack of effective upward influence was not the only cause of the explosion, it was clearly a contributing factor. Having reviewed summary 360-degree feedback results in more than sixty organizations, I was not at all surprised by this finding. This is the norm for many organizations, not the exception. NASA is but one of a great many organizations to be hurt when knowledge workers do not effectively "influence up." Organizations in all fields suffer when key employees cannot effectively influence upper management.

The ten guidelines presented in this chapter are intended to help you do a better job of influencing your upper management. I hope that you find them useful in helping you convert your good ideas into meaningful action.

> 1. When presenting ideas to upper management, realize that it is your responsibility to sell—not their responsibility to buy.

In many ways, influencing up is similar to selling products or services to external customers. They don't have to buy—you have to sell! Any good salesperson takes responsibility for achieving results. No one is impressed with salespeople who blame their customers for not buying their products.

While the importance of taking responsibility may seem obvious in external sales, an amazing number of people in large corporations waste countless hours blaming management for not buying their ideas. We can become "disempowered" when they focus on what others have done to make things wrong and not what we can do to make things right.

If more time were spent on developing our ability to present ideas and less time on blaming management for not buying our ideas, a lot more might get accomplished.

A key part of the sales process is education. To again quote Drucker, "The person of knowledge has always been expected to take responsibility for being understood. It is barbarian arrogance to assume that the layman can or should make the effort to understand the specialist."[2] The effective upward influencer needs to be a good teacher. Good teachers realize that communicating knowledge is often a greater challenge than possessing knowledge.

> 2. Focus on contribution to the larger good, not just the achievement of your objectives.

An effective salesperson would never say to a customer, "You need to buy this product because if you don't, I won't achieve my objectives!"

Effective salespeople relate to the needs of the buyers, not to their own needs. In the same way, effective upward influencers relate to the larger needs of the organization, not just to the needs of their unit or team.

When influencing up, focus on the impact of the decision on the overall corporation. In most cases, the needs of the unit and the needs of the corporation are directly connected. In some cases, they are not. Don't assume that executives can automatically make the connection between the benefit to your unit and the benefit to the larger corporation.

> 3. Strive to win the big battles. Don't waste your ammunition on small points.

Executives' time is very limited. Do a thorough analysis of ideas before "challenging the system." Don't waste time on issues that will have only a modest impact on results. Focus on issues that will make a real difference. Be willing to lose on small points.

Be especially sensitive to the need to win trivial nonbusiness arguments on things like restaurants, sports teams, or cars. People become more annoyed with us for having to be right on trivia than our need to be right on important business points. You are paid to do what makes a difference and to win on important issues. You are not paid to win arguments on the relative quality of athletic teams.

> 4. Present a realistic cost-benefit analysis of your ideas. Don't just sell benefits.

Every organization has limited resources, time, and energy. The acceptance of your idea may well mean the rejection of another idea that someone else believes is wonderful. Be prepared to have a realistic discussion of the costs of your idea. Acknowledge the fact that something else may have to be sacrificed in order to have your idea implemented.

By getting ready for a realistic discussion of costs, you can prepare for objections to your idea before they occur. You can acknowledge the sacrifice that someone else may have to make and point out how the benefits of your plan may outweigh the costs.

> 5. "Challenge up" on issues involving ethics or integrity. Never remain silent on ethics violations.

The experience of Enron, WorldCom, and other organizations has dramatically pointed out how ethics violations can destroy even the most valuable companies. The best of corporations can be severely damaged by only one violation of corporate integrity. Ideally, you will never be asked to do anything by the management of your corporation that represents a violation of corporate ethics. If you are, refuse to do it and immediately let upper management know of your concerns. This action needs to be taken for the ultimate benefit of your company, your customers, your coworkers, and yourself.

When challenging up, try not to assume that management has intentionally requested you to do something wrong. In some cases, inappropriate requests may be made because of misunderstandings or poor communication. Try to present your case in a manner that is intended to be helpful, not judgmental.

> 6. Realize that your upper managers are just as human as you are. Don't say, "I am amazed that someone at *this* level . . ."

It is realistic to expect upper managers to be competent; it is unrealistic to expect them to be better than normal humans. Is there anything in the history of the human species that indicates that when people achieve high levels of status, power, and wealth, they become more wise or more sane? How many times have we thought, "I would assume someone at this level . . ." followed by "knows what is happening," "is logical," "wouldn't make that kind of mistake," or "would never engage in such inappropriate behavior."

Even the best of leaders are human. We all make mistakes. When your managers make mistakes, focus more on helping them than on judging them.

> 7. Treat upper managers with the same courtesy that you would treat partners or customers. Don't be disrespectful.

While it is important to avoid "kissing up" to upper management, it is just as important to avoid the opposite action. A surprising number of middle managers spend hours trashing the company and its executives or making destructive comments about other coworkers. The item "Avoids destructive comments about the company or coworkers" regularly scores in the bottom ten on ratings of coworkers' satisfaction with peers.

Before speaking it is generally good to ask four questions:

1. Will this comment help our company?
2. Will this comment help our customers?
3. Will this comment help the person that I am talking to?
4. Will this comment help the person that I am talking about?

If the answers are no, no, no, and no, don't say it! There is a big difference between total honesty and dysfunctional disclosure. As noted earlier, it is always important to challenge up on integrity issues. It is often inappropriate to trash down when making personal attacks.

> 8. Support the final decision of the team. Don't say, "They made me tell you," to direct reports.

Assuming that the final decision of the team is not immoral, illegal, or unethical, go out and try to make it work! Managers who consistently say, "They told me to tell you," to their coworkers are seen as messengers, not leaders. Even worse, don't say, "Those fools told me to tell you." By demonstrating a lack of commitment to the final decision, we may sabotage the chances for effective execution.

A simple guideline for communicating difficult decisions is to ask, "How would I want others to communicate to their people if they were passing down my final decision and they disagreed with me?" Treat your manager in the same way that you would want to be treated if the roles were reversed.

> 9. Make a positive difference. Don't just try to win or be right.

We can easily become more focused on what others are doing wrong than on how we can make things better. An important guideline in influencing up is to always remember your goal—making a positive difference in the organization.

Corporations are not academic institutions. In an academic institution, the goal may be sharing ideas, not changing the world. Hours of acrimonious debate can be perfectly acceptable in academia. In a corporation, sharing ideas without having an impact is worse than useless. It is a waste of the stockholders' money and a distraction from serving customers.

When I was interviewed in the *Harvard Business Review*, I was asked, "What is the most common 'area for improvement' for the executives that you meet?" My answer was "winning too much."[3] Focus on making a difference. The more other people can be right or win with your idea, the more likely your idea is to be successfully executed.

> 10. Focus on the future—let go of the past.

One of the most important behaviors to avoid is whining about the past. Have you ever managed someone who incessantly whined about how bad things are? People who whine sabotage any possibility that they might have an impact in the future. Their managers tend to regard them as annoying. Their direct reports view them as inept. Nobody wins.

Successful people love getting ideas aimed at helping them achieve their goals for the future. They dislike being proved wrong because of mistakes in their past. By focusing on the future, you can concentrate on what can be achieved tomorrow, as opposed to what was not achieved yesterday. This future orientation may dramatically increase your odds of effectively influencing up. It will also help you build better long-term relationships with people at all levels of your organization.

In summary, think of the years that you have spent perfecting your craft. Think of all of the knowledge that you have accumulated. Think about how your knowledge can potentially benefit your organization. How much energy have you invested in acquiring all of this knowledge? How much energy have you invested in learning to present this knowledge so that you can make a real difference? My hope is that by making a small investment in learning to influence up, you can make a large difference for the future of your organization.

Marshall Goldsmith is a foremost authority in helping successful leaders achieve positive change in behavior for themselves, their people, and their teams. He has worked as a consultant with more than sixty CEOs and their management teams, and his work has been highlighted in a *Harvard Business Review* interview, a *New Yorker* profile, and a *Business Strategy Review* cover story. He has been listed in the *Wall Street Journal* as one of the top ten executive educators in the United States, in *Forbes* as one of the nation's five leading executive coaches, and in Asia's *Business Times* as one of the sixteen global thought leaders in his field. He is on the executive education faculties of Dartmouth College and Michigan State

University. He was the 2003 keynote speaker at the national Academy of Management convention, and his work has received national recognition from the Institute for Management Studies, the American Management Association, the American Society for Training and Development, and the Human Resource Planning Society. His sixteen books include *The Leader of the Future* (a *Business Week* best seller), *Coaching for Leadership*, and *Global Leadership: The Next Generation*. *The Leadership Investment* was named "Outstanding Academic Business Book" by the American Library Association, and *The Organization of the Future* was a *Library Journal* "Best Business Book." Amazon.com has ranked six of his books as most popular in their field. Goldsmith is the founding director of A4SL—the Alliance for Strategic Leadership. Contact: marshall@a4sl.com; http://www.marshallgoldsmith.com.

Chapter Four

Where "Managing Knowledge" Goes Wrong and What to Do Instead

Niko Canner

Jon R. Katzenbach

"Knowledge management" is more often than not a bad idea. We will explain why this is so and how to make better use of the underlying good ideas that got us interested in knowledge management in the first place.

In an age that has been marked by extraordinary progress in our ability to process, manipulate, and transfer information, we are naturally drawn to see the world through the lens of information. Any problem that has not been reduced to a problem of manipulating and transporting information holds within itself the apparent seed of a breakthrough in productivity. Inventory along a supply chain is managed at far lower levels as the informational content associated with orders and resource requirements is shared across multiple linked enterprises. Credit scoring can be performed effectively in real time and at a distance, given the ability to leverage models built from large databases. Amazon.com is able to deliver book recommendations far better than we would expect from most members of the staff of a local Barnes & Noble bookstore, if perhaps not as well as the proprietor of a good bookstore in a college town.

The Role of Human Judgment in Knowledge Management

Where the practice of knowledge management (indeed the very expression "knowledge management") has most frequently gone awry is in failing to see the tremendous differences between (1) what is required to take a function that has involved human judgment and reducing it to a problem of information processing (for example, Amazon's book recommendations) and (2) what is involved in supporting a function in which human judgment continues to play a central role (such as determining how to resolve a complex insurance claim).

The first problem, decision and process automation, requires that a model be able to drive usable outputs in most or all cases (potentially escalating a process to a human decision maker if certain conditions hold). The second problem is not so much about "managing knowledge" as it is about providing a context and a set of tools that enable human actors to maximize their effectiveness.

Too often, knowledge management initiatives, as distinct from decision and process automation, fall into the pattern of encouraging participants in a business process to turn their judgment and experience into documents ("codification") and then creating a technology that enables others to obtain these documents ("access knowledge") to inform decisions and actions. The stories told to obtain sponsorship for these initiatives seem plausible enough, resting as they do on the intuition that no one has available the experience base or the expertise that the full range of employees possess collectively. We can all think about situations in which someone took action without the benefit of what a colleague knew, resulting in a costly missed opportunity. The promise that such mistakes will be avoided in the future pulls powerfully on heartstrings and purse strings both.

Challenges of the Codification-Access Model

Unfortunately, this codification-access model rarely works. The knowledge management community has focused on the problems associated with incenting codification and generating awareness of the valuable knowledge to be found in their systems. These problems are real but less fundamental than three others:

1. *Experts can rarely "extract" their own knowledge.* Experts possess the ability to exercise practical judgment in context. When they try to codify what they know, they generally arrive at either something so specific that it appears to lack broader applicability or something so general that it appears obvious.

2. *Insight occurs mostly by analogy.* When someone is stuck (knowingly or not) in solving a problem, the issue most often is that the person has not seen that the problem actually resembles some other problem for which a solution could more easily be envisioned. Once someone has framed the problem right, finding the solution tends to be relatively easy. In business, however, we are constantly surrounded by tremendous amounts of potentially distracting detail. Problem framing is consequently quite difficult. The codification-access model assumes that the "user" has already framed the problem right and can now go about trying to find ideas that will help solve the problem. Unfortunately, this is often not the case.

3. *Professionals rarely want to disrupt the flow of their work.* The kinds of people to whom knowledge management is generally directed are competent, busy, and used to having to deal with complex problems quickly and efficiently. A large part of what professionals learn how to do is to take a daunting task and approach it in such a way that they can systematically and rapidly complete it at an acceptable level of performance. Professionals often fail to optimize the result of their work, but they are rarely stumped. Knowledge management systems generally require professionals to stop what they are doing ("working") and do something else ("access knowledge") that generally does not yield the feeling of rapid progress that they associate with the mastery they have achieved.

There are of course situations in which these issues have been addressed, and we would be disappointed if each of our readers failed to think of two or three right off the bat. We believe, however, that these are the exceptions that prove the rule.

To see how exceptional the conditions are in which the codifi-cation-access model works, take one success: McKinsey's use of a knowledge management system to help consultants worldwide access "practice development" materials relevant to developing proposals for new projects and to helping engagement managers structure work plans once a project starts. The conditions at McKinsey represent something of a "perfect storm":

- The hiring model and the way people develop on the job are carefully honed to ensure that people are not only good at solving problems but also at stating how they have solved problems (clients would be skeptical of purely tacit expertise). Therefore, consultants are far more able to "extract" their knowledge than many other knowledge workers.

- The vast majority of consultants are very comfortable with reading and writing, given the academic emphasis of the firm.

- Reputation is significantly a function of having disseminated ideas for which others have a high regard, creating a strong reason to publish internally.

- Expertise outside the firm in the areas most relevant to the firm's work is often not readily accessible. There is not an extensive professional literature on many of the specific questions that McKinsey consultants need to address (for example, strategy in a particular industry).

- There are strong practices focused on industries and functions, making it much easier than in most situations to know where to "file" newly codified knowledge and where to look for it.

- There are often slack resources at the end of a project that can be used to codify work that resulted from the project.

- Both the nature of the work (frequent need to solve problems perceived as unfamiliar) and the rhythm of how the work is done (a new engagement manager brought in to start up a project, in many instances) make people more receptive to conducting an initial "search" phase early in a project.

Note that even in many other kinds of professional firms, these factors are not present to the same degree as in the particular example of strategy consulting. Law firms, for example, have generally not been successful in using knowledge management to reduce duplication of efforts in research and memo writing. Firms that develop custom software applications have struggled to realize full potential from cataloguing and reusing elements of code. Based on our experience in companies in many different industries, we believe that successes of the codification-access model result from a coincidence of many enabling conditions. These successes are very much exceptions.

Five Promising Approaches to Managing Knowledge

Much of the momentum behind the knowledge management movement comes from the fact that we all believe that (1) people will perform better if they can learn things that other people in a company know and (2) the incremental performance is potentially significant enough that companies should not leave this learning to chance. These claims are undeniably true. They do not, however, imply that companies should extract knowledge, codify that knowledge, put it into systems, and encourage people to search those systems to access and act on the relevant nuggets. The metaphor of "managing knowledge" and the codification-access model that it has spawned have in fact distracted attention from other promising approaches to acting on the opportunity that we all sense arises from (1) and (2). Consequently, we would like to lay out what we believe are five ideas that have been underappreciated, given many practitioners' reflexive focus on the codification-access model.

Expanding the Boundaries of Automation

Where it is possible to automate knowledge work fully, there are tremendous returns to doing so. Certainly there are many instances in which highly complex tasks have been fully embodied in software. In our view, however, too little creativity has been applied to the question of how software can be used to replace providers of professional services, whether those providers are inside or outside the corporation. In the consumer realm, TurboTax represents probably the most impressive undertaking of this kind. TurboTax works so well partly because of the rule-based nature of tax preparation and partly because the software itself is structured as a conversation that follows the thread of a defined process or sequence. Although the software can fully substitute for the professional tax preparer, professional advice delivered by a person can complement the underlying preparation and filing system that TurboTax provides. TurboTax has the potential to focus the use of professional advisers on the areas where their expertise is genuinely needed and to enable greater specialization in the advisory realm, where a TurboTax user might consult different individuals expert on specific questions that factor into a single return.

We believe that there are many areas of professional services in which variations on the TurboTax approach could prove valuable. One venture that our firm has launched automates the process of interpreting 360-degree leadership feedback instruments, instruments for team assessment, and other management surveys. We have been able, for an investment of less than a million dollars, to build a system that delivers detailed feedback to managers from 360-degree or team surveys with each bullet point in a feedback report based on a specific micropattern in the survey data. These reports generated by our Performance Leaders system pass the "Turing Test":[1] they are as good as or better than the interpretive feedback generated by trained coaches, as judged by the designers of the instruments. Tools like TurboTax and Performance Leaders represent the very beginning of what is possible in terms of full automation of expert judgment. While we believe strongly that it is important to recognize when business problems cannot be reduced to problems of information processing, the upside, in terms of scalability, is tremendous when full automation can be achieved.

Sharing Expertise Face-to-Face

Where transfer of expertise is tremendously valuable, the limitations of technology should not be allowed to become constraints. Nearly all large companies have what we call mirror-image functions: large numbers of groups engaged in parallel tasks. Districts in a sales force, teams in a call center, and product development teams in a research and development facility are common examples of mirror-image functions. There will always be a distribution curve of performance in such mirror-image functions, and we have noticed in many of the companies we have observed that management tolerates a fairly wide performance distribution because the tools they have to narrow or shift that distribution (hiring and firing, financial incentives, process standardization) are such blunt instruments. In many of these cases, the value of narrowing the gap between current performance and internal benchmarks is astronomical. For one credit company, for instance, the value of moving each unit in their five collections sites halfway to the performance of the best site was $75 million per year.

Certainly, in cases like this, it pays to try actively to influence the process by which leaders learn the practices that enable others to achieve superior performance. What we have discovered in situation after situation is that the value is so high that sophisticated internal or external resources can be used to help groups of leaders understand one another's practices and how insights from one area can be applied in other areas. Rather than codifying the knowledge of the best practitioners, putting that knowledge into a system, and letting others access that system, we have found that the returns are far higher from having a trained facilitator engage groups in discovery and application face to face, in real time. Much of the effort spent disembodying knowledge, so that it becomes a commodity that can seemingly be "managed," could be better leveraged through increasing the quantity and quality of problem solving that takes place among peers outside the chain of command.

Connecting People with People

To spark innovative thinking, technology should focus on connecting people with people rather than on providing codified knowledge. Much professional problem solving and nearly all of the most innovative problem solving involves the perception of analogies rather than the straightforward application of a process or rule. Knowledge management systems conceived in the codification-access model focus on providing all the knowledge that a user needs in order to be able to act on someone else's idea. A system designed to support problem solving by analogy would take a very different approach. Professionals would be able to search a collection of short stories (perhaps one- or two-page case studies) that sketch out situations their peers had faced, innovations developed in those situations, and results or work in progress. The stories would be written not to enable the reader to be able immediately to apply the new technique but rather to enable the reader to understand to whom he or she might want to speak to in order to learn about ideas and analogies worth exploring. The system has done its work if the user connects with a peer or a few peers who can provide valuable dialogue (often mutually valuable).

Pfizer implemented a system of this kind in its worldwide marketing organization around the time of its merger with Warner-Lambert and was able to provide newer members in particular with a much richer connection to the organization than even a very good system to manage fully codified knowledge could have provided.

Folding Knowledge Management into Process Management

Wherever possible, systems designed to access knowledge should be integrated with systems designed to support business processes. As noted earlier, one of the factors contributing to low usage for many systems is that a professional needs to step outside the tasks that he or she does in order to access knowledge as a separate act. Again, an analogy with TurboTax helps illustrate the alternative.

Individuals working on a tax return are much more likely to follow a prompt they encounter while completing an online interview (doing the work) to learn more about a specific IRS regulation (accessing knowledge) than they would be to stop doing an online interview in one system to go to a new Web site and search for an IRS regulation that might turn out to be important. Most corporate knowledge management systems, however, follow the latter model.

This is another area in which Pfizer has successfully innovated. The Powerpath system at its global headquarters arranges all of the information and applications needed for a process, such as strategic planning, into a "pathway" that users can follow. For instance, a product team leader working on his or her strategic plan can see the timeline and steps required for a successful submission and can access templates, guidelines, analytical applications, databases, and best-practice examples needed at each step of the planning process. A single password gives the product team leader access to everything he or she needs to work on a complex project. As more of these pathways are developed, communications associated with process changes become dramatically easier—all that is necessary is to update the pathway—and usage of resources both new and previously developed has increased. Most important, significant amounts of time have been freed up from administrative tasks to focus on strategic issues.

Recognizing the Value of Simple Affirmation

Where behavior change generates business value, there is often more impact from affirmation and reinforcement than from discovery of new information. One of the implicit assumptions of many knowledge management initiatives is that if people acquire the right information, it will translate into changed behavior and improved performance. In some circumstances, this assumption holds true, even where a company is focused on an issue like best-practice sharing; however, in many cases the impact may result more from the motivating effect of hearing about best practices than from learning about fundamentally new ideas.

IBM has experimented internally with a system for managing massive virtual events on a global basis, beginning with an all-employee dialogue named WorldJam and continuing with a forum for all managers named ManagerJam. These events had multiple purposes, but at their core was the goal of capturing best practices that employees could use to drive results throughout this global corporation. A thorough review of the transcripts from the multi-day ManagerJam event revealed that although there were few instances of real-time development of true breakthrough ideas, a number of relatively straightforward but valuable management practices were discussed at length. The galvanizing effect of these dialogues is potentially significant. Hearing testimony from peers worldwide about why a management practice is important and receiving reinforcement for one's suggestions about how to implement the idea provide a strong motivation to carry through with actions that a manager already knew were good. One of the implications is that often when we think about building searchable databases of codified ideas to enable discovery of new practices, we would do better to orchestrate vivid events (online or offline) to reinforce practices that are already known but not consistently applied.

Conclusion

There are tremendous opportunities for corporations to invest in systematically managing professional problem-solving work: through automation, guided learning among peers, help in surfacing potential analogies, systems that support work processes, and events that reinforce effective work practices, as well as through traditional "knowledge management" systems. As the field that we have, for now, named knowledge management matures, we hope that the metaphor of knowledge as a commodity that can be distilled into component parts and managed is replaced by other more complex and more accurate ways of thinking. Already we have seen a number of organizations innovate in how they use both technology and face-to-face disciplines to increase the quality and impact of knowledge work. We believe that by clarifying exactly where and how traditional systems in the codification-access model will work and by expanding the range of options they consider, more organizations will begin to find breakthroughs in this critical set of problems.

Niko Canner is a founder and managing partner of Katzenbach Partners LLC, a management consulting firm that applies strategic thinking to issues of organizational and people performance. He has worked with Pfizer, IBM, and a number of other companies on how knowledge workers develop and share ideas. In addition to his consulting work, Canner has led the firm's investment to develop Performance Leaders, a venture to build assessments that provide managers and teams with highly individualized feedback based on their specific business situations. Prior to founding Katzenbach Partners, Canner was a practice leader with Mitchell Madison Group and a founding member of the McKinsey Change Center. Contact: niko.canner@katzenbach.com; http://www.katzenbach.com

Jon R. Katzenbach is a founder and senior partner of Katzenbach Partners LLC, a management consulting firm that applies strategic thinking to issues of organizational and people performance. Formerly a director of McKinsey & Company, Inc., Katzenbach has served executives of leading companies, as well as public institutions. He is a leading researcher on new approaches to organizational performance, and his perspectives on leadership, teams, and organization have been presented to numerous executive leadership groups throughout the world. His published works include *The Wisdom of Teams*, *Real Change Leaders*, *Teams at the Top*, *Peak Performance*, and *The Discipline of Teams*. His newest book is *Why Pride Matters More Than Money*. Contact: jon.katzenbach@katzenbach.com; http://www.katzenbach.com

Chapter Five

Knowledge Management Involves Neither Knowledge nor Management

Marc S. Effron

The death knell for knowledge management (KM) as a concept was sounded with a *Wall Street Journal* article chronicling McKinsey & Co.'s failure to manage its "knowledge" successfully. The article quotes from an internal McKinsey report that says despite having the requisite systems in place, "the ability of our consultants to tap into and effectively leverage our knowledge is poor. . . . Our knowledge base is mixed in quality and poorly structured. It takes much too long to find the right knowledge, and in many cases, the best existing knowledge is not identified and brought to the client."[1] If the world's most prestigious consulting firm could not successfully wrangle information, what hope was there for anyone else?

The failure at McKinsey was not its inability to categorize and retrieve the volumes of experience from its legions of Harvard-trained M.B.A.s but rather the widely held Pollyanna-like belief that knowledge can actually be managed. Even though McKinsey had published numerous articles outlining the secrets to successful knowledge management,[2] it too missed the underlying truth. What is the truth? The truth is that the sheer concept of knowledge management is fundamentally flawed—it involves neither knowledge nor management and therefore cannot be expected to succeed. Though on its face KM seemed like a great idea, it's time that we relegated it to that dustbin of history labeled "honorable intentions" and begin to focus instead on helping organizations truly share the intellectual capital their workers possess.

Before you cite the example of Company X having improved productivity when workers in Singapore explained a new way to machine a widget to workers in Seattle, let's define some terms. The sharing of "best practices," a potentially dangerous sport of its own, doesn't constitute managing "knowledge," just sharing procedures. Similarly, training one group on a skill learned or improved by another group is exactly that, training, not KM. By putting my latest presentation on CEO succession into my firm's database, I have not managed any knowledge, merely posted information, making it accessible to a larger population.

To use a tired but in this case helpful literary device, the dictionary defines *knowledge* as "the fact or condition of knowing something with familiarity gained through experience or association."[3] This makes it impossible to acquire "knowledge" without either experiencing something yourself or interacting with someone else who has. What the cheerleaders define as KM is most frequently just information sharing, which certainly has its role but doesn't achieve the original intent of its proponents.

The fundamental, undeniable fact is that knowledge is intrinsic to human beings and is gained only by participating in an experience or having contextual understanding of that experience. The typical definition of KM as an information technology (IT)–based process run by chief knowledge officers to enable global sharing of best practices is nothing more than a string of threadbare consulting clichés. Knowledge exists only in people.

However, all is not lost. The billions of dollars spent on consultants, IT systems, and training courses may still yield some small return if we're willing to take a very honest, even brutal look at the core truths about why KM doesn't work and how organizations must behave if they truly want shared knowledge.

My framework addresses KM as experienced by corporate managers and those in professional service firms, but many points would be just as applicable on the shop floor. Let's start with what doesn't work.

Why Knowledge Management Doesn't Work

It's not much of a challenge to think of a slew of clear reasons why KM is a failed concept and why organizations have not realized its lauded benefits despite the multiple billions of dollars being spent annually on the effort.[4] I can easily think of nine of them. These nine nails should serve to keep the lid on the KM coffin so that this beast never again threatens corporate-kind.

1. There's No Accountability

If knowledge is adequately managed in an organization, who gets rewarded? If it's not, who gets penalized? Those questions define accountability but cannot be answered by those who promote KM. Although everyone wanted a piece of KM when it first emerged, no one ended up with clear accountability.

The early battle for accountability pitched human resources (HR) against IT as HR fought to claim KM as its own. Jack Fitz-Enz of the HR benchmarking Saratoga Institute, stated, "The open door for HR is that KM is not a technical issue. It is a human issue. This is HR's chance to be at the heart of the most important force in the 21st century—information."[5] Yet HR had then and still has today enough challenges managing other employee data. HR was not prepared to take accountability for the information residing in every employee's head. Likewise, IT's approach to classifying and storing data, albeit potentially very efficient, ignores the fundamental human aspect of actually transferring knowledge. In the end, no one has been accountable, so little has been accomplished.

2. There's No Quality Control

To paraphrase from George Orwell's *Animal Farm*, "All knowledge is equal, but some knowledge is more equal than other knowledge." As a veteran of knowledge database experiences at a Fortune 20 bank and a leading management consulting firm, I know that all too frequently these databases become nothing more than filing cabinets for every project that the professional staff completes, regardless of quality. Although we all do great work, some of that work is, by definition, our "best," and some is the firm's "best." Without a knowledgeable human to review and screen for quality every piece of information going into a database, you're asking the rest of the organization to fish for information in a polluted pond. Let's not even start with the question of who reviews all this information as it ages to ensure that it's still fresh and still represents the current best thinking in the organization.

3. It's Not Really Knowledge

As I stated earlier, knowledge cannot be stored in a database; only information can. In case you think that this is just a semantic argument, consider this: if I search a database for key success factors in implementing succession planning, I'll likely get a raft of reports and presentations on succession planning—information. It will be my responsibility to guess at the context and nuances that generated this information. However, if I ask Bob from down the hall, who has done twenty of these projects, I'm just about guaranteed to get something closer to knowledge, thanks to the context he can provide. Even the KM experts agree with this. According to George Bailey, PricewaterhouseCoopers's North American leader for innovation, "Everybody goes there [to the database] sometimes, but when they're looking for expertise, most people go down the hall."[6]

4. It's Push, Not Pull

Information gets into a database only if people put it. It's difficult, even for those with the best of intentions, to remember to do this on a regular basis, and sometimes people don't have the best intentions. According to Robin Giang, from the technology consulting firm

International Data Corporation, "Knowledge is power, and to publish your knowledge is to relinquish it."[7] This long-acknowledged information-hoarding issue is still not adequately addressed at most companies. One highly intrusive way around this challenge is found in new "sifting" software that mines companies' e-mails to identify content expertise that isn't being shared. If I've sent ten e-mails on succession planning, I might be flagged as a knowledgeable source, whether accurate or not. Aside from the ethical questions that this technology raises, it leaves open the question "Are you getting better information or just more of it?"

5. There's No Incentive to Share

We're all team players who believe in the benefits of cooperation. We're all also very busy, and convincing busy professionals that sharing their information should be a priority must involve either a carrot or a stick. Most firms implementing KM made the false assumption that professionals would prioritize their time around stocking the database instead of pursuing the other dozen objectives that they would actually be rewarded for achieving. I know of no major corporation that measures and rewards employees' contributions to their "knowledge database."

6. The ROI Is Difficult to Prove

In a period of dramatic cutbacks in corporate discretionary spending, multimillion-dollar KM investments haven't proved their worth. Unlike customer relationship management software, in which the financial benefits of improved customer relationships can be measured through traditional financial metrics like revenue per account, KM has no tangible measures of success. "Most of the benefit of [KM] is anecdotal," says Charles Lucier, Booz Allen's chief knowledge officer. "I can't prove it, but we do better work."[8] That level of proof might not be sufficient for today's CFOs.

7. *There's Nothing for the CKO or CLO to Do*

The hiring of a chief knowledge officer (CKO) or chief learning officer (CLO) in a company provides the other corporate executives with a greater sense of job security. They now know that they won't be the first person let go in the next round of layoffs. More than 25 percent of Fortune 500 companies had CKOs at the peak of the KM craze, but less than 20 percent of them have one today. A recent *Wall Street Journal* article chronicled the profession's challenge to define its worth to corporate America.[9] An industry consultant says that "CKOs are like a vitamin pill. They make you feel good, but in a bear market the only thing that really sells is painkillers."[10] The CKO or CLO position implies that it's possible (or desirable) for an individual or department to "manage" the knowledge of others. This is the same flaw that we saw in the beginning of the quality movement, when corporate quality departments arose to preach and teach continuous quality improvement. It wasn't until leaders like Larry Bossidy of AlliedSignal (now Honeywell) and Jack Welch of GE established Six Sigma as a way of doing business, not just a department, that many firms finally saw sustainable benefits from the exact same quality tools introduced years earlier.

8. *It's Cultural*

To overcome the barriers to sharing information, a company has to modify its corporate culture to overcome the natural aversion to doing this. Carla O'Dell, president of the American Productivity and Quality Center, says that of the companies trying KM, fewer than 10 percent have succeeded in making it part of their culture.[11] Even companies with strong information-sharing systems fall into this trap.

At Ford Motor Company, the Best Practices Replication Process has delivered "billion-dollar benefits for the automaker."[12] However, this sophisticated system didn't allow Ford to spot the issues in the Firestone tires it placed on its Explorer SUVs. "Why did no one know about the [Firestone] tire problem? Two reasons. First, knowledge is best shared within communities. People with something in common talk more than strangers do. . . . Second, the more widely dispersed knowledge is, the more powerful the force required to share it."[13] Even the most sophisticated systems can't overcome the fundamental cultural behaviors in an organization.

9. It's a Fad

Not that all fads are bad, but it's important to recognize when that label rings true. KM as a concept rose and fell in lockstep with the dotcoms. It was fueled with the same excited type of "if we could just put information at people's fingertips!" naiveté. One great measure of when the KM bubble burst is the number of books published on the topic. According to the Knowledge Management Resource Center, that number fell from a high of fifty-seven in 2001 to a low of fifteen in 2002. That sound you hear is that last nail entering the KM coffin.

How Knowledge Management Can Work

Despite this dreary landscape, the potential remains to actually manage real knowledge in organizations and realize the financial benefits from doing so. What it takes to do this right however, involves more than a new Web server and a fat consulting contract. It means paying attention to how people actually acquire knowledge and how they can most effectively transfer it to others.

The definition of *knowledge* stated earlier provides the key to how organizations can improve their capability in this area. Knowledge is gained through experience or association, something no database can give you but your experienced peers, superiors, and subordinates can. True knowledge management means acknowledging that increased person-to-person contact is the only sure way to improve the shared level of knowledge in an organization.

1. *Realize Its Limitations*

Although KM may marginally improve your firm's capabilities, it is highly unlikely that it will revolutionize your business. An example of this is the promising field of data mining, in which large amounts of data are sliced and diced looking for heretofore unknown and potentially profitable correlations. As Michael Schrage of *Fortune* puts it, "Just because [you find that] single, left-handed, blond customers who drive Volvos purchase 1,450% more widgets on alternate Thursdays than their married, non-blond, right-handed, domestic car driving counterparts does not a marketing epiphany make."[14] Set realistic objectives for what you hope to achieve. Better to underpromise than to underdeliver.

2. *Hold on to Your Best*

One stated reason for developing KM is that the valuable knowledge stored in employees' heads could walk out the door tomorrow and never return. Since that's true, it seems like the most obvious solution is to retain that employee. You know which employees hold the most knowledge on key subjects. Make sure you use all the fundamental levers of employee engagement to keep them around: great developmental opportunities, a strong sense of purpose, and above-market compensation. To leverage their knowledge, set up interaction-based forums where they can share this knowledge with their peers and other interested parties. Tried and true venues, such as "lunch and learns" (or video "lunch and learns"), in which the expert presents the latest and greatest knowledge and discusses how this knowledge was gained, are likely more effective at sharing real knowledge than a search of the company's database.

3. *Use Apprenticeships*

It's difficult to argue that there is a more effective way to transfer knowledge than through an apprenticeship. You study, quietly observe, and practice your craft under the gaze of an expert until you've become skilled enough to actually do the job on your own. Although this may seem more applicable to coppersmithing than to corporations, the structure of work in most corporations provides plenty of opportunities for apprenticeship experiences. Staff junior people on projects, task forces, committees, and the other machinery of corporate life. Let them interact with the experts to gain knowledge from their more experienced colleagues and exposure to a broad range of experiences. Make them accountable to listen and learn and to participate where warranted. Provide them with clear objectives for what they're supposed to learn, give them the time to do it well, and measure whether the requisite knowledge has been acquired.

4. Anoint Experts and Set Expectations

Some people know more about certain things than others. Recognize that people like having a "go to" person, and hold your subject matter experts accountable to serving as this resource. Let everyone know who has expertise in certain areas (finally a good use for that database!), and include in the expert's performance measures the responsibility to proactively share this information. If the experts can convey their knowledge face to face, then actual knowledge, not just information, gets managed.

5. Rely on Human Interaction

You know all those company conferences and sales meetings you so efficiently moved to videoconferencing? It's time to start getting people back together, face to face, to actually share knowledge. The highly predictable answer you get from professionals evaluating nearly any conference or group get-together they have attended is that the unscheduled, interpersonal "networking" time was the most valuable. It's the interaction at venues like these that actually results in knowledge being shared.

6. *Put Accountability Where It Belongs*

Managing knowledge is a fundamental part of managing an organization, and accountability for it should rest with those in line
management. Though HR or IT may install the computer system,
line managers must be held accountable for getting quality information into the system. Line managers must also be held accountable to ensure that their team gets the experiences they need to
acquire knowledge. In Hewitt Associates' "Top 20 Companies
for Leaders" study, the use of development assignments to build
capabilities differentiated the best firms from the also-rans.[15]

7. *Sure, Have a Database*

It's easier than paper for keeping track of information that supports
knowledge. However, along with all the other conventions for storing and retrieving data, two key components must be in place for
this database to be effective. First, you must have a live, knowledgeable human being screen every piece of information that goes
into it to ensure that only the best work is accessible. While costly
and bureaucratic, there's simply no substitute for this. Second,
there must be incentives in place for sharing information. This
means that you must have a method to track who is submitting
information to the database for consideration and have a meaningful part of employees' annual incentive based on that sharing.

Is this a lot of effort? It probably is, but who ever said that
trying to extract and categorize every piece of company information into a searchable database religiously serviced by your entire
professional staff was going to be easy? Who? Oh, yeah, I guess
they did.

Conclusion

The laudatory objectives of KM should not be abandoned, despite
the significant obstacles to its success. Many other once popular
management topics have trod the well-worn path from panacea to

pariah, only to end up parked comfortably in the toolkit of management practitioners everywhere: think of reengineering or team building.

Your challenge is to cut through the consultants' hype, take a hard look at the numbers, and realize that knowledge in an organization can only be derived from people.

Marc S. Effron works with the world's leading corporations to help them build the quality and depth of their leaders. His recent efforts include developing the corporate leadership strategy for a large pharmaceutical firm, a senior team succession-management process for a global utility, the executive performance management program for a media corporation, and executive coaching for a global banking and insurance firm. He guides Hewitt Associates' research efforts on leadership, creating and now managing Hewitt's Top Companies for Leaders global research. The findings from this research were featured as the cover story of *Chief Executive* magazine's June 2002 edition. Effron coedited *HR in the 21st Century* with Marshall Goldsmith and cowrote *Building Great Leaders*. He speaks to business groups and conferences throughout the world and has recently been quoted in the *New York Times*, the *Asian Wall Street Journal*, the *Europe Wall Street Journal*, and *HR Executive*. Contact: marceffron@hewitt.com

Part Two

Processes That Work

Chapter Six

The Real Work of
Knowledge Management

Margaret J. Wheatley

We really do live in the Information Age, a revolutionary era when the availability of information is changing everything. Nothing is the same since the world was networked together and information became instantly accessible. Information has destroyed boundaries, borders, boxes, distance, roles, and rules. The availability of information has dissolved the walls of repressive governments and secretive executives, and it is creating the greatest mass empowerment of all time. Because of access to information, we are in new relationships with everyone: with medical doctors (we go to the Web and learn more than they do), with car salesmen (we know the real sticker price), and with leaders of all kinds (we know when they walk their talk). The World Wide Web has created an environment that is transparent, volatile, sensitive to the least disturbance, and choked with rumors, misinformation, truths, and passions.

This Webbed world has changed the way we work and live. "24/7" is one consequence of instant access and the dissolution of boundaries. We no longer have clear lines between work and private life—if the cell phone is on and there's a phone jack available, bosses and colleagues expect us to be available. Increasingly, it's impossible to "turn off," to find time to think, to take time to develop relationships, to even ask colleagues how they're doing.

Information has changed capitalism and the fundamental character of corporate life. Corporations now play in the global casino—focused on numbers from moment to moment, suffering instant losses or gains in trading, merging to look powerful, down-sizing to look lean, bluffing and spin-doctoring to stay in the game. In this casino environment, the long term has disappeared, thinking for the future is impossible, and developing an organization that will still be around in twenty years seems like a sentimental and wasteful notion.

These are only a few of the profound changes created by the Information Age. A September 2000 study by a futures group from the U.S. military summed it up this way: "The accelerated pace and grand breadth of information exchange is arguably beyond comprehension and certainly out of control. With so much information to choose from, each day it becomes harder to determine what is real, right, and relevant to people's' lives."[1]

Knowledge Management As a Survival Skill

In this time of profound chaos and newness, we still have to do our work. But what is our work? For those in human resources information management, there is relentless pressure to find ways for technology and people to support organizations through this tumultuous time. Organizations need to be incredibly smart, fast, agile, and responsive. They need to respond and make smart decisions at ever-increasing speed, even as the unintended consequences of speedy decisions flare up in a nanosecond and keep leaders focused only on firefighting. The old days of "continuous improvement" seem as leisurely as a picnic from the past. In this chaotic and complex twenty-first century, the pace of evolution has entered warp speed, and those who can't learn, adapt, and change from moment to moment simply won't survive.

Many of these organizational needs are bundled together today under the banner of "knowledge management." The organization that knows how to convert information into knowledge, that knows what it knows, that can act with greater intelligence and discernment—this is the organization that will make it into the future. We all know this: our organizations need to be smarter.

Knowledge management (KM) therefore should be something eagerly embraced by leaders; it should be an incredibly easy sell. Yet KM appears at a time when all organizations are battered and bruised by so much change, entering the Information Age after decades of fads, by investments in too many organizational change efforts that failed to deliver what was promised. These experiences have exhausted us all, made many cynical, and left others of us worried that we'll never learn how to create organizations that can thrive in this century.

Unlike past organizational change efforts, knowledge management is truly a survival issue. Done right, it can give us what we so desperately need—organizations that act with intelligence. Done wrong, we will, like lemmings, keep rushing into the future without using our intelligence to develop longer-term individual and organizational capacity. To continue blindly down our current path, where speed and profits are the primary values, where there is no time to think or relate, is suicidal.

Beliefs That Make KM Impossible

How can we ensure that KM doesn't fail or get swept aside as just the most recent fad? How can we treasure it for the lifesaving process it truly could be? For knowledge management to succeed, we will need to lay aside the following dangerously out-of-date beliefs:

- *Organizations are machines.* This belief becomes visible every time we create separate parts—tasks, roles, functions—and engineer (and reengineer) them to achieve predetermined performance levels. It is the manager's role to manage the parts to achieve those outcomes. Strangely, we also act as though people are machines. We attempt to "reprogram" people with new training and technology, hoping that, like good robots, they will go off and do exactly what they're told. When people resist being treated as dumb machines, we criticize them as "resistant to change."

- *Only material things are real.* A great deal of our efforts focus on trying to make invisible "things" (like knowledge, commitment, trust, and relationships) assume material form. We believe we have accomplished this when we assign numbers to them. (This belief combines with the next one.)

- *Only numbers are real.* (This belief is ancient, dating back to the sixth century B.C.) Once we assign a number to something (a grade in school; a performance index; a statistic), we relax and feel we have adequately described what's going on. (These two beliefs reinforce the next.)

- *You can only manage what you can measure.* We use numbers to manage everything: ROI, P-E ratios, inventory returns, employee morale, staff turnover. If we can't assign a number to it, we don't pay it any attention. To keep track of increasingly complex measurements, we turn to our favorite new deity, which is the next belief.

- *Technology is always the best solution.* We have increasing numbers of problems, which we try to solve using technology. However, this reliance on technology actually only increases our problems. We don't notice that the numeric information we enter in a computer cannot possibly describe the complexity of the experience or person we are trying to manage. By choosing computers (and numbers) as our primary management tool, we set ourselves up for guaranteed and repeated failures.

All of these beliefs show up strongly in knowledge management. We're trying to manage something—knowledge—that is inherently invisible, incapable of being quantified, and borne in relationships, not statistics. In addition, we are relying on technology to solve our problems with KM—we focus on constructing the right database and the most efficient storage and retrieval system and assume we have KM solved.

The Japanese approach KM differently than we do in the West. The differences in approaches expose these Western beliefs with great clarity. In the West, we have focused on explicit knowledge—knowledge one can see and document—instead of dealing with the much more important but intangible realm of "tacit" knowledge, knowledge that is present but observable only in the doing, not as a number. American and European efforts have been focused on developing measures for and assigning values to knowledge. Once we had the numbers, we assumed we could manage it, even though more and more people now acknowledge that "knowledge management" is an oxymoron.

Current approaches to KM in the West demonstrate that we believe that knowledge is a thing, a material substance that can be produced, measured, catalogued, warehoused, traded, and shipped. The language of KM is littered with this "thing" thinking. We want to "capture" knowledge, to inventory it, to push it into or pull it out from people. I don't know how this imagery affects you, but I personally don't want to have my head opened, my cork popped, my entire body tilted sideways so that what I know pours out of me into an organizational vat. This prospect is not what motivates me to notice what I know or to share it.

These language choices have serious implications. They reveal that we think knowledge is an entity, something that exists independent of person or context, capable of being moved about and manipulated for organizational advantage. We need to abandon this language and, more important, the beliefs that engender it. We need to look at knowledge—its creation, transfer, and very nature—with new eyes. As we rethink what we know about knowledge and how we handle the challenges of knowledge in organizations, our most important work is to pay serious attention to what we always want to ignore: the *human dimension*.

Think for a moment about what you know about knowledge, not from a theoretical or organizational perspective but from your own experience. In myself, I notice that knowledge is something I create because I am *in relationship*—relating to another person, an event, or an idea. Something pulls me outside of myself and forces me to react. As I figure out what's going on or what something means, I develop interpretations that make sense to me. Knowledge is something I create inside myself through my engagement with the world. Knowledge never exists independent of this process of my being in relationship with an event, an idea, or another person. This process is true for all of us: knowledge is created in relationship; it is inside thinking, reflecting human beings.

From biology, it is evident that we are not the only life form that engages in knowledge creation. Everything alive learns and creates knowledge for its survival. All living beings pay exquisite attention to what's going on in their environment, with their neighbors, offspring, predators, and even the weather. They notice something and then decide whether they need to adapt and change. Living beings never engage in this process of noticing, reacting, and changing because some boss tells them to do it. Every form of life is free to decide what to pay attention to and how to respond. This freedom lies at the heart of life, each species deciding how it will respond to its neighbors and current conditions and then living or dying as a result of its decisions.

This same autonomy describes us humans, but we tend to find it problematic, if we're the boss. We give staff detailed directions and policies on how to do something, and then they, like all life, use their autonomy to change it in some way. They fine-tune it; they adapt it to their unique context; they add their own improvements to how the task gets done. If we're the one in charge however, we don't see this behavior as creativity. We label it as resistance or disobedience. But what we are seeing is *new knowledge*. People have looked at the directive, figured out what would work better in the present context, and created a new way of doing it, one that in most cases stands a greater chance of success.

I experienced just such evidence of this knowledge creation process a few months ago as I sat on an airport commuter bus and listened as the driver trained a newly hired employee. For thirty minutes, I eavesdropped as she energetically revealed the secrets and efficiencies she had discovered for how to get to the airport in spite of severe traffic or bad weather. She wasn't describing company policy. She was giving an uninterrupted, virtuoso demonstration of what she had invented and changed in order to get her customers to their destination. I'm sure her supervisor had no idea of any of this new knowledge she'd been creating on each bus ride.

Yet this bus driver is typical. People develop better ways of doing their work all the time, and we also like to brag about it. In survey after survey, workers report that most of what they learn about their job they learn from informal conversations. They also report that they *frequently* have ideas for improving work but don't tell their bosses because they don't believe their bosses care.

Principles That Facilitate KM

Knowledge creation is natural to life, and wanting to share what we know is humanly satisfying. So what's the problem? In organizations, what sends these behaviors underground? Why do workers go dumb? Why do we fail to manage knowledge? Here are a few principles that I believe lead to answers to these questions.

Knowledge is created by human beings. If we want to succeed with KM, we must stop thinking of people as machines. Instead, we must attend to human needs and dynamics. Perhaps if we renamed it "human knowledge," we would remind ourselves of what it is and where it comes from. We would refocus our attention on the organizational conditions that support people, that foster relationships, that give people time to think and reflect. We would stop fussing with the hardware; we would cease trying to find more efficient means to "decant" us. We would notice that when we speak of such things as "assets" or "intellectual capital," it is not knowledge that is the asset or capital. People are.

It is natural for people to create and share knowledge. We have forgotten many important truths about human motivation. Study after study confirms that people are motivated by work that provides growth, recognition, meaning, and good relationships. We want our lives to mean something; we want to contribute to others; we want to learn; we want to be together. And we need to be involved in decisions that affect us. If we believed these studies and created organizations that embodied them, work would be far more productive and enjoyable. We would discover that people can be filled with positive energy. Our organization would be overwhelmed by new knowledge, innovative solutions, and great teamwork. It is essential that we begin to realize that human nature is the blessing, not the problem. As a species, we are actually very good to work with.

Everybody is a knowledge worker. This statement was an operating principle of one of my clients. If everybody is assumed to be creating knowledge, then the organization takes responsibility for supporting all its workers, not just a special few. It makes certain that everyone has easy access to anyone, anywhere in the organization, because you never know who has already invented the solution you need. The Japanese learned this and demonstrated it in their approach to KM. I learned it on that bus ride.

People choose to share their knowledge. This is an extremely important statement, and the operative word is *choose*. Most KM programs get stuck because individuals will not share their knowledge. But it's important to remember that people are making a choice not to share what they know. They *willingly share* if they feel committed to the organization, believe their leaders are worth supporting, feel encouraged to participate and learn, and value their colleagues. Knowledge sharing is going on all the time in most organizations. Every organization is filled with self-organized communities of practice, networks that people spontaneously create among colleagues to help them work more effectively or to help them survive current turbulence. These communities of practice are evidence of people's willingness to learn and to share what they know. But the organization must provide the right conditions to support people's willingness. The following are some of these necessary, nonnegotiable conditions:

- People must understand and value the objective or strategy.
- People must understand how their work adds value to the common objective.

- People must feel respected and trusted.
- People must know and care about their colleagues.
- People must value and trust their leaders.

If we compare this list to the reality in most organizations, it becomes clear how much work is needed to create the conditions for effective KM. The work of KM would be much easier if the necessity of these conditions weren't true, but that has been proved repeatedly in case studies and research. If we don't vigorously undertake creating these conditions as the real work of KM, we might as well stop wasting everyone's time and money and just abandon KM right now.

Knowledge management is not about technology. This would seem obvious from the preceding statements, but it feels important to stress because we modern managers are dazzled by technical solutions. If people aren't communicating, we just create another Web site or online conference; if we want to harvest what people know, we just create an inventoried database; if we're geographically dispersed, we just put videocams on people's desks. But these technical solutions don't solve a thing if other aspects of the culture—the human dimension—are ignored. A few years ago, British Petroleum successfully used desktop videocams to facilitate knowledge sharing among its offshore oil drilling rigs. But this wasn't *all* the company did. It also worked simultaneously to create a culture that recognized individual contribution and moved aggressively to create a bold new vision that employees could rally behind (BP came to be known as "Beyond Petroleum").

Many other organizations have learned from experience that if they want productive teams, they must bring people together in the same space several times a year. They're learning that in the absence of face-to-face meetings, people have a hard time sharing knowledge. It's important to remember that technology does not connect us. Our *relationships* connect us, and once we know the person or team, we eagerly use the technology to stay connected. We share knowledge because we are in relationship, not because we have broader band width available.

Knowledge is born in chaotic processes that take time. The irony of this principle is that it demands two things we don't have: a tolerance for messy, nonlinear processes and time. But creativity is available only when we become confused and overwhelmed, when we get so frustrated that we admit we don't know. And then, miraculously, a perfect insight suddenly appears. This is how great scientists achieve breakthrough discoveries and how teams and individuals discover transforming solutions. Great insights never appear at the end of a series of incremental steps. Nor can they be commanded to appear on schedule, no matter how desperately we need them. They present themselves only after a lot of work that culminates in so much frustration that we surrender. Only then are we humble enough and tired enough to open ourselves to entirely new solutions. They leap into view suddenly, always born in messy processes that take time.

Some companies have created architectural spaces to encourage informal conversations, mental spaces to encourage reflection, and learning spaces to encourage journal writing and other reflective thought processes. These companies are trying hard to reclaim time to think in the face of prevailing tendencies for instant answers and breathless decision making. They don't always succeed—warp speed continues its demands, and people have less time to use their journals or sit in conversation-friendly architecture.

We have to face the difficult fact that until we claim time for reflection, until we make space for thinking, we won't be able to generate knowledge or to know what knowledge we already possess. We can't argue with the demands of knowledge creation: it requires time to develop. It matures inside human relationships, which are always messy and inherently uncontrollable.

Conclusion

Although we live in a world completely revolutionized by information, it is important to remember that it is *knowledge* we are seeking, not information. Unlike information, knowledge involves us and our deeper motivations and dynamics as human beings. We interact with something or someone in our environment and then use who we are—our history, our identity, our values, habits, and beliefs—to decide what the information means. In this way, through our construction, information becomes knowledge. Knowledge is a reflection of who we are. It is impossible to disassociate the person who is creating the knowledge from the knowledge itself.

It would be good to remember this as we proceed with knowledge management. We can put down the decanting tools, we can stop focusing all our energy on database designs, and we can get on with the real work. We must recognize that knowledge is everywhere in the organization, but we won't have access to it until, and only when, we create work that is meaningful, leaders that are trustworthy, and organizations that foster everyone's contribution and support by giving staff time to think and reflect together.

This is the real work of knowledge management. It requires clarity and courage—and in stepping into it, you will be contributing to the creation of a far more intelligent and hopeful future than the one presently looming on the horizon.[2]

Margaret J. Wheatley writes, teaches, and speaks about radically new practices and ideas for organizing in chaotic times. She works to create organizations of all types in which people are known as the blessing, not the problem. She is president of the Berkana Institute, a charitable global foundation serving life-affirming leaders around the world, and she has been an organizational consultant as well as a professor of management in two graduate programs. Her latest book is *Turning to One Another: Simple Conversations to Restore Hope to the Future*. Wheatley's work also appears in two award-winning books, *Leadership and the New Science* and *A Simpler Way* (written with Myron Kellner-Rogers), and in several videos and articles. She draws many of her ideas from new science and life's ability to organize in self-organizing, systemic, and cooperative modes. Increasingly, her models for new organizations are drawn from her understanding of different cultures and spiritual traditions. Contact: info@margaretwheatley.com

Chapter Seven

Tangling with Learning Intangibles

Dave Ulrich

Norm Smallwood

Jordan Pettinger, senior vice president for human resources of a global insurance company, was frustrated. Over the past eighteen months, her company had invested hundreds of thousands of dollars in consultants and technology to improve its knowledge management capability and create a "learning organization." Jordan had spent countless hours interviewing other executives to understand what areas needed to be leveraged across the geographies. Her expectations were not even close to being fulfilled. The company, organized as a matrix by region—North America, EMEA (Europe, Middle East, and Asia), and Latin America—and by major products, continued to operate as if each region were an independent company. Knowledge sharing across regions had improved incrementally for a short period of time after the Global Learning Organizations Work! (GLOW) conference but had tapered off in the last few months. The company did not seem any further ahead, yet expectations for improvement had increased.

Jordan's frustration is not unique. In our experience, some organizations seem to have the ability to learn better than others, creating intangible value in the process. These organizations are not only able to change but also able to learn from each change experience so that cumulative progress occurs. This ability to learn has value in the marketplace. Our view of learning starts with understanding market or shareholder value. Why is a firm's stock price what it is? The easy and some would say obvious answer is that when firms make more money, their stock price goes up. Market value follows financial performance. On the surface, this makes sense, but the facts refute it. Increasingly, a firm's market value is not fully explained by financial results such as earnings. A number of studies have shown that financial results explain 50 to 70 percent of a firm's market value. The rest is explained by investors' perceptions of the firm's likelihood of achieving similar, greater, or lesser earnings in the future. This perception about future earnings is called "intangibles." Intangibles describe the capability of a company to deliver on its promises for making money in the future. Organizations that learn have more investor value because these organizations not only create new ideas but also share those ideas throughout their structure, building knowledge networks where technology and communities of practice transfer experience from one setting to another.

Three Building Blocks of a Learning Organization

In our work, we have found that the following simple equation can represent the extent to which an organization has developed its learning capability and can help leaders assess their firm's overall ability to learn:[1]

Learning capability = generate × generalize ideas with impact

Examine each element of the equation. *Generate* means creating new knowledge through discovery, invention, experimentation, or innovation. *Generalize* means moving ideas across boundaries. Some companies may seem more adept at doing new things before others, yet merely having an idea (generating) is not sufficient for learning. Learning requires that the idea transfer across a boundary, such as time, geography, or business units. *Impact* means that something substantial has changed. Learning as an intangible requires all three building blocks. True learning organizations both generate and generalize ideas and ensure that the ideas will have impact. Such learning occurs at three levels: individual, team, and organization. When each of these three learning targets employs the building blocks effectively, an organization creates intangible market value.

Fostering Individual Learning

As leaders, you have probably noticed that some individuals are predisposed to learning. By nature, they are inquisitive and curious; they're always experimenting, trying new things, and seeking ways to improve. These individuals have a constant stream of fresh insights and ideas. They see alternatives and connections not readily apparent to others. These natural learners are valuable employees because they generate new ideas and offer alternatives for the future not grounded in the past.

Leaders should identify these individuals both as they come into and as they move through the organization. Natural learners see alternatives that others don't see.

Screening the applicant pool and securing natural learners may sound enticing, but bear in mind that what makes these individuals creative on the one hand may make them difficult to manage on the other. Creative people need space to experiment and try new ideas.

Three Steps: Choice, Consequence, Correction

Even people who aren't natural learners can master the tools of learning. Any organization is well advised to help them do so, as there are never enough natural learners to fill all the available jobs.

Natural and trained learners go through a learning cycle that has three steps: choice, consequence, and correction, as shown in Figure 7.1.

Figure 7.1 The Individual Learning Cycle

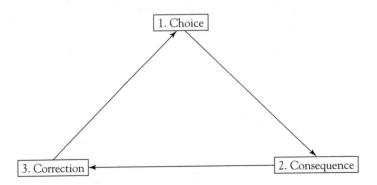

Step 1: Choice

Learners seek alternatives. They see what might be, not what has been or has to be. They brainstorm multiple ways of approaching and defining problems. Learners increase their ability to make choices in the following ways:

- *Comparing.* Learners see what others do and adopt mentors who offer formal and informal counsel about their experiences. They encourage staff to ask for advice from those who have relevant experience.

- *Experimenting.* Learners take risks by testing new ways to do things, even when the old ways are still working. They do this by setting up small experiments during which they do something one way and see the impact and by assigning staff members to projects that are not within their comfort zone.

- *Risking looking stupid.* Learners accept that they probably won't get everything right the first time. When learners make a mistake, they take it in stride, figure out why it happened, adapt, and try to not make the same mistake twice. They don't blame; they reflect.

- *Volunteering for tough assignments and projects.* Learners increase choices by taking on assignments that stretch their thinking and approaches.

- *Asking*. Learners moderate fear of failure and generate new ideas by thinking through "what if" questions, such as these:

    What if I don't succeed? What is the worst possible thing that can happen? Am I okay with that?

    What if I don't try something new? How will I feel about myself in the future?

    What if I try to do this project another way? How would someone else approach this project? What insights can I gather from seeing this project through someone else's eyes?

Individual learners create choices and seek alternatives. They exercise *agency*—a term psychologists use for acting on one's own behalf—and recognize that choices always exist. They seek novel and unusual ways to solve problems.

Step 2: Consequence

Every choice has a consequence: sometimes good, sometimes not so good. Natural learners instinctively connect choice and consequence. They see both the positive and negative impacts of their choices. They constantly play the "if X then Y" game: if I make this decision, then such and such is likely to happen. In the "if X then Y" game, they can see future consequences of present decisions. They envision a future and fold it into the present.

Often employees fail to learn when they cannot connect choices to consequences. Employees who won't work on tough projects, who won't take difficult assignments, who don't work well on teams, or who do the minimum to get by are surprised when they don't have opportunities for promotion or long-term success. These employees have not connected choice and consequence; they are not able to envision a future and fold it into the present.

Step 3: Correction

Learners adjust and adapt to the choices and consequences they experience. They constantly need to take corrective action to inform the next cycle of choices. Effective learners are *feedback junkies*—they always want to know how their work is viewed by others and the effect it has on others. They ask what worked and what didn't so that they can adapt and improve their work. Sometimes they seek formal feedback on their general behavior (as with a 360-degree survey). At other times they seek informal feedback by watching how others react to their work. They do not make the same mistake over and over. Rather than being satisfied with the status quo, they always want to improve and make things better.

Strategies and Recommendations to Promote Organizational Learning

The strategies that follow will assist leaders, teams, and individuals in developing learning organizations. In such organizations, learning is an integral part of the overall business strategy, and this exploration of new possibilities, strategies, and opportunities is paramount to their success.

Create Opportunities Where Individuals Can Generalize Ideas with Impact

Sometimes the most creative people don't have the impact that they should or would like to have. Some creative people who generate new ideas fail to generalize the ideas they create. Their personal creativity does not lead to sustained innovation. They do not see patterns, connections, or integrated solutions. They are not able to generalize their knowledge beyond isolated experiments or applications. Leaders want to harness individual creativity by ensuring that the most creative people deliver on their ideas. When those who generate also generalize their ideas, they turn energy, action, and creativity into sustained innovation and results.

Create Team Learning Opportunities

Increasingly, companies perform work through task forces, projects, groups, account teams, and the like. Teams as collectives of individuals may be scored on their ability to generate and generalize ideas with impact. High-performing teams begin their learning journey by generating new ideas, which come both from the composition of the team and from the way the team operates.

Build Teams That Generate Ideas with Impact

Teams generate ideas by having diverse members on the team, by brainstorming alternatives before reaching a conclusion, by setting stretch goals that demand new ways of doing work, by doing risk assessment to examine probabilities between actions and outcomes, by orienting new members rigorously to norms and listening to new members for new ideas, by using time well to ensure that progress is made, by allocating rewards based on team performance, and by managing their group process to promote smooth teamwork.

Create Opportunities Where Teams Can Generalize Ideas with Impact

High-performing teams not only generate new ideas but also generalize those ideas by rigorously improving their team process. Team process checks enable teams to audit and improve how well they are working. Four processes are critical for team effectiveness: defining purpose, making decisions, managing relationships, and learning. Some audit questions might include the following:

> How clear are we as a team about our purpose and direction?
>
> How effectively do we make decisions as a team?
>
> Do we make decisions too fast? Too slow?
>
> How are our interpersonal relationships?
>
> How effective are we at capturing important learning that has occurred?

Develop the Capacity for Organization Learning

Organizations as entities also have the capacity to learn. By so doing, routines or patterns become adopted and shared throughout an organization.

Build Organizations That Generate Ideas with Impact

Our research on learning organizations identified four learning styles that represent ways in which organizations generate ideas with impact: experimentation, competency acquisition, benchmarking, and continuous improvement.

Learning Style 1: Experimentation. Some organizations learn by trying many new ideas and by being receptive to experimentation with new products and processes. The primary sources of learning are direct experiences from customers and employees. They aim to achieve organizational learning through controlled experimentation, from both inside and outside, rather than through exploiting the experience of others. Sony, 3M, Hewlett-Packard, and Unilever are companies known for their experimentation strategies.

Learning Style 2: Competency Acquisition. Some organizations learn by encouraging individuals and teams to acquire new competencies. Learning is a critical aspect of business strategy and focuses on both the experience of others and the exploration of new possibilities. By investing resources in training and development, these organizations provide cutting-edge materials and concepts to their members through consultants, line managers, and faculty. The intention is to help organization members acquire relevant knowledge that may accelerate their subsequent assimilation of new knowledge and stimulate them to develop innovative products and processes. Motorola and General Electric are well known for their competency acquisition strategies.

Learning Style 3: Benchmarking. Other organizations learn by scanning how others operate and then trying to adopt and adapt this knowledge for their own organizations. Learning comes from organizations that have demonstrated excellent performance or developed the best practices in specific processes. Benchmarking companies learn primarily from the experience of others and exploit successful technologies and practices that already exist. Samsung Electronics, Xerox, and Milliken all emphasize benchmarking.

Learning Style 4: Continuous Improvement. Still other organizations learn by constantly improving on what has been done before and mastering each step before moving on to new steps through a disciplined process like Six Sigma. They often emphasize employee involvement groups, such as quality control circles or problem-solving groups, which are organized to resolve issues identified by internal and external customers. These are organizations that rely on learning through both direct experience and the exploitation of existing practices. Toyota, Honeywell, and Honda are continuous improvement companies.

Create Opportunities Where Organizations Can Generalize Ideas with Impact

Many more organizations generate ideas than generalize them, and yet from the learning capability perspective, it's not enough to be awash in new ideas. For example, too many companies have succeeded in creating pockets of excellence and then failed to transfer the achievement across boundaries to the rest of the firm. They never established best-practice forums to codify and disseminate lessons from one site to another. For generalization of ideas, implementation of what has been learned is essential.

Leaders build learning capability, therefore, not just by generating ideas but by sharing them within—and even beyond—the organization. The primary leadership task in generalizing ideas is to create an infrastructure that moves ideas across boundaries. While chief learning officer and vice president of management development of General Electric, Steve Kerr created a learning matrix that identified the source of good ideas for sharing across geographical, functional, or business boundaries and proposed a disciplined process for moving ideas across units (see Exhibit 7.1).

As your first step, identify an important initiative that is in the process of being rolled out and that the company is committed to doing well, such as service, quality (Six Sigma), customer focus, cycle time, or training. Let's call this initiative "X." Substitute this initiative for X in the proposition in step 1 of the Learning Matrix: "To be world class at X."

Exhibit 7.1 Learning Matrix

Step 1: Proposition: To be world class at X.												
		Step 2: Critical Success Factors for X: To be world class at X, we must . . .										
		a	b	c	d	e	f	g	h	i	j	k
Step 3: Locations Where Work Is Done	1											
	2											
	3											
	4											
	5											
	6											
	7											
	8											
	...											

Step 4: In each cell, score 1 (low) to 5 (high). Mark 0 if not applicable.
Step 5: Repeat for each part of the business.
Step 6: Build a plan for how to move best practices across the entire business.
Step 7: Generalize the learning capability across the organization.

Source: Adapted from a form used at General Electric Company. Used with permission.

Next, identify critical success factors for X. Complete the statement "To be world class at X, we must . . ." The outcome of this step should be the identification of eight to ten critical factors for this corporate initiative to succeed. Arriving at this outcome might involve a small research team, a task force, or another group that defines these critical success factors. Put these critical success factors in the columns labeled a. . . through j.

Next, answer the question, "In what locations are these critical success factors demonstrated?" The units are generally discrete work settings (plants, divisions, business units, or regions) where work is performed. Put these locations in the rows labeled 1. . . through 8, adding rows as necessary.

On a scale of 0 to 5, score each cell of the matrix: 0 = not applicable; 1 = we have no skills at all; 2 = we have some skills; 3 = we're average; 4 = we think we are good; 5 = others think we are good ("world class"). Either an organizational unit leader or a rating team external to the organization should do this assessment of the unit (such as a corporate group who inspects the unit or an outside rating agency). Members of the unit can provide scores of 0 to 4, but a score of 5 must come from someone outside the unit. (Scoring in this step will help a leader diagnose the extent to which the unit exhibits the specific actions required by the overarching initiative.)

The unit leader should complete the scoring of the matrix. This completed companywide matrix can help pinpoint pockets of excellence (scores of 5 in a cell) and provides an overall corporate score on any initiative. The overall score may provide feedback for a corporate person assigned to pursue initiative X. The matrix itself indicates the baseline for how ideas are generalized across these different units.

The leader can now proceed to steps 5, 6, and 7. These steps are to repeat the scoring for each part of the business, to build a plan on how to move best practices throughout the business, and to generalize the learning capabilities throughout the organization.

One beauty of Kerr's Learning Matrix is that it simply and elegantly shows where pockets of excellence exist, and it suggests how to move ideas from one unit in the firm to other units. The Learning Matrix offers a simple methodology for generating and generalizing ideas with impact within an organization. Leaders who use methods like this ensure that good ideas are not hidden within a unit but are quickly and rapidly disseminated across units.

Leadership Implications

Jordan Pettinger, the senior vice president of human resources mentioned at the beginning of this chapter, could make practical use of these ideas. She found that her leaders could build learning into their organizations by generating and generalizing ideas with impact for individuals, teams, and organizations. In addition, she found other actions that helped her to build learning into her organization:

1. Bring natural learners into the organization, and encourage all employees to learn through the choice-consequence-correction cycle.

2. Encourage employees to look for patterns and to transfer knowledge from one setting to another.

3. Provide forums (meetings, training, and the like) where people have the authority and the opportunity to reflect on better ways to do their jobs.

4. Help teams become more creative and insightful by bringing new people onto teams and by operating teams in a way that encourages debate and dialogue.

5. Allow teams to generalize learning through team audits on purpose, decision making, relationships, and learning.

6. Encourage units to create new ways of doing work through experimentation, competency acquisition, continuous learning, and benchmarking. Make sure that all of these receive at least

some attention and also that experimentation and competency acquisition are not overshadowed by the more cautious approaches.

7. Share knowledge and ideas across organization boundaries by building the right culture and a disciplined learning process.

8. Frequently audit for internal best practices in relevant areas, and find ways to export these best practices to other parts of the firm.

9. Use your intranet to create chat rooms and e-mail lists focusing on important issues, making it easy to discuss important ideas across geographical boundaries.

Dave Ulrich is president of the Canada Montreal Mission for the Church of Jesus Christ of Latter-Day Saints while on a three-year sabbatical from his position as professor of business administration at the University of Michigan. Professionally, he has studied how organizations change fast, build capabilities, learn, remove boundaries, and leverage human resource activities. He has helped generate multiple award-winning national databases on organizations that assess alignment between strategies, HR practices, and HR competencies. A prolific author, Ulrich's books include *Organizational Capability: Competing from the Inside Out* (written with Dale Lake), *The Boundaryless Organization: Breaking the Chains of Organization Structure* (with Ron Ashkenas, Steve Kerr, and Todd Jick), and *Human Resource Champions: The Next Agenda for Adding Value and Delivering Results*. He was editor of the *Human Resource Management Journal*, is a fellow in the National Academy of Human Resources; and is cofounder of the Michigan Human Resource Partnership. In 2002, *Business Week* ranked Dave the number one management educator in America. Contact: dou@umich.edu; http://www.rbl.net

Norm Smallwood is cofounder of Results-Based Leadership, Inc., which provides education and consulting services that increase leaders' capability to deliver business results consistent with organizational values. He was managing director and cofounder of Novations Group, Inc., a strategic change management and career development-consulting firm. He also worked with Procter & Gamble and Esso Resources Canada Ltd. (Exxon/Imperial Oil). At P&G, he participated in the start-up of a successful manufacturing plant in Georgia. While at Esso, he worked in research and development and then in exploration as an organization effectiveness consultant. He is coauthor of *Results-Based Leadership*, named book of the year by the Society for Human Resources Management, and of *Real Time Strategy*. His most recent book, written with Dave Ulrich, is *Why the Bottom Line Isn't: How to Build Value Through People and Organizations*. Contact: nsmallwood@rbl.net; http://www.rbl.net

Chapter Eight

When Transferring Trapped Corporate Knowledge to Suppliers Is a Winning Strategy

Larraine Segil

When should we outsource and transfer knowledge to suppliers? The answer has been the same for decades: when the knowledge or expertise required is not core to our mission and activities in providing value to our customers and shareholders.

The answer changes when knowledge management and valuation is the issue. Let's rephrase the question: When can knowledge and expertise be provided to us by our suppliers, in a superior, turnkey fashion, so that we become more competent and serve our customers better? This happens when the trapped value of our knowledge is realized and we are better served with more competent expertise than we had in-house.

The rephrasing of the question requires a different mind-set from both the outsourcing provider and the buyer. A regular supply relationship that is managed by the purchasing department will not deliver the knowledge and competency desired in the second scenario. However, if that supply or outsourcing relationship were managed as an alliance, it would generate far more value. What does this mean? Managing a supply relationship like an alliance requires the following (see Exhibit 8.1):

A supply alliance that looks costly in the first stages of development may create great returns in the last stage of development. However, if the relationship is seen purely as a supply relationship

Exhibit 8.1 Managing a Supply Relationship like an Alliance

Supply Relationship Management	Alliance Relationship Management
Pressure on price	Pressure on deliverables
Compatibility is no issue—just supply products and services at high quality, low cost	Compatibility is an issue—integrated working conditions over time require understanding of style, life cycle stage of company, personalities, goals, and market factors
Other suppliers stand ready to supplant the contracted supplier if it does not	Other providers have been screened and this supplier was chosen as the best partner; certain compromises will be made to deliver value
Mutuality is not a big issue—supplier is presumed to make some margin, and it's the suppliers problem if it doesn't	Mutuality is a big issue since both parties should be cognizant of each other's success potential
Multiple parties in the supplier mix are the responsibility of the buyer	Multiple parties in the alliance, or with whom the alliance partners are partnered, become the responsibility and concern of all parties in order to gain the most from the alliance

with its accompanying price haggling, there is little chance of its maturing into a life stage in which the maximum financial benefit is realized for all concerned. The knowledge transferred back into the organization will be limited in the early stages. The outsourcing supplier may indeed have evolving and increasing levels of competency that will be tailored to the customer's need over time. The longer the relationship is, the higher the return on the supplier's investment will be. This is because the supplier can amortize its costs of ramping up for the relationship. Furthermore, the longer the relationship, the higher the potential of knowledge transfer to the customer, if managed properly.

Managing the "Returning" Knowledge

Managing the "returning" knowledge properly is the customer's responsibility. For example, are these expectations of increased knowledge from the supplier to the customer made known to the supplier up front? Are resources, both human and capital, in place to ensure that the knowledge transfer is not one way, from customer to supplier, but also that improved knowledge will be taught to the customer? After all, the supplier is facing its customer and knows its market demands and challenges, and the supplier's products and services will improve and continue to be competitive if there is a symbiotic relationship.

A good example of this symbiosis is Flextronics. Although its revenue has diminished from its high growth increases of the past decade due to recent economic slowdowns, its market share continues to increase as it moves into becoming the outsourcing supplier for design and logistics management. Flextronics epitomizes the outsourcing supplier knowledge transfer competency. As the outsourcing provider for Motorola, Casio, Ericsson, and Nokia, Flextronics seamlessly incorporates the needs of its customers. Flextronics is learning from its customers while at the same time educating them about how to integrate their services more effectively. The result is that the ultimate customers don't realize that they may be interfacing directly with a Flextronics factory or logistics system rather than the branded company (Nokia, for example).

Supply Alliances Expense Versus Return

Many supply alliances are all expense during the initial stage. Costs include hiring people to do research and investigation; putting in capital to support the infrastructure of pilots; hiring, training, and testing; and the initial launch of the program, then remediating and relaunching it as new learning is achieved. It may be some time until the highest-margin, lowest-cost results are seen, and only then can they be incorporated into the overall relationship. It may be in the mature level of the alliance life cycle that real value is generated, so if attention is not paid throughout the early cycles of development, launch, and learning, the return on that investment may be compromised.

For example, the supply relationship could be expanded to include an online component, and this may well be in the middle stage of the alliance life cycle. Looking at supply relationships as if they were alliances with life cycles that require different resources at each stage and even different teams of managers will ensure that the relationship has the chance of reaching its fullest potential.

Toys "R" Us created an online activity for the sales of its products, the development process of the fulfillment of buying and selling and shipping toys online. Yet its in-store sales and the effective way it had of buying, selling, and serving its customers continued to be its core competency. Finally, executives at Toys "R" Us realized that the online segment of the business was not working the way they wanted it to. In fact, it was diluting the company's brand value. An alliance looked like the solution to the problem. The company that fulfilled online orders better than anyone else for Toys "R" Us was Amazon.com. Toys executives began discussing and planning the integration of facilities and the two brands on Amazon's virtual real estate. They piloted the program before rolling it out in full.

This online alliance has been highly successful, and it is an example of understanding the various stages of the alliance. As the Toys "R" Us and Amazon alliance grows and begins to reach its potential, the alliance is changing, and the market is becoming more comfortable with the joint marketing, supply, and outsourcing relationship of the two organizations. Making it transparent was the goal, and it is working. Now Amazon not only markets and sells the goods but also shares revenues as well as payment for the turnkey operation of the fulfillment process. It has been so successful that Amazon is now repeating the approach and is moving into the apparel business.

Supply Chain Management as a Strategic Alliance

Supply chain management is rarely thought of as a strategic alliance. Yet the characteristics of an alliance will generate more integrated relationships, which could leverage benefits for all concerned.

Consider the integration of Procter & Gamble (P&G) with its major customer, Wal-Mart. In this classic supplier-customer integration example, Wal-Mart gave P&G access to its supplier management processes and asked for help. P&G spent huge resources and time analyzing and designing a supplier management system that integrates customer purchases and store inventory management to the manufacturing, ordering, and shipping processes of P&G. In this way, P&G created a nearly seamless system that allows integration between two separate entities. This has worked so well that Wal-Mart asked P&G to help it integrate this as a supply chain management system for other suppliers. Wal-Mart is now known to have one of the most intimate and detailed supplier management systems, which leaves little room for inefficiency and contributes to its cost savings and overall customer promise.

Another example of supplier-customer integration is that of Starbucks and its integrated relationships with its partners Safeway and Albertsons. Contrast the DaimlerChrysler relationship, with its tier-one suppliers, with the Chrysler *keiretsu* of the past. Were Chrysler costs lower before, when it opened its *kimono* to its suppliers and said, "Work with us to save us all money," or is it better off now that it is driving cost savings into the structures of its suppliers? Certainly, tier ones are pushing the cost issues to tier-two suppliers. Yet the reality is that tier-three suppliers are going out of business.

Managing these complex relationships like alliances would have created a collaboration that would have transmuted the systems of supplier concerns and margin issues to the more collaborative discussions of customer constraints and investment issues.

Seeing the supplier relationship as an alliance positions the parties as coventurers, joint investors of both human and knowledge capital for value. Together the possibility would exist for mutual benefit, rather than an unbalanced, untrusting, and competitive relationship. Managing a supplier relationship as if it were collaboration rather than a bid gives way to outsourcing and quality enhancement, rather than suppliers who resentfully cut corners trying to squeeze profit out of a reluctant customer. It can be done. It requires a strategy, a commitment from senior management, transparency of costs and margins, and longer-term contracts.

Supplier Alliances

For example, Kansas City, Missouri–based Butler Manufacturing Company delivers its construction services for multiple-site customers on a collaborative supplier basis. (Customers include Toys "R" Us, Wal-Mart, FedEx Ground, and many other retailers, manufacturers, and distributors.) These alliances work for Butler and for its customers. Butler looks at the entire enterprise, the whole construction project or program, and the customer's needs from building concept to move-in and start-up. It shares information and value all along the value chain, and everyone benefits. This hundred-year-old market leader has the most loyal customers, who return again and again to their partner, Butler Manufacturing, to help them roll out huge chains of stores and warehouses. This process has been proved to deliver unmistakable benefits over the alternative of consistently relying on the lowest-cost material supplier. Managing a supply relationship like an alliance can leverage benefits that in traditional supply relationships seem unimaginable.

Outsourcing

Outsourcing is a trend that is increasing annually into more complicated and intricate relationships that carry huge benefits both for the suppliers of the services and products and the buyers of them.

For example, IBM is determined to make "on-demand" computing the future of the hardware, software, networked, and hi-fi environment. Sam Palmisano, chairman of the board and CEO of IBM, has stated publicly that the company is moving into a place where customers using its systems will have self-diagnosing, self-healing, and self-remediating software and hardware systems. He claims that many of these systems will be provided to customers by outsourcing providers who will incur the infrastructure cost. These providers will have state-of-the-art products and services, thus diminishing the problems for customers of legacy systems and future huge infrastructure capital investment. Of course, this scenario will increase the role of the professional service providers and systems integrators.

IBM has put its stake in the ground in this arena, but its position does have a different twist from Larry Ellison, CEO of Oracle, who stated a decade ago that it was the "network," not the computer.

Why does IBM now call it "on-demand" computing? The concept is that organizations will not need to invest in huge infrastructure capital expenses to acquire systems that become obsolete and transition into "legacy" systems with wasted cost in both capital and human resources. Rather, they will develop relationships with organizations, such as IBM and the systems integrators that they support, for on-demand hardware and software combined with services.

Is this far-fetched? Not really. Look at it this way: artificial intelligence, sensors, nanotechnology, and a variety of "self-learning" systems mean that the concept of software that self-diagnoses, self-heals, self-upgrades, and more is upon us. Smart software that works with outsourced infrastructure providers, who have the ongoing responsibility of being on the cutting edge of hardware and systems, is already a concept that buyers have accepted as a quality choice. When those services are partnered with the professional service providers and systems integrators who tie the back and front ends together, the scenario should end up like this; the buyer initiates the need, and the need is anticipated and answered even beyond the buyer's expectations.

This scenario may sound utopian, but IBM has spoken with a loud voice regarding its determination to be in the forefront of this movement. In addition, it has the resources and staying power to make it happen in part, if not in total. The bottom line in this scenario, however, will be treating these suppliers as treasured alliances. After all, outsourcing IT and systems services are not new ideas. The wholesale turnkey operation of the nature that IBM's on-demand concept envisages contemplates an entirely different supplier relationship. Now the alliance issues should be dealing with mutuality, not just price-related and commoditized bargaining methods managed by the purchasing department. These mutuality issues should be negotiated and managed at corporate headquarters. The chief alliance officer (CAO) level should work hand in hand with the chief supply officer (CSO) to distinguish between relationships that require alliance management and those that require supplier management. The question then becomes, what is the difference between supplier and alliance management? (See Exhibit 8.2.)

Exhibit 8.2 Supplier Versus Alliance Management

Suppliers That Are Not Tiered	Suppliers That Are Tiered into Alliances
Little information shared and low communication commitment	High level of information shared; excellent communication processes and attention
Low level of integration whether manufacturing, distribution, joint marketing, joint purchasing, or mutual design	High level of integration whether manufacturing, distribution, joint marketing, joint purchasing, or mutual design
Low level of relationship investing	High level of relationship investing
Negotiations take place at the purchasing department level, and relationship manager is not allocated or if allocated is seen primarily as a supply chain manager and price negotiator	Negotiations take place at the senior executive level, and relationship managers are not in the purchasing department but rather in the alliances group or at the division level

Hewlett-Packard (HP) has moved even further into the enterprise environment with its newly merged Compaq skills as well as the alliances (for instance, Disney) that Compaq added to the HP mix. Although HP is certainly a supplier for Disney, the management of the relationship is not at the purchasing level but rather at the CEO level. The relationship is seen, managed, and valued as a partnership or alliance, and that makes a substantial difference in the way it delivers results.

The differences between outsourcing suppliers and supplier alliances that are not outsourcing suppliers can be seen in Exhibit 8.3.

As you can see, the burden is greater on the buyer when working with multiple suppliers individually, especially if each is essential and viewed and managed as a supplier alliance. This means that there must be clear processes for success metrics, regularly measured mutuality, and analysis and quantification of competitive issues (for example, the supplier works with a competitor and transfers your information to the competitor). When dealing with

Exhibit 8.3 Outsourcing Suppliers Versus Supplier Alliances

Outsourcing Supplier Seen as an Alliance	Supplier Who Offers Partial Solutions and Products, Not Turnkey, but Still Seen as an Alliance
Contracts are long, with quality provisions built in, with highly integrated components and joint development	Contracts will continue to have integrated aspects and could be lengthy; loyalty and good pricing are bought by longer contracts and lack of multiple-bid programs
The evaluation and choice process of the outsourcing provider is risky and complicated, requiring research, learning, knowledge, and investment by both buyer and outsourcer	The evaluation and choice process is less onerous for both buyer and supplier-partner; however, the integration of multiple supplier-partners into the supply chain, since the total solution is not outsourced or turnkey, will place a heavier burden on the buyer to be sure that all solutions can integrate and that the separate suppliers can work together

turnkey outsourcing providers, the burden shifts to the buyer to ensure that the providers integrate and work together and can provide their self-healing and upgrading solutions whenever and wherever needed.

Conclusion

IBM's dream may seem far-fetched now, but ask your chief technology officer (CTO) and chief information officer (CIO) how their budgets have changed regarding infrastructure purchases and where they would rather put the burden of upgrade costs. Most will say on someone else. How can you argue with this approach? After all, that's the reason to be in business, to serve the customers and deliver shareholder value.

Of course, this hypothetical CIO, CTO, and even CEO would be one that would not be weighted down with internal silos, politics, territories, "not invented here" issues, and control phobias. Maybe that is where the issue will lie: Will the buyer really have the company, customer, and shareholder value in mind, or will the human failings, personal aggrandizements, ego issues, and control problems that occur in all environments prevent this utopian vision from being realized?

Being the kind of person who finds a room full of manure and just knows there is a pony in there somewhere, I am convinced that personal goals will yield to corporate good and shareholder return in the new era in which we find ourselves. This is a time of corporate accountability and when less is seen as preferable to more, when issues of building infrastructure and expense are the choice, rather than outsourcing the capital cost and expertise to others.[1]

Larraine Segil speaks on the management tools for alliances, leadership, and e-business. Author of *Measuring the Value of Partnering, Dynamic Leader, Adaptive Organization, FastAlliances: Power Your E-Business, Intelligent Business Alliances*, she also coedited (with James Belasco and Marshall Goldsmith) *Partnering: The New Face of Leadership*. Quoted as an expert in alliances by the Corporate Strategy Board and in the Corporate CFO Strategy Study, she has been featured as "The Real Internet Deal" by *Fast Company* magazine. Segil has been profiled in *Business Week*, *CEO*, *CIO*, *CFO*, *Bloomberg News*, and *Internet World*, and she is a regular commentator on CNN, CNBC, and Yahoo FinanceVision. The Financial Times Knowledge Dialogue Group named her its World Thought Leader on Alliances. She is a partner of Vantage Partners. Contact: lsegil@vantagepartners.com; http://www.vantagepartners.com

Chapter Nine

Informal Learning

Developing a Value for Discovery

Marcia L. Conner

It may surprise you to learn that more than 70 percent of learning experiences in the workplace are informal or accidental, through activities not structured or sponsored by an employer or a school.[1] This learning is continuous and all-encompassing, arising from everyday activities and events. Sometimes it is spontaneous; other times learners organize it as they do their work. It is not limited to a predefined body of knowledge (what is known) but instead emerges and is constructed from the spontaneity and serendipity of personal interactions. It happens whenever and wherever people do their work: around a conference table, on site with customers, at a laboratory bench, or on a shop floor.

For leaders to elicit its potential, they can allow for some learning of their own: they can discover how to encourage the vast amount of informal learning already going on so that they and their organizations can learn, and innovate and excel, even more.

Informal Learning on the Job

Work is profoundly social. As we work, we learn informally through listening to others, making mistakes, talking about what we've read and done, and paying attention to our daily activities. Informal learning generally arises at work as a means to achieve individual and organizational goals. Some informal learning develops from

explicit goals, such as becoming productive with a new software feature or brushing up on a particular forecasting method before writing a report. You set out to learn something specific and figure it out
through informal means. Other times informal learning occurs in a
broad and open-ended context: when you become familiar with different markets, observe a more seasoned colleague, or get a sense of
the culture in a company you've just joined. You probably find that
even when you are not aware that you need to learn something, you
accidentally learn along the way (see Figure 9.1).

If formal education fulfills its duty to help strengthen mental
pathways, build frameworks, create options, and widen perspectives,
informal learning can then support the day-in and day-out culture
building and skills development needed in a rapidly changing,
increasingly competitive global marketplace. Informal learning
enables us to adapt and adopt. More than what we learn through

**Figure 9.1 Formal and Informal Methods
People Use to Learn at Work**

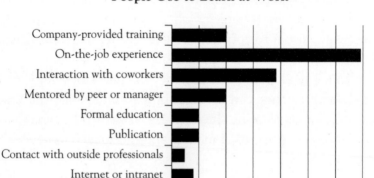

Source: CapitalWorks LLC. Used with permission.

formal means, informal learning helps us sense and respond to situations we face.

Despite such noble responsibility, informal learning receives little attention. Perhaps that's because it sounds ad hoc, inadvertent, and unmanageable. Although you cannot *schedule* informal learning, you can acknowledge, uncover, liberate, access, promote, jump-start, nurture, integrate, encourage, follow, and even celebrate it in an effort to foster a learning culture in all types and sizes of groups.

Even if informal learning is invisible, its value can be seen. In an economy fueled by sparkling innovations and distinctive information, what people learn informally can move ideas through organizations and help people generate something new.

As a leader and as a colleague, you can play an important role in nurturing informal learning with the people around you. Even though it might sound paradoxical, you can create an organizationwide discipline of informal learning without destroying the social, spontaneous, and serendipitous aspects that bring it to life by simply understanding it, paying attention to it, and valuing what it offers to everyone. Here are some steps to get you started.

Acknowledge Learning Within You

At Xerox PARC, in Palo Alto, California, former chief scientist John Seely Brown focused Friday lunch meetings with his team members on what they did well, what they did wrong, and what they learned along the way. At one meeting, some team members casually remarked that whenever they saw Brown make a certain face in response to someone's idea, it was obvious the idea didn't stand a chance. Brown had the next meeting videotaped. Sure enough, he saw for himself that he did sometimes display a disapproving expression. From then on, when that feeling washed over him, he worked at changing his facial expression and listening more attentively to what the person was saying.

Begin by asking yourself what you have learned recently and in which situations your greatest learning takes place. Did you learn more from a formal event or an impassioned conversation with colleagues? Do you learn during a walk around the block or while taking a hard look at yourself in the mirror? Challenge colleagues who tell you that you have something to learn by asking, "How can you help me learn it *now?*" Become mindful of all impromptu opportunities, and allow for moments that can become openings to learning. Express to others you see that you are learning from many sources, and show people that you are dedicated to creating a culture in which everyone learns every day.

Uncover Learning Around You

At San Diego–based WD-40 Company, people talk about what they have learned every chance they get. At a meeting of global brand managers, for example, everyone presented five or six hard lessons they had learned in the past year. People have found that when they share their learning moments—the times when they screw up and learn something as a result—everyone becomes deeply involved in one another's success and can help in unanticipated ways.[2]

Modern work relies on interaction and ingenuity, where people become *bricoleurs*, making do with whatever or whoever is at hand. Many surveys report that the typical knowledge worker spends more than 25 percent of his or her time in face-to-face encounters; for executives, this figure can reach 95 percent. When people interact, the question is not, "Is informal learning going on?" but rather "How much was learned?" and "What was learned?" Ask people what they discovered today that would enable the company to outshine its competitors tomorrow. Invite them to share what they learned since the last time you saw them and what lessons they'd like everyone to understand. Collect stories about informal learning in your organization, and post them where others might read them and add to them. Wander down hallways and listen. Get involved in impromptu conversations, whether with direct reports or with colleagues you barely know. Get a sense of where and when informal learning happens, and never pass up an opportunity to experience more.

Liberate Learning in Others

At Inland Paperboard and Packaging in Indianapolis, senior executives realized, in the middle of initiating a culture change, that they themselves were having a hard time mastering new skills. They also realized that they all learned in different and often conflicting ways. The organizational effectiveness department suggested that the company use an individual learning styles inventory to help accelerate the change effort. Assessment began with the company's CEO and his direct reports. Then, over the course of a year, all managers, from executives to frontline supervisors, learned about how they learn and how to work better with people who have different styles.

People are natural learners—asking, observing, searching, speculating, theorizing, and experimenting all the time—but many adults have little confidence in their learning abilities and feel anxious when pressured to learn more. Circulate learning-style assessments to help people understand their strengths, and ask the training department to offer follow-up discussions on learning techniques. Practice storytelling, and share what you discover. Publicize available "how to" materials, and make them easy to understand. Consider asking the research group to publish search tips and asking librarians to help people find what they need.

Access Learning Wherever You Can

A team at General Motors in Detroit is working on reducing the response time from car order to delivery. Team members post what they're doing and learning so that people not directly involved can help shape questions and make suggestions on what else needs to be explored. This practice helps the team, and it inspires others in the organization to act on what the team has learned.

Find opportunities to disseminate information already in your organization. If you use a knowledge base, ask a veteran communicator to edit entries or a recent recruit with journalistic talents to find new items to include. If your organization has an intranet, establish usability guidelines for linking and presenting information so that people can find anything fast. Encourage people to publish the department job aids and cheat sheets they create for themselves. Offer a shared space to log topical bookmarks from personal lists or communities of practice. Create frequently asked question (FAQ) lists, and make them available in a format that everyone can add to and update.[3]

Promote Learning with New Practices

At Siemens Power Transmission and Distribution in Wendell, North Carolina, executives once wondered how to stop workers from gathering in the cafeteria for chitchat about family or golf. Then leaders realized these get-togethers offered their organization an opportunity to grow through interpersonal relationships and peer-to-peer learning, so pads of paper and overhead projectors were placed on cafeteria tables to assist learning during these informal talks. By providing essential tools and then staying out of the way, those executives now support employee learning in an innovative way.

Find new ways and times for people to talk about and improve the work they share. Place a whiteboard near the water cooler, in the stairwells, and by the printer or copy machine so that people can capture and share conversations wherever they hold them. Provide an informal guide to informal learning opportunities as part of your everyday meetings and new-staff orientations.[4] Advocate for seasoned staff to become mentors and coaches. Create overlaps between shifts so that peers can begin to build rapport. Encourage, or at least don't discourage, people sending instant messages when they seek help from others in the enterprise or those they can learn from across the globe.

Jump-Start Learning with Novelty

At Microsoft, in Redmond, Washington, I worked with new employees in the product support division. After their first week of work, we sent them to the technical support lines to answer calls, some of which were from irate customers. After a few calls, each of the new employees quickly grasped that he or she had plenty to learn. From then on, they were very receptive to advice, coaching, and lessons from coworkers and instructors on how to handle difficult situations.

Stimulate the learning process by mixing in different activities. Effective informal learning activities are those that are compelling, not necessarily those that are most frequent. An activity such as cross-training may shake up everyday work, but walking in your customers' shoes, rotating jobs, or visiting the manufacturer who develops the components you use—activities that may occur less frequently and are rich with novelty and impact—may prove more insightful.

Nurture Learning Through Reflection

As Brenda Wilkins of the Montana Children's Theatre began to write her doctoral dissertation, her daughter became ill. Brenda cleaned out her home office, fearing she wouldn't be able to return to it for a long time. To keep her notes straight, she taped them around the room, and then she closed the door. Occasionally, she took a break from caring for her daughter and walked around the office, ruminating on the yellow pages covering the walls. After several long weeks, her daughter regained her strength. When Brenda returned to her computer, she discovered that her conclusions came quickly and with new clarity.

When you hurry, you can miss out on valuable contemplation and consideration. Set aside time each day to think, ruminate, and reflect. Establish a practice to produce postmortem reports (either in written form or on video) and then have people go over them and draw conclusions based on previous events. Find ways to change your perspective mentally and physically, such as asking for opinions from customers or partners and working outside or sitting on the floor. Create a productivity lab, as formal as a usability lab or as casual as a space to hold focus groups, where people can meet and reflect on what they've learned.

Integrate Informal Learning with Formal Structures

The United Nations Development Programme (UNDP) created a global network of "learning managers," all trained to be learning coaches, who serve as sources of information for issues related to staff development and performance. The result is a very informal, diversified, decentralized, and therefore responsive personalized support system. Instead of waiting for answers from headquarters, every staff member can go to a learning manager who will either help the person find the answer in himself or herself, through guided discovery, or direct the person to an external resource.

Make the distinctions between formal and informal learning more fluid. Formal learning stimulates informal learning, and informal learning often stimulates the intentionality of formal learning.[5] Consider producing recordings of information meetings and streaming them throughout the organization. Supplement formal conference calls with informal calls around a hot topic. Dedicate an intranet site to locally grown ideas, and use those materials in formal classes. Involve influential employees in formal meetings and training events. Offer educators the chance to be mentors and to be mentored by people on the front lines, too.

Encourage Learning's Many Faces

Play, a creativity consultancy in Richmond, Virginia, fashioned a four-square game court (like one seen on a schoolyard playground) right inside its front door. Visitors are encouraged to play with Play's staff. While they bounce a big red ball, they talk about what they want to do together and reflect on the situations they surface. In the larger office space, people learn in open work areas, a resource center, a quiet zone (with soundproof walls), and a kitchen where they can linger or cook a meal together.

Most informal learning occurs as a natural part of the workday, so it consumes little or no additional budget. However, if some resources (human or financial) are needed, help acquire them. Create comfortable places where people can talk and attractive spaces that draw people in. Encourage people to ask for help and to help each other. Ask for help yourself to demonstrate your participation, and provide help when others ask. Introduce groups to one another, and create e-mail dialogues between people you know outside the organization to whom your colleagues might not otherwise have access.

Follow Learning's Influence

At PeopleSoft, based in Pleasanton, California, I began a session at a sales meeting by handing out little cocktail napkins with a logo from a hotel. I then asked people to watch a demonstration, write and draw key sales points from the demo on their napkins (a technique they might actually use to make a sale), and then have the person next to them critique their napkin-based sales skills. Together they learned and assessed each other's learning in a way they could use back on the job.

Informal learning may be difficult to quantify, but you can *qualify* it. Track informal learning by keeping individual and departmental logs that answer questions such as "What have you learned today?" "How did you learn what you learned?" "Who or what helped you?" and "How will you apply what you learned?" Consider unconventional methods, such as job readiness reviews, peer appraisals, and social network analyses to measure what is being learned.[6] Initiate inventories that capture changes in content knowledge, or ask managers to report regularly not only on business metrics but also on what their groups discover and are prepared to share.

Celebrate Learning's Pervasiveness

Gartner, Inc., in Burlington, Massachusetts, has created a succession policy designed to reward and promote employees who learn continuously and share their knowledge with peers and subordinates. WD-40 Company recognized a learning superstar, a person who learned the most and from whom others learned the most over the course of a year, by paying for that family's food for a year.

Talk about the ongoing nature of informal learning and the improvements the organization has made as a result. Honor success by citing examples of learning from the executive suite to the manufacturing floor. If learning all the time is an explicit organizational goal, it then becomes a value on which people pride themselves. They are likely to increase skills and knowledge, improve performance and bottom-line results, work successfully as a team, offer timely assistance, and develop innovative approaches to work. Don't change the essence of informal learning by trying to codify too much, though; some people prefer the unbounded nature of their contributions and prefer to decide how much attention and praise they receive.

Conclusion

To create a smarter organization, discover what learning already lurks on your walls and in your halls. Then purposefully support an environment full of additional informal opportunities and experiences that ready employees for fresh challenges, create new intellectual capital, and provide greater benefit to those you serve. Along the way, you may discover that these opportunities increase employee confidence and enthusiasm, a feeling of security, personal growth, a sense of community, and rewarding relationships. Could there be any better reasons for becoming a champion of informal learning today?[7]

Marcia L. Conner is director of the Ageless Learner, cofounder of the Learnativity Alliance, and a fellow of the Batten Institute at the University of Virginia's Darden Graduate School of Business Administration. She serves as executive coach and senior counsel to curious leaders around the world. She wrote *Learn More Now* and coedited *Creating a Learning Culture*. She was information futurist as well as vice president of education services for PeopleSoft, a senior manager of worldwide training at Microsoft, and editor in chief of *Learning in the New Economy* magazine. Contact: marcia@agelesslearner.com; http://www.agelesslearner.com; http://www.learnativity.org

Chapter Ten

The Company as a Marketplace for Ideas: Simple but Not Easy

Alexander J. Ogg

Thomas Cummings

Every business leader we know struggles with how best to leverage the size and scope of his or her organization; this is particularly true of individuals who manage large multinationals. Whether they work locally and have to pay "corporate taxes" or they work at the corporate center and need to "justify their existence," the questions are "How do we take advantage of 'bigness' to compete with smaller competitors?" and "How do we benefit from 'early information' to move as fast as or faster than our more nimble adversaries?" We believe that there are three important things that can be leveraged in large companies to help take advantage of being a big organization: money, talent, and ideas.

Essentially, big organizations can almost always bring more money, better talent, and stronger ideas to the "point of attack." Unfortunately, all too often the same "bigness" that creates advantages also creates barriers to getting either enough money, the right talent, or the best ideas to the right places at the right time to win. As leaders, we need to adopt an "efficient market" perspective for our organizations if we hope to overcome the barriers.

It is our experience that business leaders need to create "efficient markets" for money, ideas, and talent in their organizations. That is to say, managers must systematically identify and eliminate the major barriers that prevent ideas, talent, and money from flowing easily to the point of "highest and best use."[1] Most of us working in large organizations have experienced the frustration of knowing we have better talent, the financial resources, or the best idea somewhere in our organization but are unable to find it or free it up in time to help us win. The popular business press is full of stories that describe how leaders have taken on the barriers to efficient internal markets—Cisco's open job posting; the way GE Capital moves money to high-leverage businesses; the approaches Intel, Cannon, or 3M use to generate ideas for manufacturing and new products, or the way Shell moves its stock of international talent across the world. In this chapter, we draw on our own experiences to focus specifically on just one of these key drivers of leverage: creating an efficient marketplace for ideas.

An Idea Marketplace

A market is made up of buyers, sellers, and brokers; there are efficient markets and there are inefficient ones. If we consider real estate markets for a moment, they are generally very efficient. Knowledge of buyers, sellers, and brokers is readily available. The value of a particular piece of real estate is fairly easy to determine at fair market rates, there are lots of safeguards to ensure that transactions go smoothly, and there are sanctions for not playing by the rules.

In contrast, the market for knowledge and ideas in most organizations is highly inefficient. Unlike our real estate example, the right "sellers" are difficult to locate and can be hard to get to even if we know where they work. It is nearly impossible to establish the right "price," because we have no clear way to establish the value of the idea or knowledge we are "buying," and different parts of the organization often play using different rules.

There are many reasons why our internal markets for ideas are so inefficient. We will focus on only a few of the most damaging and suggest that unless leaders work on these sources of inefficiency, the marketplace for ideas will not flourish.

Organizational Boundaries

In a letter to shareholders, Jack Welch, the famous former CEO of General Electric (GE), declared that he was going to make the company "boundaryless." He created an initiative called Boundarylessness. GE and many other multinationals have recognized that ideas get trapped behind organizational boundaries, boundaries between business units, geographies, or levels in the organization. "If we only knew what we know. If we could only prevent repeating known mistakes." These frequently heard laments from CEOs reveal the difficulties of getting ideas out from behind organizational boundaries. Organizational boundaries can have a debilitating impact on a leader's ability to move ideas through a company culture, structures, and processes no matter how well they are designed.

Who Gets the Credit?

Bob Galvin, legendary CEO of Motorola, once said, "Just imagine what we could accomplish if we stopped worrying about who gets the credit. . ." Idea markets are not about "buyers" exchanging cash with "sellers." These markets for intangibles are about credit. Credit is the primary medium of exchange, and if buyers take the ideas as their own without acknowledging the sellers, trust is lost and the medium of exchange breaks down. At the same time, companies are "geared" for rewarding and singling out individuals, especially where "intellectual capital" and "knowledge" are the primary currency used to gain credits.

What Is the True "Value" of the Ideas, and What "Price" Am I Willing to Pay?

Knowledge is generally very local. Most ideas flow between locals. The farther ideas have to travel, the more inefficient the markets become. The price (in terms of time) of finding, understanding, and translating the ideas, the probability that the idea will "fit locally," and overcoming "not invented here" resistance add cost to ideas and slow down their adoption locally. It is an unfortunate truth that leaders and their teams can come up with good ideas, but if the organization lacks the capacity to capture the value from the ideas, they become a low-cost supplier of intellectual capital to the rest of the industry.

Timing

Efficient markets are made up of cycles within cycles, and they are influenced by the just-in-time actions of entrepreneurs. A recent Wharton study revealed that it takes, on average, thirty-six months for a good idea to become a "best practice" in use in another part of the organization.[2] Timing is influenced by the alignment of organization processes or "cadence," the willingness and ability of managers to send and receive knowledge, and the clarity of the ideas to be adopted. Change the cycle time and you change the competitiveness of a company and the effectiveness of its leaders.

Trust

All markets are based on a foundation of trust. Just consider what has happened to the stock markets in the past couple of years when financial information was no longer considered trustworthy. Trust is the biggest single factor affecting the marketplace for ideas within organizations. When individuals lack trust in other individuals, teams, and organizations, ideas simply will not flow between them.[3] Trust can take years to build and minutes to destroy. The founder of Southwest Airlines knew that the willingness of an organization to listen and act on a leader's ideas is built on a lifelong foundation of trustworthiness. There are three important components of trust—reliability, competence, and sincerity—that together will determine the legitimacy of a leader's good ideas and intentions.

Making Ideas Move

We would like to focus on five concepts leaders can apply to make their organizations more efficient marketplaces for ideas.

Leaders as Idea "Brokers"

In our experience, the single biggest factor contributing to the movement of ideas is the mind-set of the leaders, exemplified by their behavior. The higher leaders rise in their organizations, the more their primary role becomes creating leverage: how to make their organizations more effective "markets" for capital, talent, and ideas. Consider Rob Poulet, business group president for Unilever's $8 billion global ice-cream business. Rob and his core team visit all the major units of the ice-cream business each year. Following each visit, he and his team sit and discuss where else in the world of Unilever ice cream can the great growth ideas they just discovered in, say, Brazil be used. They then take it upon themselves, as idea brokers, to connect the other teams in the world that could benefit from these ideas. They even go so far as to designate "sister cities" where there are two diverse geographies that could benefit from each other's growth ideas. This has proved to be a highly effective way to get great ideas flowing between the two local companies. Effective leaders as brokers are in tune with both the speed of the transaction and the value of the content knowledge they provide. They are validated in the organization because they connect rather than control those whom they serve—the front line and the customers.

Meetings as "Marketplaces"

Most meetings and high-level gatherings (workshops, forums, and conferences) can be a terrible use of organizational resources because all too often they are held at the wrong place with the wrong people at the wrong time. Some leaders have figured out that meetings can be incredibly leveraged occasions that become markets for talent and ideas. Mike Zafirovski joined Motorola as the general manager of the mobile phone division of GE. Taking his knowledge of the operating "cadence" of GE, he quickly took charge of the calendar and divided the year into three trimesters: T1 (January through April), T2 (May through July), and T3 (August through December). In T1, he pulled all of the HR discussions into focused Talent Management meetings together. T2 is about strategy, and T3 is about next year's plan. In these meetings, his top team visits, or is visited by, operating units in a focused way. Following each meeting, Mike, with the help of his team, drafts a personal letter that is sent to each business leader summarizing key actions and learning. At senior leadership team meetings following T1, T2, and T3 meetings, Mike asks each business leader to share with colleagues a best practice that he or she is proud of. In fact, all the major meetings Mike runs are opportunities for sharing great ideas and reinforcing the organization's operating cadence.

Reducing Resistance Through Infrastructure

It is essential to get the infrastructure right to create efficient markets for ideas. This means "digitizing" key knowledge-sharing tools with good information technologies. We all know that technology is necessary but not sufficient. It is important to connect people in order to establish the relationships and trust necessary to create meaning and a context for ideas to be shared. Technology facilitates and leverages the sharing. During the rollout of a Web tool at Motorola, Carey Dassatti, corporate vice president for human resources, established a weekly conference-call regimen that was frequently attended by forty or more individuals. This global team jointly invented each screen shot of the Web tool and discussed the various issues surrounding implementation. These somewhat formal conference calls went on for over a year and built an informal network of HR professionals who could be leveraged as new applications were introduced.

Creating a Tipping Point

Ideas and knowledge reside in people. The culture of a company is essentially its *habits*—norms of behaviors and values. Companies, like individuals, have good and bad habits. In his best seller *The Tipping Point*, Malcolm Gladwell describes large-scale changes as "epidemics."[4] These epidemics are often brought on by small things that represent a "tipping point," and then things move very quickly. Leaders can create a culture of sharing ideas and knowledge if they establish the necessary conditions of a tipping point. Following Goldman Sachs's IPO, the partnership started to lose its famous ability to leverage its knowledge and team-based culture around the world. Company directors Henry Paulson, John Thain, and John Thornton established the Pine Street leadership initiative (Goldman's first offices were on Pine Street, around the corner from Wall Street) to rekindle a sense of partnership and to reestablish the value of "culture carriers" in the company. They hired Steve Kerr, the former head of GE Crotonville, to make visible their promise of rapidly deploying intensive leadership and coaching for senior partners. By acting quickly, they achieved a tipping point that turned the tide on company morale and partner performance at a critical moment in the company's history.

The Goldman Sachs experience showed that it takes responsive and insightful leaders to harness and leverage the power of a marketplace for ideas in an organization. From their past success at focusing the partnership and teamwork on the most critical organization campaigns, these leaders know the value of creating "tipping points" to propel the company forward.

Recasting the Learning and Talent Management

Far too often, corporate universities, skills courses, topical initiatives, and recruiting drives think that their own brochure, a Web site, and a new competence framework can suffice for a company-wide learning and development strategy. When each division produces its own brand, when ideas are not shared and knowledge is compartmentalized, the transfer of ideas across the organization is stifled, thereby reducing the alignment needed to achieve corporate renewal. In addition, when initiatives such as coaching and change management are outsourced to consultants, the forgetting curve of the organization moves faster than the learning curve. Steve Mercer at the new Boeing Leadership Center boasts that the center has had full managing board involvement over the past two years on every event. Leaders at the center have redesigned all general management programs to focus on business-driven action learning and benchmarking against world-class companies. They align program schedules to reinforce the strategy, to encourage formal and informal contacts between program delegates, and to develop coaches that are professional enough to work part time in other companies. When recast as a networked marketplace and a crossroads for ideas, the overall mind-set of the leaders is shifted to just-in-time learning on demand, where leaders take an active role in design, delivery, and coaching.

How Effective Are Your Leaders at Guiding the Internal Marketplace?

In a world of fast-moving and changing relationships, where leveraging knowledge and information in a global arena is the ticket to play, leaders must reorient their attention to the internal marketplace for money, talent, and ideas if they hope to capture the benefits of bigness. Simply put, of these three markets, ideas are the most important source of competitive uniqueness. When ideas get locked up in organizational boundaries, point-scoring, not-invented-here resistance, and slow cycle times, the whole system of trust and informal sharing breaks down. When leaders act as brokers, when they use meetings as a marketplace and an opportunity for alignment, and when they build proper infrastructures and trusting leadership support, ideas can move quickly to reinforce alignment and tipping points in the organization.

Alexander J. Ogg is senior vice president of the Foods Division at Unilever. He is responsible for leadership, learning, and performance within the organization. Prior to joining Unilever, he held the change management/organization effectiveness role for Motorola. In this position, he assisted in the transformation of all communications businesses. Before joining Motorola, Ogg spent fifteen years as a leadership development and change management consultant. He also held positions of president at the Center for Leadership Studies, managing director at Dove Associates, and founder of Via Consulting Group. He began his career as a line officer for the U.S. Coast Guard. He held various positions, was involved in search and rescue activities, and became a highly decorated commanding officer. Contact: Sandy.Ogg@unilever.com; www.unilever.nl

Thomas Cummings is the newly appointed global head of learning and organization for Unilever. During the past three years, he served as executive vice president for leadership development at ABN AMRO Bank and prior to that was a founding partner of Leading Ventures and Executive Learning Partnership, a European-based organization advisory and leadership development firm. Cummings's client engagements are typically built through long-term, trust-based collaborative agreements between a business and its external partners. He has completed corporate change and leadership development assignments for management teams in a range of companies. As a research fellow and then teaching faculty at IMD International in Lausanne, Switzerland, he conducted research, taught, and codirected the Programme on International Business Alliances. While at IMD, he wrote two award-winning case studies on international strategic management and authored several case studies on strategy, innovation, change, and leadership. Contact: Tom.Cummings@unilever.com; www.unilever.nl

Chapter Eleven

Knowledge Mapping

An Application Model for Organizations

Spencer Clark
Richard Mirabile

By now it should be abundantly clear to everyone that the world of work has dramatically changed. Here are just a few of the realities that are fundamentally reshaping the workplace.

- Work itself is being redefined. More emphasis is placed on lifelong learning, higher-order thinking, and an ever-increasing demand for innovation.
- The war for talent is an explicit condition of strategic business operations.
- Executive positions with responsibility for knowledge management, intellectual assets, and corporate learning are now appearing in the most respected Fortune 1000 companies.
- Companies specializing in some form of online training or knowledge management that did not exist five years ago have burst into the technology and service marketplace.

These examples, among many others, are indicators of an important phenomenon that is sweeping through business in ever-vigilant attempts to increase market share, improve economic performance, and expand shareholder value. Simply stated, it is the trend toward leveraging intellectual capital vis-à-vis knowledge capture and dissemination as a strategy for business survival. The rationale for this very deliberate emphasis is succinctly stated in *The New Organizational Wealth,* in which author Karl Erik Sveiby claims that "people are the only true assets in business."[1] In this context, people are viewed as the repositories of *knowledge capital,* which is subsequently defined as the cumulative wealth of an organization as measured by its collective knowledge, skills, and talent.

Evidence of this phenomenon is all around us. Here's one that should strike a chord for most people in today's workforce: "Faster, better, cheaper!" This pronouncement has become a mantra of business in the twenty-first century. Any CEO will tell you that finding ways to develop and deliver products and services in less time, with increased quality, and for less money is a cornerstone of success. CEOs know this to be true because the free market dictates a higher performance bar than ever before. "Faster, better, cheaper!" ultimately translates into speed, innovation, quality, and operational excellence, and it is our contention that these metrics can only be realized through the intelligent management of knowledge capital. Said another way, because virtually every business mission, strategy, initiative, or goal requires the use of some form of human competence, the faster, more reliably, and more intelligently that competence can be developed and deployed, the more likely it is that a business will achieve its objectives. In addition, translating competence into performance requires knowledge in various forms.

Consider these additional realities:

• A Macintosh PowerBook 5300c weighs 6.2 pounds, has 8 megabytes of RAM, and sports a 500-megabyte hard drive. The original IBM personal computer tipped the scales at 44 pounds, and the keyboard alone weighed 6 pounds. It contained something called "user memory," 16 kilobytes' worth. The Mac has 500 times more brainpower than the original IBM computer but is one-seventh the size. That's a 3,500-fold higher ratio of intelligence to physical matter.

- The new Boeing 777 airliner, designed entirely with computers, is powered by petroleum; more than half the cost of finding and extracting petroleum lies in the information required to perform these tasks.

- A typical automobile, powered by petroleum, has more microchips than spark plugs. A car's electronics cost more than the steel to build the vehicle.

- It used to require three to four hours of labor to make a ton of steel. Now it can be done with sophisticated computer programs in forty-five minutes. The intellectual or knowledge component has grown, and the physical component has shrunk.[2]

The Challenge

In today's global and technological economies, knowledge is being made available to people at exponential rates. While the best processes and mechanisms for capturing and distributing knowledge are still being debated, there is another aspect to the issue that has yet to be discussed. To pose it in the form of a question: Is it possible to efficiently organize and categorize knowledge that is being made available to us in order to facilitate decision making regarding its use? Asked another way: Can we develop methods to help people determine both if a particular piece of knowledge is useful to them and, if so, where in their respective organizational systems it would have the most application and impact? If methods could be developed to deliver on that capability, the drive for faster, better, and cheaper might suddenly shift into high gear.

Herein lies the meat of our chapter. We're suggesting that it is possible to develop such a method, and although the one we will propose is by no means a final solution, our intent is to stimulate the dialogue that is required for innovation to occur. It is in this process that we hope others will step forward to expand on the ideas and knowledge presented and to move this discussion to further application and development.

An Application Model

The task we've selected is to develop a framework and a process that would enable companies, quickly and with a high degree of consistency, to organize and categorize the streams of knowledge that are made available to them. Further, this would need to be done in such a way as to result in an enabled decision-making process. Although each company would likely create categories specific to its particular environment, the fundamental principles behind the system would hold for most organizations, regardless of size or industry.

For a preliminary version, this task can be divided into three parts. First, it's necessary to devise a framework of categories into which knowledge streams could be logically placed. Second, one would have to create some method of determining how to "map" the knowledge, that is, how to determine in which category the knowledge logically belongs. Finally, we believe it would be important to create some metrics to determine impact or relevance to the organization and to seek revisions and upgrades on some periodic basis.

Categories

The assumption behind a category framework is that every company has some reasonably clear and consistent language that is used to operate and manage the business. Such language is already used in everyday communications and planning but is probably not considered a repository for knowledge mapping. Here's a list of some of the common words, labels, and other linguistic indicators that would work as a starting point for the category requirement. (The definitions offered are meant to provide some measure of distinction between the categories and are not intended to imply an absolute or consensus meaning.)

Vision: A compelling image or description of a desired future state

Mission, purpose, charter: The core reason for a company's existence

Values: Unchanging beliefs or principles on which a company's actions are based

Strategy: Directionally based actions designed to achieve the vision and mission

Culture: A company's underlying values, beliefs, and assumptions, in their entirety

Structure: The way in which a company chooses to organize itself

Policies: The rules and procedures for operating in a particular business setting

Processes: Ways in which actions are grouped to achieve some end result

Goals: Specific and desired end results of actions

Objectives: High-level end states achieved through a combination of actions

Competition: Other companies that compete in the same market

Reorganization: A change in structure and reporting relationships

Coaching: A process intended to facilitate improved performance and development

There are undoubtedly many other potential categories that could be used, but the point should be clear. One immediate challenge with the category requirement would be to determine not only which ones to incorporate but also perhaps how many. Further, it would be helpful to create some sort of cross-referencing system for knowledge streams that might logically map to more than one category. Again, each company would determine what's in its own best interests.

Knowledge Mapping

To create an efficient process for this portion of the task, a mapping strategy would require triggers of some sort that represented clear and consistent signals alerting anyone as to the logical category or categories into which knowledge streams might be mapped. For example, an e-mail is circulated that describes the outcomes and follow-up actions related to a recent offsite event. Depending on the particular categories a company has established, this could fall into one of several categories. One might be strategy; another might be mission. The point is that for clear and consistent mapping to occur, one would need to identify the triggers—words, topical labels, or some other key indicators of the subject matter.

It also seems reasonable to assume that over some period of time, a listing of such keywords or triggers would be produced by the company and become a dictionary of categories. Further, much like a keyword search capability in some software programs, this capability would enable anyone to quickly identify the likely categories into which the information would be mapped by simply recognizing the triggers for category mappings. It also seems plausible that after some period of stabilizing such a system, any knowledge stream, e-mails, memos, handouts, and other distributed information could be coded with the appropriate knowledge map category or categories. Over time, this type of process would become part of the natural way of communicating and distributing information throughout the company.

Metrics

As with any new initiative, some form of evaluation should be considered in order to determine its true value. In this regard, each company would need to determine the appropriate value proposition for itself, but here are some suggested questions that might be addressed in an effort to make that determination.

- Does the categorization and mapping strategy add anything substantive to the business? In other words, does it facilitate knowledge dissemination and application across the company?
- Does the process facilitate improved decision making in any way? Does it enable individuals and teams to come to better decisions in less time, or does it provoke more meaningful debate regarding programs, processes, or other initiatives?
- Is there a better way to provide the categorization and mapping outcomes to the company in order to achieve the goal of efficient knowledge classification and improved decision making?
- Is there a way to demonstrate measurable impact from using a system and process such as this, and if so, what kind of metrics would be used? Faster response time to mission critical activities? Improved customer service levels? Improved team performance? Reduced time to market with products and services? These and other indicators are possible yardsticks to be used in more rigorous evaluation processes. Simpler versions could merely ask employees whether or not they found the process useful to them in any way. If not, would there be value in revising it, or should it be abandoned altogether?

Conclusions

Our purpose has been to propose an idea that might have benefit in the increasingly difficult challenge of efficiently managing the abundance of knowledge that is being made available to us all. The issue seems less how to collect and disseminate knowledge than how to quickly and effectively organize and categorize it in ways that facilitate decision making at all levels. If knowledge is power, then real-time access to the most relevant streams of knowledge is the most potent form of this new-age engine.

As Thomas Stewart writes in *Intellectual Capital*, "Knowledge and information are the competitive weapons of our time."[3] If one believes his premise, then the more quickly and more reliably we can direct knowledge toward decision makers who can leverage it for application purposes, the more likely it will be that those organizations will achieve the competitive advantage all organizations seek. Although the model we've proposed here is by no means the best solution to this complicated challenge, it is intended to stimulate a dialogue that will lead us all in the direction of possibilities.[4]

Spencer Clark is chief learning officer of Cadence Design Systems, the industry leader in the electronic design automation space. In this role, he is building Cadence University and driving global implementation of technical, professional, executive, and leadership development. He is responsible for implementing an organizational development practice within the Cadence Culture. His responsibilities also include the development and integration of an explicit talent development program into the Cadence succession-planning process. For the five years preceding Cadence, Clark was president of his own consulting company, where he used his skills to improve the performance in a variety of industries and disciplines, including power, defense, security, and manufacturing. He is a member of the board of directors for the China Institute of Software Technology, RFI Enterprises, the Chief Learning Officers Network, the advisory board for Leavy School of Business at Santa Clara University, and a member of the American Nuclear Society. Contact: sclark@cadence.com

Richard Mirabile is an organizational psychologist with more than two decades of diverse business and academic experience. In his current role, he works with many top companies. He specializes in leadership and executive development, large-scale organizational change, high-performance teaming, and assessment. Earlier in his career, he was an assistant professor at Purdue University and an adjunct faculty member at the University of Texas at Austin, the California School of Professional Psychology, and John F. Kennedy University. Contact: rjmirabile@aol.com

Chapter Twelve

Just-in-Time Guidance

Calhoun W. Wick
Roy V. H. Pollock

Knowledge in motion is a product of the digital revolution—the extraordinary progress in microelectronics that has transformed our ability to gather, process, store, and disseminate information. That progress is measured in orders of magnitude and necessitates a reexamination of the way in which knowledge is organized and conveyed.

Thirty years ago, Gordon Moore, cofounder of Intel, observed that the number of transistors that could be placed in a given area and the number of computations that could be performed per second had doubled roughly every year. He predicted that this trend would continue. His prediction, now known as "Moore's law," has proved uncannily correct.

When Moore made his prediction in 1965, his laboratory held the most complex computer chip ever built: it contained 64 transistors. In contrast, the Pentium III chip, introduced in 2000, contained 28 million transistors. At the time of Moore's prediction, a hard disk system capable of storing two megabytes (million bytes) of information cost $50,000 and was the size of a filing cabinet. Today, disks costing one one-hundredth as much store 10,000 times more information and fit in laptop computers. Despite the daunting technical challenges to continued progress—for one thing, components have become so small that they are running up against the laws of quantum physics—most computer scientists believe that Moore's law will apply for another decade.

Unfortunately, progress in making information available has far outstripped advances in making information useful. This is especially true with respect to knowledge about leadership and management. Storage has become so cheap that companies have compiled ever more encyclopedic databases. Braggadocio among learning organizations too often concerns who has the greatest number of items, vendors, and gigabytes, rather than the extent to which the information is actually used to benefit the business. More is not necessarily better; managers are already suffering from information overload.

Our contention is that information technology has an important role to play in leadership and management development. To achieve its full promise, however, the way in which information is organized and made available must be rethought. In this chapter, we explore the need and opportunity to use information technology and the Internet to support leadership development more effectively, using illustrations from our own work and that of others.

The Challenge

While there is little doubt that ignorance of management and leadership principles is an impediment to greater effectiveness, the converse is not necessarily true. That is, knowledge of principles and methods does not necessarily lead to their application. As Jeffrey Pfeffer and Robert Sutton explain in their book *The Knowing-Doing Gap*, "Regardless of the quality of content, the delivery, or the frequency of repetition, management education is often ineffective in changing organizational practices. . . . We came to call this the knowing-doing problem—the challenge of turning knowledge . . . into actions consistent with that knowledge."[1]

The challenge, then, is not merely making knowledge available but doing so in a way that encourages and ensures its application.

Follow-Up

Marshall Goldsmith and colleagues compared five different leadership development programs involving more than twenty thousand individuals in five corporations.[2] Programs varied in length from one day to one week. All of them included 360-degree feedback. Some offered coaching from external advisers, some offered coaching from internal HR, and some provided no formal coaching.

Three to six months following the leadership development experience, contributors to the original 360-degree feedback were asked to complete a short new survey. The survey included their assessment of the degree of change (from −3 to +3) in the program participant's effectiveness and the extent to which the participant had "followed up" (from "no follow-up" to "consistent or repeated follow-up").

In every program, some individuals were rated as having significantly (+2) to markedly (+3) improved, indicating that leadership development programs can and do produce meaningful changes in effectiveness. Others were rated as unchanged or worse.

In every program studied, the degree of improvement correlated directly to the extent of the individual's follow-up. Those who were perceived to have done "no follow-up" were also judged to have made no improvement in leadership effectiveness. Those who the raters felt had done "consistent or periodic follow-up" were almost uniformly rated as improved, the majority as significantly or markedly improved. Goldsmith and his colleagues concluded that regardless of the instruction method, program length, or source of coaching, the amount of follow-up is the single most important determinant of change in leadership effectiveness.

These findings are consistent with David Goleman's work on the role of emotional intelligence in business and leadership success. Effective leadership requires a range of complex skills that depend on emotional intelligence as much as or more than knowledge and intellectual ability. For most managers, improving leadership effectiveness requires unlearning old behaviors and practicing new ones. Practice is of key importance because of the way in which behaviors are learned and incorporated:

> The limbic system evolved much earlier than the neocortex (the "conscious" or "thinking brain") and it learns more slowly. While the neocortex absorbs new cognitive skills (rational thinking) very rapidly, the emotional centers require repetition over time to internalize new behaviors and affects. Improving emotional intelligence requires "unlearning" old habits and patterns of response and replacing them with the new, more effective reactions. Brain circuits are strengthened with each repetition so that if a behavioral sequence is repeated often enough, it no longer requires conscious effort, but becomes the new "default." Executive education should provide learners the support they need to fully incorporate new, more effective patterns of behavior in their leadership style.[3]

The Need for Ongoing Guidance

Given the importance of follow-up and practice over time, we have developed a follow-through reminder and support system known as Friday5s that helps ensure that leadership training is put in action to produce results. We have shown that structured follow-through increases both postcourse effort and return on the training investment.[4] In the course of that work, however, we discovered that leaders often had difficulty translating a general goal—for example, to improve their listening or delegation skills—into concrete actions they could apply to the conduct of their daily work. They benefit from ongoing guidance in the application of course principles.

A number of texts have been published to fill this need, including *FYI*, the *Successful Manager's Handbook*, and the *Essential Manager's Manual*.[5] We believe, however, that information technology and the Internet offer the potential to get this kind of knowledge "on the move" and used more effectively. Merely dumping existing texts to an electronic database is not the answer and indeed potentially makes the problem worse. Today's managers are pressed for time and are already overwhelmed by information. Providing even more is not the answer. The challenge is to redesign leadership guidance and present it in a manner that reflects the time demands on today's managers.

We suggest that to be effective, a leadership behavior guidance system needs to have the following characteristics:

1. The information needs to be readily available "just in time," at the place and moment it is needed, and integrated into the ongoing development effort.
2. The access has to be simple, fast, and specific.
3. The suggestions need to be concrete and actionable.
4. The information has to be in "bite-sized pieces" without being superficial.
5. The knowledge system itself needs to learn and grow over time.

Information That Is Readily Available "Just in Time"

Just-in-time inventory management has revolutionized manufacturing; instead of stockpiling huge quantities of components in anticipation of future demand, manufacturers work with their suppliers to ensure that parts arrive at the time and place they are needed. The same principles can be applied to revolutionize learning.

Information is most valuable and best remembered when it is received in the context of an immediate and pressing problem. Unfortunately, most traditional education is like traditional inventory management: trying to stockpile solutions in advance of future applications—giving people answers to questions they haven't yet asked. The problem is compounded because knowledge inventory is perishable; if it isn't used promptly, it rapidly decays.

In the context of leadership development, then, the ideal guidance system would present the learner with ideas "just in time," at the moment he or she is planning future action. It should be fully integrated into the ongoing development effort, as opposed to being a separate activity or resource. Books on shelves and notes in binders are too easily forgotten.

Virtually all leadership development programs require participants to set goals to apply what they have learned, but goals are not sufficient. Thirty years ago, Peter Drucker observed that "unless objectives are converted to action, they are not objectives; they are dreams."[6] The most effective leadership development programs maximize the value of goal setting by having participants translate their objectives into concrete plans for action. Books of development suggestions are useful in this context; participants can consult them while preparing their development plans. However, the physical limitations of books (constraints on length, organization, indexing, and reprinting) limit their effectiveness in supporting an iterative process of planning and action.

Guidance regarding steps to take to improve skills should be available throughout the development process. It ought to be integrated into a follow-through process that periodically asks individuals to reflect on their progress and plan their continued development. Computer-based systems offer significant advantages over books for this purpose:

- Computer-based suggestions can be integrated into an online follow-through system so that reporting, planning, and seeking guidance are all part of one activity.
- Computer-based suggestions can be tailored to the specific objectives of the program and individual, rather than being static "one size fits all" answers.
- In a computer-based system, a single activity can be indexed to any number of the competencies to which it applies. This is difficult to achieve in books.

By way of example, we have created a development support system called GuideMe for use in conjunction with follow-through management. To ensure that the information in GuideMe is available at the time and place it is needed, it is Internet-based and linked to a follow-through management system using hypertext. The link to GuideMe is positioned on the form used to record progress and plan future actions. In this way, potentially helpful suggestions are only "a click away" at the time and in the context of the planning process.

It should be possible to apply the principle of immediate availability to any Internet- or intranet-based knowledge system. Hypertext transfer protocol (http) supports any number of links to the same resource. Designers should consider where additional information would be most valuable and place links to the knowledge system in these locations. As will be discussed shortly, the links should be "smart" and should direct the user to specific, relevant information, rather than to the general information site as a whole.

Access That Is Simple, Fast, and Specific

The most common complaint of today's managers is their lack of time. The continuous influx of information via e-mail, cell phones, voice mail, faxes, memorandums, and so forth is overwhelming. We surveyed 115 participants at a Lominger User's Conference regarding the impediments to putting learning into action. Time constraints and conflicting priorities topped the list.

Any system that purports to provide knowledge to support ongoing development has to be simple, fast, and specific. The system must be easy to use without special training or expertise. Given the time pressure on managers, they will reject a system that requires an upfront investment of time to learn. Barriers to entry must be minimized as much as possible. A single sign-on should suffice for all learning-related activities. Navigation must be clear and intuitive; avoid the Web designer's penchant for clever but ambiguous symbols.

Don't try to impress users with the size of the database. Managers do not have time to hunt for information or to browse a

database in the belief that "there has to be a pony in there somewhere." Make the information as specific as possible.

To satisfy the principle of specificity and focus, for example, we
made the links to GuideMe dynamic, based on the user's objectives. That is, instead of directing the user to the general index and
in essence saying, "You find it," the link directs the user to the relevant sections and items based on the type of objective (delegation,
time management, and so on). The generalization of this principle
to other systems means ensuring that links to content are always as
specific as possible and relevant to the user's objectives or areas of
interest.

A further refinement would be to take into consideration the
user's level of development or managerial responsibility; guidance
appropriate for a person in a first managerial position are likely too
elementary for a senior manager. A single list that attempts to satisfy the full spectrum of development will contain a large number
of items irrelevant for any one user. Irrelevant or unusable items
represent "noise" in the system that slows down use and impedes
getting knowledge in motion.

Guidance systems should be specific to the program as well as
the user and his or her objectives. They should employ and reinforce
the terminology, models, and concepts used in the feedback and
instruction. Corporations are increasingly developing their own
leadership models and values. The ideal guidance system should
reinforce the company's values and principles by using the same
concepts and terms, thus minimizing the need for "translation."

Properly organized electronic versions can be filtered to "separate the wheat from the chaff" by showing only suggestions relevant
to the particular skill and (ideally) the person's current level of
development and responsibility (frontline supervisor versus enterprise manager, for example). Obviously, this is easier to do in an
electronic system than a mass-produced printing, which must necessarily be "generic." Here, too, appropriately designed computer-
based systems are superior to printed materials because they can be
readily revised or reorganized to reflect specific program objectives
and content.

Suggestions That Are Concrete and Actionable

The third criterion for a truly effective guidance system is the nature of the advice. It must be specific and actionable. For a time-challenged executive seeking to improve his or her performance, nothing is more frustrating than to invest the time seeking knowledge only to receive vague and general platitudes such as "Listening is important for success."

Improving leadership effectiveness requires doing things differently and better. Einstein is reported to have said that one definition of insanity is to continue to do the same thing but expect a different result. Thus a system to support future action needs to provide concrete, actionable suggestions: practical steps people can take to improve their performance in a given competency.[7] Some of the existing texts are very good in this regard; others speak only of the overall importance of the area or provide general platitudes without ever offering clear direction. To help ensure actionable advice, we have written the guidance in our system in the first person future: "I will . . ." This has forced us to provide concrete actions people can take. We were surprised at how difficult it was to find well-supported examples in our review of the management literature. There is a pressing need for more and better research to document the most helpful actions that people can take to improve their effectiveness in given competencies.

Information in "Bite-Sized Pieces"

The pace of today's business has heightened managers' sense of urgency, their impatience, and their need to "get to the point" quickly. A crisp, concise guide will see more day-to-day use than an exhaustive treatise, however scholarly and beautifully written. The need for conciseness is further heightened when the information is presented electronically. Large blocks of text are difficult to read on computer monitors. People tend to scan and "chunk" information presented on Web pages, skipping over long paragraphs and clicking off pages of dense text.

For this reason, most books and articles are ineffective when they are simply posted to an electronic knowledge system "as is." To be effective, they must be extensively reworked to suit the way in which information is accessed and read on computers. The text must be broken up to provide much more "white space," and the key concepts must be presented in short segments or as bulleted items. This is the key concept behind Ninth House's Instant Advice, which consists of a large series of very short (one-minute) videos and text on individual leadership topics.[8]

Brevity, however, carries the attendant risk of superficiality. A savvy manager will be skeptical of unsupported one-liners of "things to do" or guides that reduce the complex tasks of management to superficial "sound bites." The solution is to give the user control, presenting top-line information succinctly and unadorned but providing "drill-down" capability through hypertext links. In this way, the user can quickly review a large amount of information but still have the option of pursuing knowledge in depth in areas of special interest. We have implemented these concepts in GuideMe by providing the first level of suggestions as short action statements keyed to objectives but offering a "Tell Me More" option for each that links to more in-depth information, background, and references to additional resources.

A Knowledge System That Learns and Grows over Time

The importance of printed paper in human history is undeniable; the invention of the printing press produced a quantum leap in human development by making it possible to preserve accumulated knowledge and disseminate it inexpensively across distance and time. Books will continue to play a vital role for the foreseeable future; their demise has been greatly exaggerated. However, once a book is printed, its knowledge is static until the next edition. A great advantage of knowledge in electronic form is that it can be revised, expanded, and repurposed more quickly and more inexpensively than printed material.

The ideal guidance system should itself learn and grow over time. It should accumulate the "best practices" for each organization, based on the real-world experiences of its users. Such best practices would have the advantage of being specific to the organization and its culture and proven in actual application.

To satisfy this principle, the guidance system must have a mechanism to capture these best practices and a simple way to add them to the database and indexes. An example of such a system is Meridian Global's GlobalSmart program, which is designed to provide tips and insights executives need to be effective in cultures different than their own.[9] The system continues to get smarter not only as a result of research by the company but also by inviting executives experienced in transnational business to contribute ideas and insights. These are checked, edited, and added to the database so that over time the system becomes increasingly rich, deep, and specific. Similarly, in our work with Home Depot's Store Manager Learning Forum, we ask each store manager to identify his or her most effective action during a three-month follow-up period. These best practices then become the source of GuideMe items for subsequent groups, which accelerates organizational learning and knowledge dissemination.

Conclusion

The digital revolution and the electronic media it has spawned offer new and exciting opportunities for disseminating knowledge. We believe that in the field of management development, more effective knowledge dissemination is at least as important as new knowledge generation.

In this chapter, we have outlined opportunities and principles for applying information technology to leadership development guidance. New systems and constructs are needed to make the information available at the time and place it is needed and to make it more specific and more concise. We believe strongly that improved knowledge application, especially in the postprogram follow-through period, offers great potential for increasing the overall effectiveness of leadership programs.

Calhoun W. Wick, founder and chairman of Fort Hill Company, has spent more than two decades studying how managers develop and businesses learn new capabilities. His research led to the development of Friday5s, a unique Web-based solution that helps companies motivate follow-through action from learning and development events and measure results. Wick is a nationally recognized expert in turning corporate education into improved business results and has published a book on the subject. Contact: wick@forthillcompany.com; http://www.ifollowthrough.com

Roy V. H. Pollock is president and chief operating officer for Fort Hill Company. Prior to joining Fort Hill, he served as a member of the global management teams for SmithKline Beecham Animal Health, Pfizer Animal Health, and IDEXX Laboratories and was a corporate officer at IDEXX. Earlier in his career, Pollock was for eight years a faculty member at Cornell University, where he served as assistant professor and assistant dean of the College of Veterinary Medicine. He is a Fellow of the Kellogg Foundation National Leadership Program. Contact: pollock@forthillcompany.com; http://www.ifollowthrough.com

Part Three

Leaders Who Make a Difference

Chapter Thirteen

What Leading Executives Know— and You Need to Learn

Howard J. Morgan

Until the 1980s, being a successful executive meant that you possessed superior industry knowledge and the most relevant technical expertise. Of course, it went without saying that your loyalty to the company was unquestioned. You were promoted by being better at what you did than your colleagues in the company were. We all remember early charts on management practices that graphically presented the need, as we advanced in the organization, to prioritize time spent on strategic initiatives while decreasing our day-to-day tactical focus. It meant getting financial and competitive results on a consistent basis year-over-year. Of course, these were also the times when changing your company's relative ranking among your competitors was a slow process at best and difficult to accomplish. Holding the number one position in your industry meant that you had better distribution channels and more organizational depth and that customers liked the perceived reliability that dealing with the largest supplier represented.

Then came dramatic increases in information technology. We now had the ability to view critical operations within an organization through the computer on our desk. This advance finally resolved the long-standing debate over centralization versus decentralization: it became irrelevant. Technology allowed us to make quicker and more comprehensive decisions. Unfortunately, it allowed our competitors to do the same thing. In fact, technology facilitated great advances in virtually all operations of the business, particularly in distribution, manufacturing methodology, and even the geographical determination of plant sites. With the advent of this innovation, once-leading companies now faced the challenge of determining "competitive advantage." After years of enjoying the benefits of size and volume, executives were now charged with finding solutions for their businesses that would allow them to maintain and even build on their standing in an increasingly competitive marketplace. Although several avenues were explored, the "opportunity" that drew the most attention was the idea of investing in human capital.

After taking a back seat to technology and systems in many companies, the individual began to draw increased attention as a variable that could play a significant role. Thought leaders spent the 1990s helping organizations grow from good to excellent through the effective use of human resources. Executives who focused on achieving results through values-driven leadership appeared to have great success in charging to the front of the competitive marketplace. However, they then faced the dilemma of how to manage senior leaders in their organizations who had successfully led their businesses to record earnings in the past using outdated business practices. It was difficult to simply fire them— after all, they were a major part of the past success of the company.

This need to "retrain" senior leaders in organizations led to a new focus on leadership development. Granted, leadership development was not a new concept, but its importance increased as an organizational priority. It was also being offered internally at executive levels for the first time. While historically most companies valued and rewarded loyal, committed employees that spent their entire careers in one organization, outside hires were now considered a refreshing way to obtain new thinking on critical issues. Indeed, the movement of executives between organizations was becoming more common as a mechanism to ensure that companies had the best talent they could afford. This movement once again altered the focus on executive development, both in direction and in content. The "new" CEO had things to learn about the organization, and in turn he or she set the strategic direction for learning and people within the company.

Today we see another shift—and what a difference just a few years can make! After a prosperous economic decade in the 1990s, the recession that followed forced shareholders to reevaluate what they expected from the executives of the companies in which they had invested. Shareholders also expected quicker responses to business challenges and grew increasingly impatient waiting for business results. Executives had gone from being judged using a measure of five- to ten-year periods to having their achievements assessed in mere months, in business quarters. The business environment today is even more competitive, and executives are under increasing pressure to bring in short-term results to ensure shareholder confidence while also ensuring that dividends are paid.

Moreover, increased scrutiny is being focused on "executive behavior," which makes it more interesting for us to examine what today's executive needs in order to be successful. In addition, there is money at issue—big money—beyond the expected bottom line. With over $50 billion spent annually on leadership education and development, defining the knowledge and attributes integral to the success of today's executive appears to be prudent.

Integrity

There was a time when integrity was taken for granted, when it was assumed behavior. No longer. The events of the past several years have put a new focus on integrity and have defined its importance as an integral organizational value. The living definition of integrity for executives requires that they conduct themselves in a manner consistent with the organization's value and ethics. Recent history has taught us that executives safeguard the livelihood of the entire employee population through their effective or ineffective handling of issues as interpreted by shareholders, regulatory bodies, or the media. It is also important to recognize that executives are expected to hold themselves to a higher standard of behavior than employees at lower levels in the organization. There is added pressure for these executives to mirror behaviors that leave no room for ambiguity or interpretation. Put another way, it is easy to talk about values; it is far more difficult to actually live values in a dynamic, competitive business environment.

Forward-Looking Vision

Today more than ever before, a critical attribute of successful executives is the ability to anticipate future trends in their industry and make decisions that allow them to be first to market. It is the instinct to see the great opportunities among myriad good ideas. However, simply seeing the vision is no longer enough. Today's executives must have the ability to inspire. They must fall in love with their vision and have the skill to articulate it clearly to others. Truly gifted executives possess the art of making their vision come alive for other leaders, employees, and shareholders in a way that builds confidence and demands patience during the journey. It is the ability to increase the knowledge and understanding of each of these constituents that allows leaders to "buy the time" necessary to stay the course. Over the past several years, a number of executives from large organizations have been given the time necessary to implement their vision. These leaders have achieved this by having the wherewithal to accurately predict the steps in the process and to deliver against those predictions. The successful executive must not only have the ability to see the vision but must also be able to paint the path for all to understand and follow.

Attracting and Retaining Top Talent

For those of us with an understanding of the sales process, it is apparent that keeping and building business with an existing customer is significantly easier than is bringing a new customer on board. The same is true for a company's employees. Great employees are always in demand and in short supply. Part of the executive's role is to build a culture and an organization that prospective employees find appealing and want to join. The inspiring leader who knows where he or she is going and how to get there and who creates a learning organization where everyone feels challenged to be better has founded an exciting place to work. It is important, however, that the executive articulate these benefits in detail to the prospective recruit. The second part of the challenge for today's executive is to retain the talent that the organization already has. Part of ensuring that your top people are committed to their leaders is letting them know that they are valued. Many executives never think about interacting with their top talent on a regular basis and acknowledging the impact that these people have on the organization and how greatly their work is appreciated. This is especially true of talented people in leadership positions. The impact that their good work and leadership capability has is felt throughout the organization. The disruptive effect that their leaving could have, though not easily measured, is nonetheless very apparent.

Culture Carriers

It is becoming increasingly important for executives to both define the culture of their companies and to implement the steps necessary to create the desired culture. Leaders, by definition, should be visible within the organization so that employees will learn to achieve by emulating their demonstrated behaviors. The old saying "Do as I say, not as I do" does not apply to organizations. Most organizational behavior is copied from the senior leadership. Indeed, learning by example is one of the most successful ways to transmit cultural behavior, and it offers the highest probability for success. Whether we want to admit it or not, organizations are political, and the most effective way to get ahead is to demonstrate like-minded attitudes and behavior. Therefore, how executives handle questions, risk, and other issues form the backdrop for the corporate culture. In many cases, decision making and other internal procedural and policy issues mirror those of the executives. It is not enough for them to talk about the importance of culture; executives must consistently model the desired behaviors.

Commitment to Self-Improvement

The business world has changed dramatically. Fifty years ago, your broad-based knowledge was perhaps the most important characteristic governing whether you were promoted in an organization or not. Today, the technical and technological components of the workplace are changing at such a fast pace that it is unrealistic to expect an executive to have the time or the resources to stay current. However, those who are seen to be committed to improving their leadership skills are perceived to have great credibility inside their organizations. Consequently, the focus in recent years has been directed to building "learning organizations." Billions of dollars have been spent to find better and more cost-effective ways to increase customer satisfaction through initiatives such as Six Sigma, TQM, and just-in-time inventory management. As these programs continue to drive savings and customer satisfaction with the business, it is becoming increasingly apparent that improving the capabilities and talent of the workforce offers similar, if not greater, potential benefits to the bottom line. Executives who establish a company culture that encourages continuous improvement will create a more personally rewarding workplace as well as an environment that fosters innovation and creativity. Without focusing on self-improvement as a valued part of the attitudes and behaviors of the company, the focus will be on what people know rather than what they have the potential to learn. Similarly, talented employees, eager to learn and to grow, will be less satisfied with their company and more likely to leave. Most important, there is a strong correlation between employees' satisfaction and long-term shareholder return and stock appreciation.

Ability to Inspire

Inspiration has long been viewed as analogous with charisma. Although charisma can indeed be inspiring, you can have the ability to inspire others without being charismatic. The ability to inspire is central to an executive's ability to create passion, commitment, and unqualified enthusiasm to go in a given direction. If an executive does not possess the skills to inspire in today's business climate, it may have a negative effect on the company's ability to succeed, given the economic pressures in the marketplace. For an executive to cultivate this enthusiasm within an organization, he or she first needs to be inspired. Consequently, the ability to inspire is closely linked to an executive's ability to craft a meaningful, vital vision for the business. It is widely understood that a salesperson cannot sell something that he or she does not believe in. The same is true for executives. If they have developed a cohesive vision, they need to fall in love with it. They then need to convey it to others with the same passion that they feel. They also need to talk specifically about what excites them about the direction or vision. Finally, they need to make sure that the message is clear and concise—that the path is visible for all to follow. People like having something exciting happening at work. An executive who conveys enthusiasm through his or her message provides the foundation for pride and self-satisfaction at all levels of the company.

Dealing with Ambiguity

Executives may have signed up for their jobs knowing that change is inherently a part of the situation, but no one could have anticipated the economic and political turmoil in which we currently find ourselves. Certainty has become the dinosaur of the business world, and having all of the facts before making a decision is nowadays a luxury that few executives can afford. For most initiatives, executives begin the journey knowing that the end will very likely look quite different from what they had envisioned. As they chart their course, required modifications and outside influences necessitate twists and turns. Given that most people find greater comfort in stability than in constant change, it is important for executives to lead in a purposeful and deliberate fashion. Indeed, it is not that people dislike change itself but rather that they dislike the uncertainty that change brings. Even as organizations change, people take comfort in a predictable workplace. This yearning for stability is driven by life responsibilities, such as mortgage payments and the raising of children. Therefore, the challenge is to bring a sense of comfort to the organization that the executive himself or herself may not enjoy. The most crucial task for executives to undertake during change-intensive times is to establish a direction, even though it is very likely that the direction will change as time goes on. The next most crucial task is to communicate the direction clearly and repeatedly so that employees will know the next steps in the plan. People are more comfortable with a direction that changes in ways they been led to anticipate than with the uncertainty that the unknown presents.

Knowing How to Deploy Resources

One of the key attributes of today's successful executive is the strategic sense that he or she possesses on where and how to deploy resources so as to ensure the greatest return. These executives have an ability to look at a project or an initiative and see its true value and worth—not just the obvious benefits but the potential that lies beneath the surface. It is this combination of wisdom and business instinct that facilitates entry into new markets or infusions of capital where there is the greatest possibility of growth. Many times we question these executives on the logic of their decisions only to find out later that their intuition was not only right but actually helped make a stellar year for the company. The same aptitude for putting resources in the right places applies to human capital as well. It is recognizing the right person for the right job. Generally, there is more than one person who could do a specific job. It is the executive's ability to assess what will be required six to twelve months down the road that allows the executive to make the best decision in asset allocation.

Building Relationships

The current business environment presents a significant challenge to talented executives. On the one hand, they need to develop a cohesive strategy and vision and inspire their people to tactically execute the strategy and share the vision. On the other hand, events in recent years have put significant pressure on executives to produce short-term results. Many boards of directors have increased their involvement and their fiduciary responsibility in company operations to ensure that dividends are paid and short-term financial results are solid. To achieve the "right" balance, an executive must be able to command the respect of the board and the shareholders in order to mitigate any lack of confidence. As mentioned previously, it is incumbent on the executive to have a vital vision and tactical plans to provide direction. Moreover, the executive must communicate this confidence to all concerned stakeholders to ensure their buy-in and continued support. This will happen when the executive demonstrates that his or her business or function is producing a financial scorecard that exceeds stakeholder expectations. This confidence can be built by accomplishing two main objectives: communicating enough to build a comfort in the strategy and avoiding any surprises that negatively affect financial performance. In other words, it is the credibility that the executive earns that has the greatest positive effect on his or her plan's sustainability.

Leaving the Past Behind and Making the Future the Goal

The world's greatest leaders have the ability to learn from the past without dwelling on it. We are all told that we should learn from our mistakes and move on, but we often keep revisiting corporate stumbles when making decisions about the future. Care needs to be taken that a past failed initiative is not labeled as a permanent failure, because new circumstances may make this the best solution or development. It may have been a great idea at the wrong time. It is about having the courage to fail, learn from the failure, and determine what would need to be changed to make it successful. Further, it is also recognizing when an idea has been exhausted and should be dropped. Many executives hang on to an initiative too long because they do not want to be perceived as having failed. A failure is taking a good idea that isn't working and letting it hurt corporate performance by supporting it too long. Moving on and exploring new possibilities is an important step for executives today. Similarly, successful executives know the importance of rewarding creativity and innovation. If a leader under their direction fails at a venture with inherent risk, the executive ensures that the leader is positioned in a new role that will be good for both the individual's career and the overall organization. It is essential that the leader not be punished for a well-conceived high-risk venture that fails. To do so would be to kill all innovation in the organization. This philosophy is particularly important given the current economic reality. We must constantly look ahead and remain solidly competitive; we must be proactive in seeking new opportunities while mitigating unnecessary risk. In most companies, the executives hold both the responsibility and authority for that direction.

Being an executive today is perhaps both the most exciting challenge and the most tenuous position in the organization. Rarely in history have executives been under as much pressure to perform or have they assumed so much accountability for the health and welfare of their organization. With that responsibility comes an obligation to protect both the internal stakeholders (employees) and the external stakeholders (shareholders). To reach that goal, executives need to learn the lessons of the past, do more of what they do well, and reinvent themselves to do that which they have not done before. Future leaders will follow suit.

As an executive coach, **Howard J. Morgan** has led major organizational change initiatives in partnership with top leaders and executives at numerous international organizations. His insights into the demands of executive leadership come from seventeen years of experience as a line executive and executive vice president in industry and government. Morgan has operated major businesses with full profit-and-loss responsibility; managed the people side of mergers and acquisitions; led international expansions and start-ups; and gained the respect of unions and corporations when negotiating agreements in volatile labor environments. He knows what it means to structure an organization, lead people, and manage a business to achieve quarterly objectives. This practical background, along with an understanding of the politics of leadership and the competitive pressures of today's global marketplace, is embodied in the roll-up-your-sleeves coaching work he does with executives. The dramatic impact of Morgan's approach is drawn from his ability to communicate the significance of people and performance issues in the context of business objectives. He has been a pioneer in the practical understanding of how motivation, productivity, and behavior are linked to organizational values, leadership approach, and employee satisfaction. He has done significant work on measuring the impact of leaders on long-term profitability and growth. He has helped leaders understand that the nuances of people management are a major influence on corporate success. Morgan is a managing director of the Leadership Research Institute and a member of the Alliance for Strategic Leadership. He specializes in executive coaching as a strategic change management tool leading to improved customer and employee satisfaction and overall corporate performance. Contact: howardmo@att.net

Chapter Fourteen

Rethinking Our Leadership Thinking

Choosing a More Authentic Path

Gary Heil

Linda Alepin

Simple truths are the hardest to come by, and they are often the most powerful in practice. Simple, powerful truths about leading people more effectively, about changing the nature of work, and about redefining our roles in the workplace are well known. For more than a half a century, Maslow, McGregor, Argyris, Bennis, and others have consistently described more enlightened ways to lead people. In fact, it is the consistency of their messages and the ubiquity of their views that makes it curious that most leaders continue to talk a better game of leadership than they choose to play.

The reasons why we have been slow to embrace research that describes better, simpler, and more effective ways to lead are many. They range from the lack of a sense of urgency for experimenting with new ideas to a lack of good role models. The main obstacle, however, may be the fact that the best leadership ideas are based on assumptions that are very different from the beliefs that are fundamental to present practices. Few challenges are as difficult for a leader as examining basic beliefs about people and finding the best ways to organize our collective efforts. Yet that is exactly what is required.

To become more effective leaders of inspired teams, we will have to unlearn many of our past practices. We will have to find new ways of challenging our beliefs. We will have to create a compelling value proposition for change. We will have to build a process that helps us anticipate and deal with the resistance that is encountered when the best knowledge available differs from the basic assumptions that support our past successes. We will have to adopt a mind-set that helps foster more fulfilling relationships in our organizations, and we will have to believe that it is not only possible to find a more enlightened path but it is also our responsibility.

This chapter does not claim to introduce new ideas about leadership or knowledge management; rather, it is a call to action. It is a call to create a dialogue to challenge the context in which we view leadership information and help us discover a more effective way to lead people. It is a plea for leaders to do the following:

- Begin a process of self-examination and self-discovery
- Resist the temptation to seek simple answers (we must seek clarity, not simplicity)
- Examine the choices we make in order to better understand how our espoused values differ from our values in use
- Choose a different set of beliefs—one that is more consistent with building inspired teams

The good news is that today, for the first time, leaders may find that authentic leadership and inspired teams are prerequisites to organizational survival. A rapidly changing world demands speed, flexibility, and responsiveness. Past systems of command and control, strict hierarchical structures, and dictated actions are inadequate to the task.

Choosing a Path of Self-Examination

Knowledge can be defined as information in a context that renders it useful. Simply put, it may be that our context for viewing information about leadership may significantly reduce or even preclude its effective use. Often our mind-set stands as an invisible obstacle to innovation and learning and renders us informed but not knowledgeable. To become more knowledgeable, we will have to accelerate a process of self-examination and resist the temptation to seek simple answers.

This process is a difficult one. Even for the leader who is willing to challenge his or her mind-set, the task can be daunting. We simply don't have good methods for challenging the way we think. Without good methods, many leaders have opted not to explore their own assumptions and have instead chosen to experiment with behavioral models that are easy to understand and apply and give them a greater sense of predictability and control. For many, these approaches have represented a pragmatic solution to the question of how they will upgrade leadership. Predictably, these methods rarely engender meaningful improvement beyond a quick but fleeting jolt in productivity.

We need look no further than the list of the most popular leadership books on Amazon.com to see our addiction to easy, quick answers. Three of the top twenty best sellers are *More Than a Pink Cadillac: Mary Kay, Inc.'s Nine Leadership Lessons; The One Minute Manager Meets the Monkey;* and *Leadership Shock . . . and How to Triumph over It: Eight Revolutionary Rules for Becoming a Powerful and Exhilarated Leader,* and all are given a rating of four or more stars by readers.

At times in the past half-century, the arguments for reexamining our leadership thinking have been compelling. Douglas McGregor made it his lifelong work to help leaders down a path of self-examination and discovery.[1] Even though he was recognized as the foremost thinker of his time, much of his message has been misinterpreted or ignored.

McGregor realized the complexities involved in challenging one's own context for viewing leadership information and suggested a number of methods to begin the process. He believed that leaders might find it easier to examine their thinking if they had a construct that could provide a comparison. He suggested Theory X and Theory Y, two very different sets of assumptions about the nature of people. He asked leaders to compare their beliefs to the fictitious beliefs outlined in X and Y. His queries remain highly relevant today:

- Are people naturally motivated to work, or must they be given incentives to get them to give their best?
- Is it natural for people to seek rewards for the least amount of effort, or are demotivated workers a symptom of stifling organizational and leadership practices?
- Can we realistically expect people to act unemotionally on the job, or are emotional reactions part of the human spirit that can be suppressed but never left behind?

Theory X and Theory Y are still recognizable terms for most. However, McGregor's hopes for these constructs were quickly frustrated decades ago. Discussions of X and Y devolved into conversations of style. In fact, most people in the 1960s, like most today, think that a Theory X leader has authoritative tendencies and that a Theory Y leader has a more democratic style. This bastardization of his ideas frustrated McGregor. He was hopeful, however, that a time would come when it would be necessary for leaders to challenge who they are. Fifty years later, the time is near. The major business crises of the recent past are forcing just such a reevaluation.

We Are What We Choose: Authenticity Is the Clear Choice

As Abraham Maslow pointed out, "A musician must make music; and an artist must paint; and a poet must write; if he is to be ultimately at peace with himself. What a man can be, he must be."[2]

Even though our willingness and ability to challenge our leadership mind-set has not gathered significant momentum in the five decades since McGregor, the need for us to take action is more apparent. Productivity improvements in almost every industry have led to a worldwide overcapacity of almost everything from crackers to jet engines. Overcapacity has shifted more power into the hands of customers, who have learned to be more demanding. At the same time, every market has grown more competitive as nearly every product has been cloned as soon as it is released. Furthermore, the lines have become blurred between what in the past was "sacred" internal information and what the consumer sees and hears about the companies with which they choose to do business. Simply log on to the Internet and see how much is available through Web sites, chat rooms, and message boards. For most companies, attracting and retaining knowledgeable people with pride in their organization and the ability to execute at world-class levels is the only path to future profitability.

This may mean that the search for a more effective way of leading inspired teams may no longer be optional. More effective leadership may be the key strategic differentiator for most. Leadership's impact on the bottom line is dramatic. According to a study by the Accenture Institute for Strategic Change, the stock price of companies perceived as being well led grew 900 percent over a ten-year period, compared to 74 percent growth in companies perceived to lack good leadership.[3] In its 1998 roundup of America's most admired companies, *Fortune* identified the common denominator of exemplary organizations. "The truth is that no one factor makes a company admirable, but if you were forced to pick the one that makes the most difference, you'd pick leadership."[4] The time may be fast approaching when leaders will be more motivated to look in the mirror in search of ways to improve their abilities to lead. We must be ready with a more concrete method if we hope to accelerate the improvement process.

The challenges inherent in past methods are compounded by our need to feel proud of our present activities. This has led many of us to confuse the values that we espouse with the values that guide our day-to-day leadership actions. The process of aligning our words and actions can help leaders challenge their beliefs.

For example, nearly every leader we have met says that customer service is important to their businesses. Yet as consumers, we
are frustrated, and rightly so. Service simply isn't very good, and the
ways most companies are led make it more likely that customers
will end up disappointed than well served. "People are our most
important asset" is reiterated in nearly every corporate speech, yet
we live in an era when the most motivated day at work for most
workers is the first day. The list of such duplicity in organizations is
a long one. Consider the differences between how we describe our
beliefs and how we choose to act when our career is on the line.
We need to ask the following questions:

- Why is it that nearly every employee understands the demoti-
  vational effects of most traditional performance appraisal
  systems, but few of these appraisal systems are changing
  significantly? Most still perpetuate an illusion that performance management processes can be both developmental
  and evaluative.

- Why is it that we talk of "empowerment," but we cannot call
  a company without hearing that the call will be "monitored
  for quality"? Do we really believe that these people feel
  empowered by the process?

- Why is it that we invest in off-sites to help build teamwork
  but perpetuate human resource practices that are built on the
  assumption that better performance will result when people
  inside a company compete with each other?

- Why is it that we talk of the need for committed, passionate
  employees but seem addicted to a system that attempts to
  gain motivation by manipulating stock options, compensation, or other rewards?

- Why is it that we say we value employee loyalty and then
  consistently fire the bottom 10 to 20 percent of the company
  annually, no matter how competent, hardworking, and loyal
  they have been?

Simply put, the choices we make and our espoused beliefs are very different. Our talk is often consistent with effective leadership theory. However, it may be a description of who we wished we were. In most cases, when push comes to shove, we opt for a more traditional, mechanical set of beliefs that appears more predictable. To be successful in building a new context, we will have to find a process that forces us to challenge our real beliefs.

This can be done by examining the choices that we make. We believe that we are our choices. If we perpetuate an ineffective performance appraisal system, we have beliefs that are consistent with that action (or inaction). If we set up internally competitive environments, we must believe that such an environment is consistent with peak performance. If our "calls are monitored for quality," there is a reason. Are we aware of our reasoning? Are we aware of the unintended consequences of our actions? To be knowledgeable leaders, we must be aware of our reasons and willing to challenge them by continuing to ask "Why?" until we identify the fundamental assumptions that define us as leaders. It is simply harder to dodge the tough questions when we are examining what we do. Once we are forced to face the duplicity of our words and actions, and when we challenge ourselves to be authentic in word and deed, we may begin to understand how much we will have to change in order to build an organization in which people can reach their potential.

Choosing to Believe Differently

We were on a plane recently talking to a principal in a large training company. When we asked him to describe his view of the future, he told us that the future of his business could be described in one word. The word was no longer *plastics* (as in the movie *The Graduate*). "The word today," he said, "is *leadership*." He told us that almost all organizational failures could be tracked to a failure in leadership and that his company was going to emphasize leadership development above all else. When we asked him what he intended to teach, he described the need for a situational approach that taught leaders how to behave appropriately, depending on the circumstances. Not only was there no mention of a leader's mind-set or assumptions, but he went out of his way to explain to us how leadership development must become more practical and behavioral. We can only hope that his message will not resonate. It is not that our behaviors don't matter. They do matter. But over time, our behaviors will always follow our beliefs.

People have great radar for detecting duplicity. They can tell whether a leader is passionate or is merely spouting the party line. They know when a leader's words are authentic and when a leader is parroting someone else's message.

More important, people can tell whether the leader cares about them or only cares about meeting his or her own goals and capturing the benefits of other people's performance. As followers, we look for respect, authenticity, honesty, and caring. When a leader is authentic, we know it. We can see it in the leader's eyes. We can feel it in the leader's presence. We look quickly beyond words or style and into the leader's heart. We care whether our leaders believe in us and whether they trust us to make a significant contribution. We care about their motives, and we should.

For example, compliments and praise can be a way of saying thank-you or can be given in the hope of getting something in return (usually better work). People can smell the difference in the motives of the leader instantaneously. No matter how practiced a leader's style, behavior exhibited in an attempt to get something in return will appear manipulative. Manipulation erodes trust and undermines the development of relationships. "Catch people doing something right," we have been told. Rarely have we been asked to think about why. Do we believe that by praising people we will get more of the desired behavior, or do we praise people because we want to say we care? The difference is everything.

We have seen leaders of all shapes and styles who are successful with their teams. Some had charisma; some did not. Some sought consensus; some did not. Some had quick tempers; others had great patience. What they did have in common, however, were similar beliefs about people that allowed them to see the possibilities. They had a unique context for viewing information. What was merely data to some leaders was profound knowledge in others' hands. Interview these leaders, as we have, and many of them will tell you that they believe deeply in the potential of people to make a commitment. They believe that in the right environment, ordinary people will naturally do extraordinary things. They have a commitment to the people who trust them to lead. They provide an environment where people can learn while engaging in meaningful work. They are perceived as authentic because their actions are consistent with their espoused beliefs.

Although no set of beliefs is universally held by all leaders, we have found that those listed in this chapter are frequently embraced by the best leaders that we have met. The words come easily for many. Consistent action and complementary management practices are less common. Authenticity in leadership has always come before all else. However, we are entering an era when people will not tolerate duplicity. Although the following ideas have been debated for generations, most of us have not made the choices required to authentically build organizations based on these assumptions. We need to ask ourselves, "How are our current practices and behaviors consistent or inconsistent with these beliefs?" Do we disagree with these assumptions? Are they impractical? Is it risky to try? Maybe we can finally ask, "Why not? Why not me? Why not now?" Today, authenticity is the clear mandate. It is no longer optional.

A Different Set of Beliefs

• *Trust is given, not earned.* People don't trust people who do not trust them. If we want people to trust us, we must trust them first. If we can't trust them, why should they trust us? Why do we expect others to earn our trust yet they are supposed to trust us because of our position? When people truly trust each other, the team dynamics flow so much more easily and openly.

• *People want to do the right thing.* People want to live values that are consistent with their aspirations. Values are a common ground by which dialogue flows and decisions are pondered. People have an implicit understanding of lines not to be crossed.

• *Freedom is the essence of motivation.* The freedom to choose is a fundamental human need. The more that need is restricted unnecessarily, the more frustrated a person will become. Only when we create environments based on self-direction and mutual accountability will we capture the potential of people. Organizations are organic and capable of evolving naturally.

• *People are naturally driven to make things better and seek meaning in their work.* Just challenge a group to make a contribution and watch the level of energy rise. There is a yearning for meaning in life and in work. People will do things for a cause that they will not do for money. Watch how people work when they are proud to tell people where they work and how they contribute.

• *People have great capacity and need to learn and grow.* The need to learn and grow is as natural as the need to eat. Unfortunately, many jobs have been designed to limit training costs and to ensure control. Abraham Maslow noted after one of his first days working in a company that "any job not worth doing is not worth doing well."[5] Jobs must be designed so that every person, regardless of pay level, can learn, grow, and make a substantial contribution. Higher expectations will lead to higher performance in the right environment, but not if the leader's expectations of a group communicates a vision of mediocrity. Dare to be great.

• *People prefer responsibility to dependency and interest to boredom.* In the right conditions, work is as natural as play. We need to be engaged and responsible. Too many management practices rob people of the ability to be responsible. Empowerment too often means that "I have the power, and if I trust you, I'll share power with you." Effective renewal is not about getting people to change in order to conform. It's about getting people to take responsibility for creating a different future. People want to be engaged. People want to be passionate. It is the leader's responsibility to create the environment and the opportunity.

- *People seek to be led, not managed.* People don't want to be managed. No one wants to be planned, organized, and controlled. People want to be part of a team. They want to participate. They want to be a partner in the process of value creation. Participation is not a tactic. It is the way people work best. However, there is power in an inspired leader of a team who drives with passion, integrity, and has the courage to make decisions and provide direction as needed. As people can be frustrated by micromanagement, they can be just as frustrated when leadership or direction is lacking.

- *People want to work cooperatively toward a shared goal.* People have a need to be part of a group and to help others. This natural tendency is often lost when people are "incented" to compete with other members of the team. This may be the biggest value subtractor in many organizations. We need to overcome our belief that internal competition leads to better performance. We need to experiment with team-based organizations. Manufacturers learned out of necessity. The rest of us must follow.

- *We must communicate as much as possible to as many people as possible.* Can you remember the last time you were asked to do something and had no idea why you were doing it? Can you remember how excited you were? We simply cannot commit to what we don't understand. Widely distributed information and a shared context for understanding that information should be the right of every employee. Jan Carlzon said it best: "People without information cannot take responsibility. People with information can hardly help but take responsibility."[6] People want to take responsibility and make good decisions. People want to live values that are consistent with their aspirations. However, too often people in organizations remain uninformed and are therefore unable to discern what is best for the organization.

- *People want to belong and feel a sense of pride in their jobs, organizations, and associates.* People come to work hoping that this company will be a great company where they will be able to make a maximum contribution. Initial experiences are compelling, and people need to see that the company is worthy of their commitment. At times they will turn down promotions, transfers, or new jobs based on a desire to stay a part of something they are proud of or to avoid moving to a place where the opposite is true.

- *People are diverse and desire to be treated as unique individuals in the workplace.* They crave to be recognized and appreciated for the individual strengths and talents they bring to the team. Too often organizations look at people with the approach of what works for the majority or who most closely fits the "organizational mold." Harnessing the energy that comes from individual strengths can make a formidable team more capable of delivering results at a phenomenal level.

- *People desire to feel important, needed, useful, confident, successful, proud, and respected.* People do not like to feel unimportant, interchangeable, useless, fearful, anonymous, or expendable.

The Time for Action: Now

The evidence is overwhelming that building more inspired teams will require most leaders to rethink their leadership. To do so, they will have to resist the temptation to seek out simple contingency models and instead opt for a career filled with self-examination and self-discovery. Because good methods for examining our thinking have not fully evolved, leaders must participate in a dialogue that can help them challenge their basic assumptions about effective leadership.

This journey must begin with a comparison of espoused beliefs and day-to-day leadership choices. By evaluating the inconsistencies in words and actions, they will be better able to identify the changes they must make in order to lead authentically. Our fervent hope is that the time that McGregor envisioned, when significant changes in leadership philosophy would become a requirement for survival, is fast approaching. This will not only enable us as leaders to build more effective, more human organizations, but it will also enable us to enrich the lives of every person who gives us permission to lead.

Gary Heil is an author, educator, lawyer, consultant, and coach. For the past three decades, he has been an ardent student of the human side of organizations. He was a pioneer in the study of loyal customer relationships and how they are affected by employee motivation. He is the coauthor of *Leadership and the Customer Revolution, One Size Fits One, Maslow on Management,* and *Revisiting the Human Side of Enterprise.* He is the cofounder of the Webcast "Leadership Lessons from the FastLane," has served as an examiner for the Malcolm Baldrige National Quality Award, and founded the Center for Innovative Leadership. Heil has served on the boards of several technology companies and remains an adviser to world-class leaders in a number of industries. Contact: garyheil@attbi.com; http://www.centerfornewfutures.com

Linda Alepin is a partner at Center for New Futures, a leadership consulting firm. She has more than thirty years of experience in the field of high technology. As a consultant, she focuses on helping her clients achieve breakthrough results through shifts in their thinking. She spent more than ten years as a vice president and officer of a Fortune 300 information technology company, and she was CEO and founder of an early Internet start-up in the e-learning space. Alepin is a noted public speaker on leadership and management. She is currently head of the leadership initiative at Santa Clara University and a founder of Open Capital Network, a nonprofit that links entrepreneurs worldwide with Silicon Valley expertise. Contact: lalepin@interjacent.com; http://www.centerfornewfutures.com

Chapter Fifteen

Learning at the Top

How CEOs Set the Tone for the Knowledge Organization

James F. Bolt

Charles Brassard

Chief executive officers sit atop huge knowledge creation and distribution systems within their organization. They have the power to shape these systems and integrate them within the operations of the company. Their decisions influence what investments will be made in technology and in people to set knowledge into motion throughout and outside their organization. Sharing with their people a compelling vision for how knowledge can be a source of competitive advantage for the company, and implementing the operating systems that will deliver on this vision are key levers for CEOs. More important, however, the beliefs, commitments, and behaviors of CEOs toward learning and knowledge sharing are what will ultimately drive changes in the culture of the organization and produce sustained results. This is because CEOs are the most watched people in any organization. What they do sends ripples down the whole line. Understandably, without a clear statement of shared values and a continuous demonstration of how learning and sharing knowledge contribute to delivering the corporate strategy, CEOs cannot create the momentum needed to fully leverage the collective intelligence of the organization.

How do CEOs learn? How do they demonstrate their commitment to learning and knowledge sharing in their organization? This chapter presents a wide range of practices used successfully by CEOs and top executive leaders to support their learning and to demonstrate their commitment to learning and knowledge sharing in the organizations they lead.[1] It also describes some of the challenges and opportunities inherent to learning at the CEO level. It provides ideas on how to integrate learning into the fast-paced lives of top executives and how to support these executives better.

What CEOs Need to Be Effective Learning and Knowledge Leaders

CEOs have considerable resources at their disposal to learn but are working under constant pressure and competing demands for their time. Their success depends largely on their ability to learn from experience and to reflect on these experiences. CEOs also have a unique vantage point from which to access and connect ideas quickly. Their learning depends on their ability to filter information and knowledge efficiently from within and outside the organization. Finally, CEOs are literally alone at the top. Their peers are outside the boundaries of the organization. Their learning depends on their ability to forge formal and informal networks with people outside their organization.

Here are some of the most important leadership attributes or behaviors that support CEOs in their learning and knowledge management agenda:

- *They have a desire to learn.* They openly acknowledge the fact that they are constantly learning. To do so, they integrate learning into all aspects of their lives (work, family time, social activities, travel), and they constantly reach out to learn from others. They adopt the attitude that there is something new to learn in every situation and from every person.

- *They have an open and curious mind.* They are not only open to diverse perspectives and points of view; they also actively seek out people and ideas that challenge their way of seeing the world. They ask questions that generate insights and new possibilities for action.

- *They show humility.* They have the ability to see themselves in action and to openly talk about their mistakes. Their ego doesn't get in the way of learning. They accept the position of not knowing and respect others for recognizing the same.

- *They make their learning public.* They invite feedback at every opportunity. They are proactive in having people observe them and are public about the development issues on which they are working. They use every opportunity to share stories about their experiences and what they have learned from them.

- *They tolerate risk.* They are tolerant of mistakes as long as there is a commitment to learning. They believe that to be successful, learning in the organization must be greater than the rate of change.

- *They "walk the talk."* Not only are they vocal about their support of learning, but they also sustain the resources dedicated by the organization for learning in good and bad times. They model what they preach and ask others to do the same.

How CEOs Acquire and Share Their Knowledge

CEOs acquire knowledge in a multitude of ways, and they don't just keep it to themselves.

CEOs Learn on the Job

CEOs see every transaction, conversation, and forum as an opportunity to learn. They are intentional about it through the process of reflection. They stop periodically to consider what and how they might learn. They invite people to trigger their reflection process through questions that challenge the way they see the business and the organization.

They intentionally use the business agenda to ground their learning and foster the sharing of knowledge. Here are four real examples of how this is done.

- *Strategic business dialogue*. The CEO identifies a critical business issue (such as the future business model for the company or doing business in a new country) and the key questions for which he or she needs answers. A few key people (such as a CEO with extensive experience in the area, outside thinkers, consultants, or partners) meet face to face in a structured conversation to consider analyses done by participants, as well as perspectives and ideas, on this particular issue. This is a dialogue for learning and opening possibilities, not for immediate decisions.

- *Business review process*. Several times during the year, CEOs meet with their top executives (in a functional or geographical area or across the company) to consider business results and future goals. They and their teams use these opportunities to assess their performance and learn from both their successes and their failures. The reviews keep the focus on learning at the practical level and foster open dialogue. CEOs use these sessions with different business units as a way to cross-pollinate ideas and best practices across the organization. In addition, these best practices are documented and integrated in the training and education programs of the organization.

- *Executive or board meetings*. CEOs use these opportunities to get continuous feedback on their performance and that of their organization. They also want to hear how the organization is perceived from the outside.

- *Regular business and project meetings*. CEOs integrate a particular focus for learning as a part of all of these meetings (for example, bringing a business outsider to share best practices or having a structured dialogue on teamwork). They also use after-action reviews in every possible business setting. An *after-action review* is a dedicated period of time at the end of every meeting in which teams may reflect on and discuss what they have accomplished, what they have learned in the process, what they could have done differently to be more effective, and how they can share what they have learned in the organization.

CEOs Learn from Feedback

They give and get feedback from multiple sources, such as 360-degree feedback, interviews with customers and employees, and surveys. They model the importance of feedback by using every opportunity to give feedback to others. They seek and receive feedback with enthusiasm, but even more important, they say what they will do about it and give credit to those who provide it to them. They publicly communicate what development areas they are working on and encourage others to emulate their commitment to learning through feedback.

They surround themselves with strong people who can give them feedback honestly and powerfully. They use their board of directors as peer respondents (in 360-degree assessments) and set time aside during every board meeting for personal feedback. They seek out people within the organization (beyond their immediate entourage of top executives) on whom they can rely for honest feedback. In other words, they drive a culture that enables people to speak up as opposed to telling them what they want to hear.

CEOs Learn from Coaches

CEOs use coaches for specific and distinct purposes. Here are three examples of how they use coaches:

- *To support the strategic agenda.* This answers the question "Where are we going?" Coaches work at this level to help CEOs in their leadership capacity, for example, to focus on an organizational priority or to implement specific change initiatives. The coaching process aims to open new perspectives and insights that can guide them in their strategic agendas. Coaches stimulate new thinking by using books, research reports, and other resources, and they challenge CEOs to approach the priority or initiative in innovative ways. The desired outcome is enhanced leadership effectiveness in the context of a successful change initiative.

- *To enhance a specific domain of expertise.* This form of coaching provides access to expertise and insights in specific areas of operations (such as financial acumen and strategy execution). CEOs often access the best resources in the world to support them in such domains. Learning in this context is "just in time" and is carefully framed so as to maximize time and performance. CEOs can be ruthless about what they need to learn and what is not useful to them.

- *To enhance their leadership effectiveness.* This typically involves coaching that focuses on building specific competencies and changing behaviors (such as managing specific relationships more effectively). This form of coaching focuses on achieving specific and measurable results (that can be observed by others).

CEOs Learn from Mentors

CEOs seek out mentors to support their learning and development. In this context, mentors are role models or "wise people." They learn by observing other leaders (for example, by joining the board of another organization to observe the CEO in action). They use mentors as sounding boards for decisions (such as regarding their careers) and to share their assessments, moods, and dilemmas. The trust and respect with which they regard these people enables them to share personal issues as well.

CEOs Learn from Their Peers

Because of their relative isolation at the helm of their organizations, CEOs mostly connect with their peers in informal or social settings. Some belong to small groups that meet a few times a year to share knowledge and insights and to discuss issues common to the industry, business, and CEOs. They also look for opportunities to connect with people from other sectors of society through their involvement in community and charitable causes. The relationships they develop enable them to call each other for advice or to test ideas. Some CEOs connect informally with key industry or business counterparts to explore opportunities and scenarios for partnerships, alliances, or mergers. They use these "explorations" as learning opportunities, gaining new strategic perspectives on their business and on potential new directions for growth.

CEOs Learn from Positive Deviants

They constantly expose themselves to new ideas and perspectives. They surround themselves with people who think differently, who can help them reframe what they see and think, or who can make connections that they would not spontaneously make. They do that, for example, by inviting people to be on their boards and by networking with people who have drastically different backgrounds. They connect with people outside of their traditional playing field (for instance, in social settings) to engage their senses in different ways (as opposed to the intellectual mode that they rely on almost exclusively in their business setting). They also stretch their thinking by spending time with creative people within their organization in "blue-sky" conversations around emerging issues or challenges.

CEOs Cast Their Knowledge Net Widely

They are avid readers who explore topics well outside their own business domain. They encourage their executive team members to stretch their minds in similar ways. They draw on summaries from articles, books, and reports to keep up on trends, developments, and issues. They create networks of people across the organization that exchange information and intelligence in areas they have identified as key to their knowledge and effectiveness. This "executive information system" is designed for them and their teams to stay current and to learn from a wide variety of sources. They access this information in bite-size pieces at the time and point of need. Technology plays a big role in meeting these needs. (CEOs are typically technology-savvy.) In this context, they recognize how important it is for them to develop their own capacity to filter and process information. They value those competencies in the people who feed them information.

CEOs expose themselves to many different conversations and perspectives. One way they do that is by "walking the hallways" of the organization (the nonexecutive floors, the shop floor, retail outlets). Such practices breed a culture of access, disclosure, and open dialogue. "Store walks" enable CEOs to get a feel for the customer experience and to assess how corporate policies and programs pan out in the real world. This provides a rich source of learning for CEOs and grounds their dialogues at the executive table.

CEOs Learn by Putting Some Skin in the Game

Few CEOs take part in formal external "institutional" learning programs. (There are few that would be appropriate for CEOs.) Those who do get involved in such programs sometimes do so with their top teams so that they can focus together on a specific issue or challenge of critical importance to the organization.

CEOs actively sponsor in-company action-learning programs, where people work on real business problems for development purposes. They define the problems or challenges to be tackled by their high-potential leaders and set expectations that recommendations resulting from their work will be implemented. They dedicate quality time kicking off such programs at the front end and receiving recommendations at the back end. CEOs learn by listening and engaging their executives in the context of solving real problems and opportunities. CEOs give credit to the teams for what they learn and for achieving breakthroughs for the business. They demonstrate in tangible ways how they act on the results of the program.

CEOs learn from shaping the content of executive development programs and by teaching in these programs. This forces them to reflect on and to clarify their vision and "teachable" points of view. They also ensure that best practices are constantly embedded into company training and education programs.

CEOs use management and executive programs to give and receive feedback. They learn the most by leading dialogues in which lots of questions are asked and there is a license to speak openly and frankly about issues and concerns (as opposed to where knowledge is imparted from on high). They learn from spending time and debriefing with program facilitators and coaches following the program.

How CEOs Demonstrate Their Commitment to Learning and Knowledge Sharing

In order for individuals throughout the organization to understand the value of learning, CEOs must be role models for learning and knowledge sharing. Following are some methods they use to demonstrate their commitment to learning.

CEOs Are Champions

They invest adequate financial and human resources into learning and knowledge sharing. They always push to have more done. They champion one or two strategic initiatives annually, for which they set performance targets and learning goals. They regard these investments and the infrastructure supporting learning and knowledge management as critical to the long-term excellent performance and competitive advantage of their organizations.

They get personally involved in the design of executive development programs; even more important, they attend programs as participants, just like every other executive. This sends a clear message about the importance they put on the development of people and the use of corporate programs as instruments of change and business development.

CEOs Have a People Agenda

CEOs demonstrate their commitment to learning and development by playing an active role in succession planning and by constantly reinforcing the importance of recruiting and retaining top talent. They are intimately involved in performance and talent reviews and the development planning associated with the top management. They ask their direct reports to do the same.

They have integrated their people agenda into the business planning process. For example, they make learning a part of the performance system by assessing their management team on the results achieved in supporting the development of their people. They teach their top executives how to be effective around feedback and encourage them to do more of it. They spend quality time with their direct reports to plan their development. They insist on documenting the impact of these efforts in positively changing behaviors and improving long-term performance. They recognize the importance of learning and adaptability to change as competencies in and of themselves.

CEOs Have a Knowledge Agenda

CEOs demand that the organization have a plan around the growth of intellectual capital. They see one of their roles as fostering the development of the collective IQ of the organization. They put a lot of faith in mobilizing the collective intelligence of the organization as a means of sustaining competitive advantage. To do this, they set up mechanisms (such as networks, after-action reviews, and dialogues) to foster the dissemination of "actionable knowledge" throughout the organization.

CEOs Tell Stories

CEOs share their personal experiences through storytelling. They use stories in a wide variety of settings (such as during executive learning programs, employee or town hall meetings, management meetings, and site visits) to talk about their mistakes, what they have learned, and how they learned. The stories and the dialogues created around them help foster the sharing of values, culture, and best practices across the organization. They use many direct and virtual channels (such as weekly e-mail, broadcast voice mail, and video) to communicate their insights and learning throughout their organizations and to harvest ideas and intelligence on organizational progress.

CEOs Exemplify Lifelong Learning

Their behavior and actions toward learning and development allow others to practice the same approach to life. They not only promote learning policies but also demonstrate how they learn. They demand that others be committed to and engaged in executive and management development processes to the same degree that they are. CEOs are "coaches at large," supporting people who seek to improve their performance and attending to their development. They encourage learning by asking questions that disturb, generate insight, and uncover knowledge and new possibilities.

Obstacles to Learning That CEOs Face

CEOs who invest in their learning and that of their people create a systemic and strategic capacity for knowledge creation and distribution in their organizations. In large part, embodying the values and the practices that can drive a learning culture starts at the top. This cannot be done successfully without having the right operating mechanisms supported by the right kind of dialogues and working relationships among people who promote learning and knowledge sharing as means of achieving the business strategy of the organization. CEOs who don't recognize the importance of modeling these behaviors face many potential setbacks. The following obstacles are most often seen as deterring CEOs in their learning and development efforts and in their ability to enroll their top teams and the rest of their organizations in this agenda.

• They are captured by their own success and are reluctant to expose their vulnerabilities and weaknesses. Their arrogance and perception of self-importance create few openings for learning. Self-knowledge and self-awareness are their biggest blind spot.

• Like all successful people, they are overcommitted. Learning to them is important but not urgent. Since they have to deal with so many crises, they find it hard to make a sustained investment in their learning. They don't protect any time for learning.

• They are impatient. Few people can get their attention, and their attention span is limited (for example, many CEOs find it difficult to listen without interrupting). They create few openings to learn from other people.

• They are driven by the need to win. If the conversation topic is trivial to them (with no perceived impact on winning), they will pay little attention to it. Wanting to be right can impede their learning.

• They are under family pressures. They dedicate any "free time" to being with their families in an attempt to balance their heavy work commitment with family life.

• They are surrounded by thick filters, which can make it difficult to get real information to them. This "heavy protection shield" may close them off from possibilities for learning. Internal beliefs and myths about what can be said to the CEO also act as similar filters for learning.

• Near the end of their career, CEOs may be hesitant to let go. This can get in the way of learning about what lies ahead for them beyond their current position and frustrate the learning process for potential incumbents.

Conclusion

All in all, our survey shows that despite formidable obstacles, CEOs play a crucial role in learning, as well as knowledge creation and

distribution, in their organizations. The critical factor in their success is how they personally learn and share their learning. Some of
the keys to their success are the following:

- Their personal thirst for learning. They see every activity,
event, and business challenge as an opportunity to learn. Their
egos don't get in the way. They are not afraid to let people know
that they need and want to learn.
- They integrate learning into the agenda of every business
meeting, board meeting, and strategy or planning session. They do
this through techniques such as after-action reviews.
- They role-model learning in every conceivable way; for
instance, they receive 360-degree feedback on their leadership
effectiveness, they tell stories that include mistakes they've made
and what they learned from them, they have coaches and mentors,
they go out of their way to expose themselves to people who think
totally differently, they attend their organizations' executive development programs as students and teachers, and they coach others
frequently.
- They personally champion and drive executive and leadership development efforts, and they ensure that their organizations'
learning and development resources are above average and
sustained in good economic times and bad.
- They fully integrate their people development and strategy
development processes.
- They have a well-thought-out plan for the growth of their
organizations' intellectual capital and the development of
their organizations' collective IQ and wisdom.

Our survey clearly showed that this important leadership task
can be achieved and that there is no magic to it beyond the personal beliefs and commitment of the CEO.

James F. Bolt is chairman of Executive Development Associates
(EDA). EDA develops high-impact, custom-designed, in-company
executive development strategies, systems, and programs that help

organizations achieve their strategic objectives and make leadership talent a competitive advantage. EDA's clients have included Fortune 100 companies and leading organizations around the world. Bolt was selected by the *Financial Times* as one of the top experts in executive leadership development. He is cofounder of the Alliance for Strategic Leadership (A4SL) and the Learning Network; he also founded and manages the Chief Learning Officer Forum. He is the author of *Executive Development: A Strategy for Corporate Competitiveness*. He has contributed to several books, including the best seller *The Leader of the Future*, and written many articles, including "Tailor Executive Development to Strategy," published in the *Harvard Business Review*. Contact: jbolt@executivedevelopment.com

Charles Brassard is a certified professional integral coach and a teacher in the field of coaching. Through his company, Impact Coaching, Inc., Brassard works with private and public sector clients in Canada and around the world. He applies innovative methods to support the development of senior executives, particularly through action learning and coaching. He also designs and delivers custom programs in the area of executive and leadership development through his affiliation with Executive Development Associates. He is a frequent guest speaker and workshop leader on the topics of action learning, coaching, and professional effectiveness, and he has published a number of articles about these subjects. Contact: impact.coaching@sympatico.ca

Chapter Sixteen

Unleash the Learning Epidemic

James Belasco

The following "help wanted" advertisement recently appeared in one of the world's leading business magazines.

> We provide leading-edge solutions to many of the world's largest institutions. . . . Our continued growth is based on an unmatched knowledge of customers' business needs—and the ability to create solutions to meet them. It's an environment that encourages the desire to grow knowledge and give of our best. And that's where you'll be chartered to realize that aim. . . . You will help us maximize the business advantage we gain from the finest minds we employ.[1]

I've seen similar ads in other leading newspapers. Many organizations are looking at learner-leaders (L^2s) to fill both management and staff leadership positions. More important, there are discussions about learning in boardrooms and offices across the world.

Developing the learning "epidemic" in your organization all begins with you, regardless of your position. Leaders cast long shadows, and everyone is a leader of some type of organization, whether it is Intergalactic Motors, an accounts payable team, a family, or even the one-person organization known as ME, Inc. Cast a long learning shadow! Set the gold standard that expects learning to be a major part of everyone's life by making it a major part of yours. Demonstrate your commitment to learning in every way possible so that others will be encouraged to follow your example. Then build the systems framework that will turn your L^2 focus into an organizationwide epidemic!

Learning Is a Personal Contact Sport

Learning doesn't happen to you; it happens through you. You are not an empty vessel that some teacher fills with learning. You must be an actor on the stage, completely immersed in the play of your life, not a spectator in the second row. You "gotta wanna," a motivational speaker once said. She's absolutely correct. You must want to learn something very badly so that you're willing to invest the personal effort to truly be different. And your "gotta wanna" will encourage the "gotta wanna" in others.

An executive I know knew things weren't going as well as he wanted in his business. He tried many "new" approaches to engage his people in the business. After listening to a tape recording of one of his meetings, he developed a strong case of "gotta wanna" that began a multiyear journey during which he committed to learning new ways of dealing with people. Today he's a different leader whose business has grown many times over and who has been chosen Executive of the Year by several leading business publications. His "gotta wanna" learning disease infected his entire organization.

Show Up in the Learning Arena Ready to Participate

Leaders go first. No one in an organization will participate in learning activities if the leaders do not lead the way. This means being an example, being enthusiastic, and being positive about learning opportunities.

Learn-by-Doing Is the Learning Arena

Doing activities are great learning "arenas" because people learn best from doing. So find opportunities to do for yourself and others, and then make certain that you and everyone learn from the doing.

Kurt was a talented design engineer working for a large oil-refining company in the Netherlands. He wanted to learn more about hydrogen-based fuel cells so that he could become an expert in designing manufacturing facilities to produce them. He believed that hydrogen fuel cells would take a large portion of the current hydrocarbon gasoline market, so he wanted to be ready when that happened. He visited several of his friends who worked for automobile companies that were developing fuel cell engines. He proposed a six-month assignment to intern at two companies to learn more about their hydrogen fuel cell technology and how these cells might be manufactured. The board recognized the opportunities and threats that Kurt had uncovered and saw the need to play in this newly emerging arena. They met with him both during and after his internship to ensure that both he and they maximized the learning from his assignment. Today Kurt leads the company's fuel cell program and reports directly to the board of directors. He took the risk, his leaders encouraged him with time and resources, and he and they all learned and gained.

Use on-the-Job Assignments as Valuable Learn-by-Doing Activities

Job assignments are great L^2 opportunities. Seize the opportunities they provide for real-time learning-by-doing for yourself, and encourage others to do the same.

Recently, I watched a great L^2 in action. Lui, head of the Toronto office of a $2 billion company, had transferred to Toronto because he wanted "a North American leadership experience" to add to his background. During the first day, Lui, Richard, the executive vice president, and I visited several potential customers and partners. On the way back to the hotel that night, Lui said to Richard, "It's really exciting to watch how you always ask how their business is going, what they do personally, and what things are important to them. In my previous assignments, I've always tried to overwhelm the other person with the long list of benefits they'd get from working with us. You turn it around and listen to them first. I learned more today in these conversations than I could have learned in years using my old system. I'd like to learn that skill."

The next morning, Richard worked with Lui on the question-asking approach. Lui was a fast learner, and by the end of the day, he was effectively leading the interviews. Several weeks later, Richard played for me a voice mail message from Lui in which Lui shared his success in landing a big new contract with a major Canadian customer. "Funny thing," Richard said to me, "I really learned a lot in the process of teaching Lui. In fact, I feel that I was the big learner in our exchange." Now that's a real L^2 at work! Richard used learn-by-doing assignments not only to help others learn but to help himself learn as well.

Whether it's in a family, a friendship, a neighborhood, a business, or a church, great L^2s leverage learn-by-doing activities, like job assignments, to help ordinary people do extraordinary things, and they start with themselves.

Training Activities Work When They Meet the "I've Got to Do It Now!" Test

Training sessions can provide valuable learn-by-doing activities, provided the learning is immediately relevant to the individual's life. I recently visited a large warehouse location with another L^2 president. Before she joined the organization, people probably managed their training activities in the typical way: the "suits" at the top decided what people needed and provided it to them. For instance, the warehouse site manager scheduled a teamwork training class because he felt that "they" needed it.

As she talked with folks in the warehouse, she asked them, "What do you need to do your job better? Is it a tool? Is it training? What kind of training?" Not surprisingly, teamwork was not high on the list of frequently mentioned topics. For instance, the production control manager said he needed an MRP (manufacturers' representative profile) system in order to meet his performance objective of 100 percent guaranteed correct output and reduced turnaround time from forty-eight to twenty-four hours. Then he said, "Give me a training day with all the associates who touch the system, so I can show them how to use the system to help them do a more effective job."

Listening to the training, which focused on meeting pressing business needs, provided immediate benefits and involved specific on-the-job activities, helped associates do a better job! No wonder the center is now the world-class gold standard in its field.

Keep Looking over the Walls to Find Great Models to Learn From

It's easy to be blinded by the brilliance of our own successes. "If it ain't broke, don't fix it!" is a popular management saying. For example, one property of a hotel chain was the consistent top performer. Workers at the property developed an arrogant "We know how to do things" attitude. In the course of the chain's annual planning process, we discovered that the high-performing hotel was actually losing market share. What a shock!

The general manager of the property, a born again L^2, immediately shifted into learning mode and urged the staff to start "shopping the competition." She set up a fund to pay for all staff members, from housekeepers to front desk people, to eat or stay overnight at competitive hotels. Within weeks, the staff accumulated enough data to begin redesigning their own hotel. Everyone took part; everyone contributed. The next six-month competitive market report showed a six-point share growth.

You can never do enough looking over the wall to learn how others do things. Your doing so will encourage everyone else to do the same, at all levels in the organization. Seeing excellence in action helps individuals visualize how they can do it for themselves.

Make Time for Learning

Most people are so busy "doing," rushing from project to project and meeting to meeting, that they don't have time to learn from all their doing. Build in learning as a part of every activity. L^2s seamlessly integrate work and learning, and they set that example for everyone else. Build time into every meeting, every project, and every day to reflect on what you've learned and how you can use that learning to do better next time.

Have Learning Objectives for Every Meeting

Start every meeting by agreeing on the major learning for that meeting. It's Stephen Covey's idea of "beginning with the end in mind." Take time at the end of every meeting to check whether all participants have accomplished their learning purposes.

Practice the "Five-Minute Rule"

For every hour of a meeting, take five minutes to debrief what you learned that can help you be more effective in the next meeting. Focus first on learning about the process—for instance, how you work together, how the meeting was structured, and how you used (or misused) various tools. Then explore what you learned about the content. The military uses this method to keep everyone focused on becoming consistently more effective as both technicians and leaders.

Use the "Hallway Challenge" to Keep the Learning Fire Blazing

Make it a practice to stop folks in the hallways and ask, "What did you learn this week, and how are you going to apply it?" Not only will this keep you up to date, but it will also keep everyone else on their learning toes. I recall a lunch with Stephen Covey when he asked his nearest tablemate, "What was the most surprising thing you learned this year?" The answer led to a very stimulating and educational conversation involving the whole table.

Spread the L^2 Epidemic: Build Your Learning Infrastructure

Nothing valuable grows in an uncultivated garden. If you want roses in your garden, it takes frequent watering, spraying, and fertilizer. It's the same with learning. In theory, everyone's in favor of learning. No one we know of campaigns for ignorance. Yet like roses in your garden, learning doesn't happen automatically. It takes lots of hard work and a system that proactively facilitates the learning equivalent of regular watering, spraying, and fertilization. That's the "learning infrastructure."

Build Learning into the Management Systems

Incorporate learning into the ongoing management system, the heart of which is the objective, measurement, and reward systems. Most organizations have annual performance goals and monthly, quarterly, or semiannual action plans to achieve those goals. In addition to the traditional financial goals, L^{2}s build in a learning objective as well. Then expect, measure, and reward learning by making the learning objective as important as financial, productivity, and market share objectives. That way everyone can add a "to learn" list to the traditional "to do" list.

Some learning objectives can be developmental or personal. For example, the vice president of sales at AT&T undertook a factory superintendent assignment as part of her learning about the manufacturing side of the business. That particular experience came in handy when she later became vice president of the entire business unit. In another, more personal example, the CFO's learning objective at Square D one year was to learn how to take a continuous two-week vacation with his family, leave the office before 7:00 at night, and write out his Christmas cards at home with his wife instead of at the office two nights before Christmas.

Reward and Recognize Learning and Learners

There are many ways to reward learning. Many organizations include the achievement of learning objectives as part of their incentive compensation plan. Many others use individual recognition as a reward. One company I know has a recognition program for employees who bring new and valuable outside learning into their organization. Much like the rewards it gives to sales staff, the company invites forty to fifty of its best L^2s to a resort for a few days, where they share their learning experiences. This is one way in which the company encourages its people to develop L^2 capabilities.

Make Knowledge More Powerful Than Rank

Who makes the best decisions? It used to be the people in charge: parents, teachers, bosses. Today it's not so simple. Getting the best decision often means getting the person with the best knowledge, not necessarily the person in charge, to make the decision.

Sam, a mid-level engineer for Minneapolis-Honeywell, a manufacturer of temperature controllers, led the accounting team for the company's largest customer. In an effort to reduce costs, the customer requested a reduction in the controller's temperature sensitivity. Sam refused the request, since granting it would mean putting an inferior product on the market. The customer called Honeywell's president and demanded that Sam make the adjustment. Honeywell's president explained that Sam was in charge and knew the situation best. He urged the customer's engineers to work with Sam to come up with a cost-effective way to solve the problem. The story ended happily: the engineers found a win-win solution, much along the lines that Sam originally proposed.

Today's organizations are looking for L^2s who demonstrate that knowledge is more powerful than rank in an effort to develop a learning infrastructure for an entire organization of L^2s who create, capture, share, and use knowledge ". . . maximize the business advantage we gain from the finest minds we employ."

In tomorrow's world, knowledge will not only supersede rank but will also redefine and redistribute it. Your challenge as a putative L^2 is to spread the epidemic of learning among all the learners in your life and to build the infrastructure that will ensure that the epidemic will be your lasting legacy.

James Belasco is an entrepreneur, best-selling author, and internationally known consultant. He is currently co–executive director of the Financial Times Knowledge Dialogue, a joint venture that connects the world's leading consultants with global executives in a videoconferencing network. Belasco founded and led a highly successful specialty chemical company and software and services organization. He is one of the top ten business authors, having written nine books, several of which made the best-seller lists. As a consultant, he coaches executives in developing and implementing breakthrough strategies, creating new cultures, and achieving higher levels of performance. He currently coaches leaders of six of the Fortune 20 companies. Contact: jim@aol.com; http://www.belasco.com

Chapter Seventeen

Leading

A Performing Learning Art

Alexander B. Horniman

The Information Age has brought with it numerous challenges and considerable change. Emphasis on knowledge and knowledge working has been increasing, yet many of the hoped-for expectations have not been realized. Knowledge and knowledge work alone are not enough. Knowledge by itself is passive, and knowledge working is only a bit more active. The time is right for a different leadership perspective, a perspective based on learning. Individuals willing to step into the role of learning leaders can play a vital leadership role in the days to come.

Leading by its very nature is an action-oriented concept. It is about doing. It is about translating ideas into actions and then learning from the results of these actions. Leading is about performing, and leaders are performing artists. *Performing* is used here not in the dramatic role sense but rather as Peter Vail describes performing, "learning as being."[1] *Learning* is about being personally engaged and through this engagement process creating a unique (artistic) experience that will deliver value. The behavior of learning leaders is necessary if knowledge work is to achieve its potential. Leaders who understand and practice learning-leading engagement can and will make a difference.

Learning is perhaps best illustrated by the actions of little children. Little children are constantly learning. They explore, push, poke, prod, and engage in hundreds of different activities a day.

Their learning behaviors tend to be uninhibited. Inhibition seems to occur with the formal knowledge patterns that emerge. The hope is that all this unfettered learning behavior will build a knowledge repertoire that will be benefited by those early childhood learning activities and will create a knowledge base that will continue to inform and inspire learning and doing behaviors. The problem is that knowing gets in the way.

Knowing is the platform for learning, but if knowing is left unchecked and unexamined, it tends to slow down, if not drive out, learning. The now well described knowing-doing gap is the consequence of this knowing-dominating process.[2]

The Knowing-Learning Dynamic

The process of being engaged is the activity essential to learning. It is doing, exploring, experimenting, designing, and creating. The individual challenge is to shape and sustain the knowing-learning dynamic throughout a person's lifetime. The challenge is exacerbated because knowing rather than knowing-learning has become the primary focus of much of our formal education process. Beginning in first grade, the emphasis is on knowing, facts, figures, and specific answers. Knowing the answer is more important than understanding why the answer is what it is. The issue is not that one is more necessary than the other but rather how the knowing-learning dynamic can be kept alive and vibrant (see Figure 17.1). There are many knowing organizations and institutions. Colleges and universities come quickly to mind, followed by law firms, engineering firms, accounting practices, and countless knowledge-based enterprises. These organizations play a vital role in our contemporary lives, and yet they have a tendency to become stuck in their knowing and hence less effective than they might be. Knowing requires less energy and is more efficient than learning, which by its nature is unpredictable, imaginative, and often incomplete.

Figure 17.1 The Knowing-Learning Dynamic

Learning is the beginning developmental stage for all of us. We begin our lives as little learners, hence little doers. Regrettably, we are expected to grow up, which often means subordinating our youthful learning to adult knowing. Herein lies a real dilemma. It's not that knowledge and knowing are unimportant; quite the contrary—they are vital. It is that learning contributes to knowing and knowing is the platform for future learning. The problem is that knowing often trumps learning. Rather than continue to learn, knowing often holds learning hostage. Leading today requires a personal commitment to the knowing-learning process.

The individual who understands this knowing-learning dynamic is in a better position to become a learning leader. Learning leaders are like performing artists: the way they lead (perform) demonstrates their art form, and their unique behaviors illustrate the knowing-learning dynamic. Business leaders like Max De Pree, former CEO of Herman Miller, clearly demonstrated mastery of the knowing-learning dynamic. He constantly extended solid business practices with innovative ideas. Richard Branson of Virgin Airlines demonstrates the knowing-learning dynamic as he challenges the assumptions that limit the travel and media industries. Herb Kelleher and Jim Parker of Southwest Airlines have artistically crafted the airline's success. In an industry that seems stuck in knowing, these men have used the knowing-learning dynamic to get "unstuck" and remain profitable. These leaders have behaved as effective learning-leading artists: they certainly know the basics of their businesses and have effectively extended these basics with their unique versions of learning.

In his book *The Fifth Discipline*, Peter Senge illustrates the dilemmas of events and how they can dominate thought and action if they remain unexamined.[3] The following learning cycle, inspired by Senge's work, is suggested for learning leaders.

The knowing stage is the first in a four-stage process that contributes to systems thinking. Figure 17.2 illustrates the four-stage learning cycle, which in turn defines some of the behaviors performed by learning leaders. Learning leaders are curious, restless, and energized by action. They see almost every opportunity as having a learning possibility. They have integrated a learning attitude into their being. Learning is truly a way of leading for them.

Knowing is all about facts, figures, events, and data. Knowing is about how, what, where, and when, and it is vital. Knowing becomes knowledge, which is an essential element in the learning cycle. It is also a phase where many people stop: the world is full of knowers.

Figure 17.2 The Four-Stage Learning Cycle

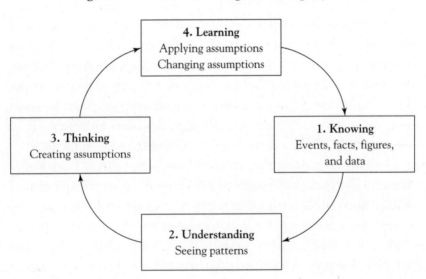

Knowing contributes to understanding, which is the discovery of patterns and form. The phrase "I've got it" often refers to the discovery of a pattern that makes problem solving possible. Understanding also provides the person who gets it with more power. Seeing patterns and relationships creates more power than can be found in events, facts, and figures.

Understanding provides the basis for deeper insight, which is realized in the next phase as underlying assumptions are discovered. The discovery and the articulation of assumptions reflect a deepening of the learning process. This is the thinking stage. Thinking is necessary for the next state, which is learning.

Learning is made possible by understanding, which leads to underlying assumption framing. Learning can be thought of as occurring at two levels. Level 1 learning is the transforming of assumptions into effective actions that solve problems and create value. Level 1 learning is demonstrated by leaders who translate assumptions into enterprise-enriching actions. Level 2 learning is performed by leaders who create and change the assumption and in so doing change the rules of the game.

Michael Dell, Steve Jobs, and Bill Gates are examples of learning leaders. These people took a solid knowledge base and through significant actions extended their knowledge to innovative heights. Dell changed the game in computer delivery systems. Jobs, of Apple fame, used his knowledge to reframe the personal computing world. Gates extended knowing and dominated computing. Each of these leaders demonstrated knowledge extension (action) and the essence of being a learning leader.

Learning leaders play a vital role in shaping and moving knowledge in organizations. The actual doing of learning levels 1 and 2 assumes that additional knowledge will be added to the knowledge base. The expanded knowledge base will provide the support for additional learning. People can and do lead from each of the four positions. However, persons leading from learning behave quite differently from persons leading from understanding or thinking (see

Figure 17.2.). Learning leaders' behaviors contribute to the creative and entrepreneurial activities that define their organizations. Although our society is enamored with learning behaviors, such as "out of the box" thinking and acting (risk taking), our education processes and reward systems are oriented toward "in the box" knowing behaviors.

Today's organizations, facing economic and market turbulence and chaos, are in need of people who are capable of being learning leaders. These will be people who are willing and able to create and apply new assumptions to challenging problems and in some cases to change assumptions, which will lead to innovative actions. As times and events become more dynamic and complex, leaders who are learners will be more crucial. Just as knowing equips people well for yesterday, a learning attitude equips leaders to confront present and future challenges. Knowing is an essential stage in the learning cycle, and yet it is not enough. The other stages must be achieved. Learning is a "contact sport." Learning is about proactive behavior that has the learner engage the context. Learning is about being fully engaged, in the same way that little kids are. Engagement is a possibility available to most people but chosen by few.

Learning as an Engagement Process

Learning leaders are people who are powerfully engaged. In our information-based economy, many experts view the ability to learn quickly and continuously as the greatest competitive weapon. How do we teach adults and companies to learn at the speed of light?[4] The answer to this question will shape the future for many leaders and organizations.

To begin responding to this question, let's return one more time to childhood learning as an opportunity to reflect on what is possible. "Small children are the definition of nonstop learning in large part because they ask millions of obvious and amazing questions and never take no for an answer. They teach us that learning is not an assignment but a way of life."[5] Taken a step further, Peter Vail offers the following: "Learning as a way of being is foundational to all efforts to enhance the learning of managerial leaders."[6] Building on these two ideas, it seems that learning is about being engaged in ways that ensure that leaders add or create value. Learning leaders are people who are powerfully engaged and consequently aware of the fact that everything they say and do matters. They seem to view every action as a learning opportunity for themselves and others in the organization. They combine childlike focus, energy, and curiosity with their adult knowledge. Being engaged means behaving in ways that reflect the integration of the four elements of engagement: physical, intellectual, spiritual, and emotional.

Physical engagement has to do with how people listen, how they speak, and the types of questions they ask. When engaged people speak, they do so in the present, not the past. They speak to solve problems and add value rather than to advance personal agendas. Engaging leaders teach in ways that inform and inspire. When engaged people listen, they do so in ways that convey respect and regard toward others. Given the chaotic times and the accompanying noise, it is difficult to listen. It takes a great deal of energy and focus. Former President Bill Clinton was said to be a powerfully engaged listener. If you were in his presence, he made you feel like you were the only person in the room and what you had to say mattered a great deal. Learning through engaged listening is a powerful process. It is a vital learning-leader process. It is also a physically demanding process requiring considerable energy. This may explain why we have so few learning leaders.

Physically engaged leaders ask questions that challenge others to learn and develop.

Physically engaged leaders are "doing learning" through their actions. They are being learners.

Intellectual engagement means being engaged in a "mindful way." Ellen Langer points out that mindful learners are constantly expanding their categories in order to effectively engage the dynamic circumstances that they are confronting. *Categories, mental models, beliefs,* and *frames of reference* are all related terms, and mindful people are constantly expanding and enriching these in order to learn and lead. Langer's wonderful phrase "premature cognitive commitment" captures the power and danger of past knowing.[7] Much of the knowing-doing gap can be understood by applying the notion of premature cognitive commitment, because it becomes the basis of "believing is seeing," which tends to have a negative effect on learning. We don't believe what we see; we see what we believe. Herein lies the knowing trap.

Intellectually engaged also means being open to new information and ideas. This is an easy phrase to express and a difficult one to do. Learning leaders are people with open and inquisitive minds.

Being intellectually engaged means being able to absorb and integrate different perspectives. The value of diversity is in bringing different perspectives to bear on situations. Intellectually engaged learners are capable of synthesizing and integrating these perspectives as a basis for future value-creating actions. The inability to integrate different perspectives traps people into simple knowing, and consequently, the learning process is inhibited. Learning leaders are people who seek out and welcome diverse thought and action and use these to inspire and innovate.

Emotional engagement means bringing the relevant emotions into the learning process. Learning is not an emotionally neutral activity. Quite the contrary, attitudes and feeling about what is being learned are a vital dimension of being engaged. In *Learning as a Way of Being*, Peter Vail notes that "learning as a way of being is learned by the whole person (fully engaged), and that means feeling the learning as well as possessing it intellectually."[8] Feeling learning is captured in the phrase "having a love of learning." Little kids have an innate love of learning, and it is important that as adults those feelings be recaptured in order to sustain the learning-leading process. Learning leaders reflect this love of learning in their daily behaviors.

Spiritual engagement is about values, principles, and beliefs. Spiritually engaged leaders behave in ways such that their important values, principles, and beliefs are evidenced in their day-to-day behavior. Spiritual engagement establishes the platform on which physical, intellectual, and emotional engagement can be played out. Leaders, and learning leaders in particular, are truly performing artists. Values such as keeping promises, telling the truth, fairness, and respect for the individual are each and collectively demonstrated in the learning leader's day-to-day performance. Every behavior makes a value statement of some sort. Value-defining behaviors provide the platform of integrity that is essential for sustained learning to occur at both the individual and the organizational level.

Each of these engagement areas is interrelated with the others, and integrating all four into a personal performance provides a unique (artistic) engagement experience. Engagement and learning are inextricably intertwined processes. When people are fully engaged in learning and leading, they tend to provide a model and by doing so extend an invitation to others to learn and lead following their example. It is difficult to be fully engaged, yet it is essential in order to advance the knowledge agenda.

Each person is unique, and hence the degree of each person's engagement will reflect his or her personal idiosyncrasies. Each person has the potential to be a performing learning artist. Knowing can be acquired with limited engagement; learning requires full engagement. Being fully engaged makes a profound difference. If they choose to be learning leaders, people who occupy leadership positions can profoundly alter the nature of organizations.

Each of us gets to choose our degree of engagement and our willingness to be learning leaders. The extent to which knowledge will be on the move is dependent on the extent to which people will be willing to make the choice to become learning leaders. The good news is that there is a choice.

Alexander B. Horniman has been a member of the Darden School faculty at the University of Virginia since 1967. During his time at the university, he has taught courses in organizational behavior, managerial psychology, leading strategic change, leadership and diversity in literature, and industrial psychology. He was the creator of what is now the Olsson Center for Applied Ethics, and he serves as Senior Fellow to the center. He has been a developer, teacher, and faculty leader of numerous executive education offerings. Prior to coming to the University of Virginia, he served in the U.S. Army as a regular Army officer. He then joined North American Aviation, during which time he worked on the Apollo program. He maintains an active consulting practice in the United States and overseas. Contact: HornimanA@Darden.virginia.edu

Chapter Eighteen

What's the Big Idea?

The "Little Things" That Build Great Leadership in Organizations

Lauren A. Cantlon

Robert P. Gandossy

As James Kouzes and Barry Posner have pointed out, "Leadership isn't the private reserve of a few charismatic men and women. It's a process ordinary people use when they're bringing forth the best from themselves and others. Liberate the leader in everyone, and extraordinary things happen."[1]

It all begins in graduate school. Case studies are clear: leaders lead; others follow; change happens. Organizational life seems straightforward and uncomplicated. As practitioners and consultants, later in our careers, benchmark studies and descriptions of best companies begin to make us feel inadequate. We design and implement the "right" interventions, but they never quite work the way we intended or the way the best are chronicled. We lead organizational change efforts that aren't ever smooth but rather are tough, hard work. Change management becomes more like wrestling jellyfish than the four- or five-step process we studied. Something is missing. Why does it always feel like we're "muddling through"?

The Little Things *Are* the Big Things

After twenty-five years of combined experience, we have reached a startling conclusion—the little things *are* the big things. What separates the best companies, the best leaders, and the best programs from the rest are often subtle nuances. It is the combination of little things that amount to a very *big* difference in organizational life.

Over the past several years, we've embarked on a number of studies to help us understand "best companies" around the world. What makes them "best"? What do they do that distinguishes them from the rest? As one piece of this larger body of work, we've focused on understanding the best companies for leaders and what they do that makes them so good. We surveyed hundreds of companies and interviewed well over a hundred senior executives, human resource leaders, and high potentials in some of the world's greatest companies, including IBM, Federal Express, Colgate-Palmolive, Home Depot, Dell Computer, UPS, Southwest Airlines, and Honeywell International.

We learned a ton. What separates these great companies from others in terms of developing leaders is clear and compelling. Those results have been reported elsewhere.[2] We also uncovered the "little" differences that somehow get lost in the tabulations of practices and programs. Some of this nuance and subtlety is hard to capture in words. The intensity, the feeling, or the collective sixth sense that some leaders or cultures seem to have about what matters when cannot be easily conveyed or depicted through words.

This chapter is an attempt at capturing some of that subtlety. With great humility after reading and editing this chapter several times, we acknowledge that we still have not fully portrayed on these pages what we've seen and what we've heard from some of the best. Most of what great companies have is clear and effortlessly described, but much is elusive. It is not something we can draw, nor is it easily articulated. Like beauty, it's something that is difficult to explain but is easily recognized. We hope that we've captured enough here so that it resonates with your experiences and provides you with a glimpse of what we've seen.

Little Ideas That Make a Big Difference

There are five overlapping clusters of little ideas that make a big difference:

It's Not the Programs—It's the Underlying Belief System

IBM's Lou Gerstner once wisely observed, "You're never done. And when you think you're done, you're in trouble."[3]

The facts are indisputable: great leadership teams build trust and confidence among their people. They motivate and inspire. They anticipate challenges and redirect the enterprise in timely and appropriate ways, unifying the workforce behind a single cause and driving the kind of performance that enabled Southwest Airlines to soar and IBM to reboot itself. Leadership, however, isn't just about what leaders do. It's something that they are, which then drives what they do. Genuine leadership comes from within. It's authentic and based on values, such as honesty, integrity, and trust. Programs and practices are the manifestations of these beliefs and values. They become the embodiment of how leaders believe the enterprise ought to be run. Without this foundation, programs and practices become sterile exercises, lacking meaning. They become modern-day bureaucracies that actually lower the credibility of leaders and further disengage associates.

Leaders' ability to create and ensure consistency between their values matters more than the programs that are in place. The strong personal values of leaders bring life to initiatives; they provide the teeth and an "in your gut" feeling that the activities provide a meaningful contribution to both individuals and the organization. Deeply embedded in programs and practices, these values and beliefs provide enduring life traveling through the enterprise and over time; they represent how things are done.

When we looked for patterns in these belief systems across a number of great companies, at least three themes emerged:

> 1. You must possess an element of commitment and passion to growing talent.

When we asked leaders why they did the things they did around developing leaders and why they spent 50 to 60 percent of their time doing so, we often received incredulous stares. Either they did not know or could not conceive of another way to run an enterprise. To them, we were asking dumb questions.

One chief operations officer (COO) whom we spoke with devotes much of her time and passion to developing future leaders, both informally and formally. Sometimes the more informal situations, she believes, are those that make the biggest impact. She invites young, high-potential employees to travel with her on business trips so that they can spend time together and so that she can get to know them on a personal level. She also arranges meetings with local high-potential employees when she travels so that they have an opportunity to present to her. She gets to see them in action and to see how they think. Not only does this COO believe that such contact is essential, but she also approaches it as fun. She believes that there is nothing better than to see people learn and grow and to help them in that process.

Many executives at these great companies showed a visible increase in their energy level and enthusiasm as they described similar experiences. Their eyes sparkled, they moved forward in their chairs, and they became more animated and intense. They find working with emerging talent refreshing and energizing and, yes, many described it as fun.

> 2. You must connect on a personal level.

A number of years ago, one of us was working in manufacturing at a microelectronics plant for IBM. In the bay for which I was responsible, dozens of silicon chips had fallen to the floor. A senior vice president for the division happened to pass by. He pulled me aside, put his arm on my shoulder, and started to educate me about the quality and the value of each silicon chip strewn on the floor. Through his patience and line of questioning, he was teaching me important lessons. In the coming months, he invested more time educating and developing me.

Across the best companies for leaders, we heard about numerous examples just like this. Leaders lead—and it's personal. One senior executive we spoke with at IBM mentors more than thirty people beyond his own direct reports. He makes a point of spending at least thirty minutes each quarter with each of them. He also initiated a reverse mentoring process, whereby someone who has been with the company less than two years has the opportunity to coach him. He believes that this provides him the benefit of learning and receiving feedback from a different perspective, and he finds this process personally inspiring, as well motivating for the younger coaches.

> 3. You must subordinate the unit for the greater whole.

In an era when we constantly hear about executive greed, one of the most fascinating—and encouraging—themes that surfaced in a number of our conversations is that leaders in top companies consistently subordinate their business unit for the good of the larger organization. What leader would really want to give away great talent once it was identified and nurtured? Surprisingly, the answer is all of them. A senior executive at IBM said, "I would give up my best person today if I knew it would serve a group goal. . . . I would give [that person] up this afternoon."[4] A CEO we met echoed these sentiments: "It's a plus to move people. It's a minus to hoard them . . . and we are keeping score. . . . It would be a bad thing for a leader to hold on to a great person. . . . If you prime the pump, when you give up a good leader you'll get another. . ."

As simplistic as these three themes are, they are the critical and differentiating values and principles of the leaders at the top companies for developing leaders. These leaders don't think twice about these things; this is the DNA of a well-oiled leadership development culture. We heard numerous anecdotes and examples of how these executives use their superior leadership skills to engage and develop future leaders and to foster an effective leadership culture within their organizations. What became increasingly evident as we spoke with these leaders is that they truly believe that if they choose the right people, set the right strategy, provide opportunities, coach, mentor, communicate, and set appropriate long- and short-term stretch goals, the cycle of great leadership will be maintained.

The leaders we spoke with run some of the world's most successful organizations; what makes them so successful is that they recognize that running the business *is* building leadership capability. They have an underlying belief system in the importance and impact of developing leaders that relentlessly shines through time and again.

How You Communicate Is as Important as What You Communicate

A Chinese proverb says, "Not the cry but the flight of the wild duck leads the flock to fly and follow."

Every senior executive knows that communication is important. Priorities, updates, and target goals need to be reinforced and communicated on a continual and consistent basis. In the vast majority of companies, these things do get done; they just don't get done well. Too many leaders delegate these tasks to corporate communications specialists who spit out, with great regularity and consistency, messages, themes, and updates to a workforce already numbed by the banality of it all. The *Wall Street Journal* offers more a more passionate and personal connection.

What differentiates the great leaders from the merely good? The innovative and passionate manner in which essential messages are conveyed. Great leaders have an incredible sense of timing. Their points are clear, concise, and candid. There is an element of surprise in how they deliver key messages—not always in an outrageous way, but just enough to skirt what's expected, just enough to get the appropriate level of attention. They work hard at simple and repetitive messages: they eliminate "corporate-speak." One senior executive reported that when he communicates either in written form or orally, he has a standard test for clarity: ". . . If there are questions as to my intent, I was not clear enough."

The senior vice president of human resources at one of the top companies for leaders claims that the CEO of his company is the "best communicator" he has ever seen. What is it that this CEO does to earn this compliment? "He takes complexity and simplifies it, and he demands this of all of his leaders. He constantly reinforces the importance of focusing on simple but dynamic communication . . ." A senior executive from another company reinforced this point regarding the importance of clear and simple communication: ". . . Communicate, communicate, communicate—very repetitively and very simply—what we are trying to do. We are trying to figure out where we are going. No matter what is happening in the environment, to keep that clear . . . [we must] keep a set of high-beam headlights as to where we are going."

One of the important messages that we consistently heard throughout our interviews was that communication is about more than *what* is said. It is about *how*. It begins at the top of an organization. The CEO who chooses to send out the same predictable communications to all employees worldwide time and again is not likely to have the messages stick. These sterile, passionless messages, crafted by the corporate communication machine, will not increase engagement among employees or enhance their connection to the company, and they certainly won't convey a sense of pride, passion, or commitment to the organization. On the other hand, there are the CEOs like the late Sam Walton, founder of Wal-Mart, who declared that if his company hit the numbers, he would do a hula dance on Wall Street. They did, and he did. Herb Kelleher created an open and communicative environment at Southwest Airlines by agreeing to do some similarly zany things. Lou Gerstner "invited people to change" and encouraged the employees of IBM to change the ways they thought and worked. Leaders such as these practice what they preach and exemplify the art of motivational, committed, and passionate communication, all of which promotes a strong leadership culture.

Leaders at the top companies also provide visible, tangible support for their priorities. For instance, many leaders struggle trying to empower employees. Empowerment promotes innovation, continuous improvement, and quality. An endless number of programs, campaigns, themes, messages, and other approaches are employed. One CEO at one of the top companies tried another tactic. He pulled together a group of high potentials and told them, "We don't have all the answers. I want you to go on a discovery mission. I want you to go around the company—all over the world. Talk to people. Talk to our customers. Observe. Discover the two to three things we need to do differently. Report back to the executive team in three months, and we'll get them done!" All the communication campaigns you can imagine would not break nearly as much ground as this did. There is just no substitute for such an initiative. "Employees don't want to be ruled," said the CEO. "They want to be involved and to make decisions. . . . We don't tell them what to do; we ask them what is right."

Taking Risks Is Less Risky Than Not Taking Risks

"The person who risks nothing does nothing, has nothing, and is nothing."[5]

There are two levels of risk that the best companies for developing leaders take. One is at the organizational level: moving the best people across the organization into functional areas or geographies for which they have little experience. The second is at an individual level: choosing to move into functional areas or geographies for which they have little experience.

The leaders we spoke with emphasized the importance of taking people and putting them outside of their comfort zone in a role where they need to develop. "If you keep doing the same thing, you'll likely get pretty good at it, but you're not likely to become a leader," one executive explained. "Becoming a leader requires a variety of experiences, honing a number of skills and capabilities, and, just as important, building confidence along the way." These are risks that some organizations and individuals would not be willing to take. Building great leaders requires that these risks be taken. One executive believes that risk taking is a big part of his company's great leadership culture. "You talk to many leaders in the company. You know they'll throw out any number of big risks they took . . . some successful, some not. I remember sitting with the CEO and the senior team. . . . The CEO looks you in the eyeball and says, 'If I give you this money, are you going to deliver? And remember, I have a long memory.' That's a serious bet. . ."

The ability and willingness of these organizations to continuously throw opportunities at people requires taking chances. These opportunities foster a different kind of learning than any formal education program could possibly address, but developing leaders on the job is risky both for the individual and the institution. What we heard is that this is not just about the risk; it's also about trust and confidence on the part of the organization and the individual. When presented with a challenge, people often rise to the occasion, knowing that a certain level of trust and confidence in their capability must exist. Realizing that your leaders are supporting you can be incredibly motivational. "It's inspiring to know you've been singled out. I wouldn't have picked me for the job," one person told us. "And I wasn't going to let them down." Succeeding also fosters the necessary self-confidence to take further risks and the confidence to take on larger, broader roles. This, according to one senior vice president and group executive, is "the only way to get to the top. . ."

Fostering Reciprocity Is Not Equal to an Incentive Scheme

"We make a living by what we get," Winston Churchill once said; "we make a life by what we give."[6]

According to the dictionary, *reciprocity* is established when there is a "shared feeling on both sides." It implies a "mutual or equivalent exchange or giving back of what has been received." In many leaders' eyes, this sense of giving back is emotional; it is a duty, an obligation to give back more than was given.

"I felt privileged to be singled out—to be moved into key jobs early in my career," one group leader reported. "They sent me to Harvard and our own executive development programs. My mentors are now running the company. I had the benefit of great coaches. Of course, others in the company were singled out, too. But somehow you were made to feel it was just you, it was personal. It's now my turn to give back."

Over and over again, we heard executives describe the opportunities given them, the risks their bosses took with them, and the faith and confidence others had—thereby obligating them, solidifying a relationship that no incentive scheme can replicate. There is a key difference between an incentive or reward scheme and the kind of emotional, obligatory sense of responsibility their reciprocal arrangements bring. Both are effective, and both are probably necessary in organizations today. However, the latter is more enduring and, in the end, more powerful.

Both are based on an exchange—an exchange of monetary rewards or opportunities for current or future performance. Reward schemes can be motivational and have been shown to change behavior, but the recipient believes that he or she has earned what was given. In these reciprocal arrangements, by contrast, the recipient feels special, "handpicked," not yet deserving of the offer bestowed. In these reciprocal relationships, there is a genuine caring about the whole person, the individual. It is less mechanical than reward systems.

Reciprocity instills a strong sense of pride and desire to give something back to the organization, to foster what was provided for you. One executive we interviewed talked at length about his "responsibility to make sure that the company is optimizing the talent identified to make sure that we are establishing the future technical or management leaders." The leaders we spoke with view their jobs as twofold: to meet a set of financial objectives and to *build an organization*, not just their own unit but a larger whole that can get the job done. There is a sense of pride on the part of the employees that is created in an organization that has developed its leaders, presented them with challenging opportunities, and invested not only time and money in them but also confidence and trust in their capability to bring the business to the next level. All of this leads to a desire to give back to the organization through building and growing the next generation of great leaders and to a determined spirit that fosters confidence and fortitude throughout the organization.

Social Networks Provide the Channels for DNA

Evenius observed, "The crowd gives the leader new strength."[7]

There is a critically important by-product of this "movement" of talent—the consistent, regular movement of people across geographies and functions, the deliberate efforts of leaders to spend time with people as they travel or in learning—and that is the social network that is formed. Even the most prescient leader would surely underestimate the organizational power this brings.

Social networks pave the way for the belief systems, the communication, the risk taking, and the reciprocity. Through the continuous movement of people, and mentoring programs that extend beyond one's own organization, employees have an opportunity to network and build relationships with people all over the organization. These networks allow great companies to better identify talent everywhere. Decision making and, even more important, execution are faster. Individuals are more able to take pride in the accomplishments of the large enterprise if they have some connection, such as a mentor or coach, or if they have worked in a number of areas.

One executive said, "Very early on, leaders meet their peers, spend time with them in both formal and informal forums, and have the opportunity to build a rapport with this group of people. This is as important as the classes themselves." A COO we met with talked about similar experiences and opportunities at her company through leadership development classes that expose high potentials to their peers as well as senior executives.

These social networks provide the right platform for each of these little ideas that make for a great leadership culture. The challenge, however, as every executive that we met with reiterated, is striking the right balance that incorporates each of these in combination.

Conclusion

The way in which these leaders have institutionalized these five clusters of little ideas is what has made them effective. This is not about just going through the motions and checking items off a list. It is about a much deeper, almost innate sense and belief in what these actions stand for and how they follow through on their promises and responsibilities. Through their strong belief and support of developing great leaders, the executives that we spoke with have ensured that their organizations will have a legacy of developing and encouraging the growth of great leaders long after they're gone. They have ingrained these processes and mind-sets into the next generation, ensuring that this leadership culture will continue indefinitely.

Lauren A. Cantlon is a research consultant in the Talent and Organization Consulting Group at Hewitt Associates' Connecticut Center. Recent projects have included research in the areas of top companies for leaders, HR executives as trusted advisers, and the people practices of top financially performing companies. Prior to joining the Talent and Organization Consulting Group, Cantlon worked in Hewitt's internal human resource function as a staffing consultant. Contact: lauren.cantlon@hewitt.com; http://www.hewitt.com

Robert P. Gandossy is a global practice leader for Talent and Organization Consulting at Hewitt Associates' Connecticut Center. He is a member of Hewitt's Global Council, and he has special expertise in improving organizational effectiveness, human resource strategy, leadership, managing large-scale change, mergers and acquisitions, and increasing growth through innovation. He was one of the project managers of a major research effort, *The Changing American Workforce in the 1980s,* and his book *Bad Business* was called a "masterful job" by Tom Peters and "high drama and a fascinating story" by Rosabeth Moss Kanter. He coedited the book *HR in the 21st Century,* which features chapters by the world's thought leaders in leadership and human resources. Gandossy is coauthor of *Best Companies for Leaders,* and he has been a speaker for a number of groups, including the Harvard Business School. Contact: robert.gandossy@hewitt.com; http://www.hewitt.com

Part Four

Changes for the Future

Chapter Nineteen

Learning Stored Forward

A Priceless Legacy

Betsy Jacobson
Beverly Kaye

In today's economy, it is common knowledge that organizational worth is not caught up only in material assets but is to be found in human assets as well. Organizations invest heavily in protecting their material assets but surprisingly less so in safeguarding their human assets. Though a reduction of investment in the former can cause great problems for companies, minimizing or cutting investment in the latter can have even more serious implications.

An organization's most valuable human asset is also among its most intangible—the vast bank of knowledge contained within its ranks. Many organizations have sought to capture the *explicit knowledge*—knowledge that is easily codified and conveyed to others, such as in business plans, procedures, customer lists, and market research—of their technical and management leaders in complex information systems and databases. To a large extent, these systems function well, but definitive results of their direct contributions and usefulness are still being studied.

Going a layer deeper in that vast bank of knowledge, we come to the *tacit knowledge*—experiential, how-to information based on clues, hunches, instinct, and personal insight—that individuals have acquired over time and now hold "in their bones." This learning gives clues and cues about how to do the work and deliver on promises. If an organization is to ensure its survival, it is this tacit or implicit knowledge that needs collecting. In fact, we believe it is this tacit knowledge that becomes the legacy that managers and leaders must bequeath to the organization before they leave or before they move from one position to another within an organization.

Leaving Learning Behind

Leaving something of enduring value to an organization—at the end of each month, each year, or an entire career—should be the ideal of every manager. At any one point in time, it is only when contributions made by individuals can be sustained or applied to future issues and problems that they can achieve their full potential for the organization. This can happen when inventions or innovations revolutionize operations for years to come. More often, however, sustained improvements occur when highly effective managers pass on their learning to others. In truth, this doesn't happen often enough.

We believe that an organization can capture the valuable learning experiences and intellectual capital of its high-performing talent for sustained excellence in future years if the organization encourages the long-term, ongoing building, living, and leaving of legacies. By leaving knowledge behind, an individual's legacy becomes the ability to build new ways of thinking and learning in others. This in turn improves the ways in which daily business is conducted so that new levels of organizational and individual maturity can be achieved.

Legacy Defined

Although the concept of a legacy has traditionally been linked to money or property, we suggest that a legacy does not have to be something tangible. Unlike an heirloom, a legacy in our sense is something that must be digested, processed, and absorbed by someone else before it can be considered "passed on."

We define *legacy* as "the valuable contribution of enhanced thinking and capacity for learning that an individual or team transfers to others so that it is available both in the present and going forward into the organization's future."

Building legacy, living it, and leaving it is crucial to leadership. It is learning in action, and it occurs at all levels of the corporate hierarchy. It is meaning culled from reflection and from interaction with others.

Legacy: Passing Learning On

What exactly gets passed along as a person's legacy? We believe it is the sum of knowledge, experience, and understanding turned into action, along with the ability to create new meaning from one's own actions and the actions of others. Of course, many people use their knowledge and can draw on past experience. But far fewer can truly reflect on their actions and translate them into new understandings, new assumptions, or new beliefs. The ability to do this is a kind of wisdom that begs to be shared.

For example, in a mentoring program we conducted, a senior manager spoke about the importance of setting personal boundaries and the ability to say no in the face of organizational pressure. He supported his message with his own personal stories and track record. When participants challenged him about the consequences of saying no, his response was that of course there are consequences, but consequences don't signal failure and don't negate the importance of taking the right stand. At that moment, he became a role model for this message—and made a hefty contribution to his legacy.

We saw another example in a biotech company. One of the engineers had a reputation for poor interpersonal skills, and by his own admission, he was a man of few words. He had an unorthodox way of running tests, but the results he achieved were consistent and accurate. He possessed intuition and insight that might never have been captured had he not been assigned a young college intern who studiously learned and then shared his methods.

Through her, his unique way of working became common practice in the lab. Despite his lack of effectiveness as a communicator, he was able to leave his legacy when someone else perceived that he had something to offer to the organization.

There are myriad opportunities to build legacy daily. Often in our own consulting practice, the question is asked, "How did you know that?" or "Why did you make that intervention then?" The answer comes out of our experience, which we've reflected on and derived particular meaning from in order to integrate theory and practice. What we give our clients in part could probably be found in a variety of textbooks. Still, how and why we do what we do is our unique twist. It is our meaning grown out of our own learning and then passed along. Over time, this includes the books, programs, failures, successes, and ideas that came before us, and it also includes our own "spin" on each of these. Our legacy is our capacity to articulate this spin and transfer it to our clients, our protégés, and our colleagues.

The Loss of Learning

When a difficult problem is addressed by an organization, it generates valuable learning. Although this happens regularly in business, it is only rarely and then generally by accident or anecdote that leaders and managers cull this learning, discuss it, and perhaps pass it on to others. In most organizations, there is little or no commitment to establishing an awareness of "how we did what we did" or "why it didn't work" before the arrival of another important thing to do.

When such learning is lost, managers miss the opportunity to more effectively address future issues and to help develop leaders who will benefit from this experience in the future. In other words, bypassed learning opportunities translate readily into risks and costs:

Failure to leverage intellectual capital for future gains

A risk of re-creating past problems

An inability to build capacity and "bench strength" through the ranks of the organization

It doesn't have to be this way. Organizations can develop ways to capture the experiences and insights of their employees. Even though a great deal of what we call legacy is embodied in the singular spin and style of the individual or team, the organization can absorb this as part of its culture.

Organizational Perks

When individuals build and leave legacies, the most obvious payoff is for the organization. By encouraging the process of building and leaving a legacy, the store of individual talent that exists within every corporation is activated in a practical way. As people join together to reflect on and discuss issues, an essential foundation is formed for building current depth and assuring future intellectual assets.

Learning grows when the organization uses more of what people know. As more individuals gain greater knowledge, the organization continually absorbs the learning. This affects policies and practices that have an impact on the whole.

The corporate world has a tendency to overlook the important brain trust on which organizations have become dependent. The organization that does not begin to cull and disseminate its intellectual capital will miss out on an important and valuable opportunity with long-range implications: the opportunity to capture legacy.

Personal Perks

Beyond the organization's needs, there are enormous personal benefits to be gained by those who can transform learning into legacy. The process of building the asset of wisdom is in itself challenging and gratifying. The act of disseminating it to build a legacy for the next generation rewards individuals with a perception of greater self-worth.

When people feel needed, their sense of purpose changes. They are no longer working simply for the paycheck but because they have something to offer others, which is a valuable reframing. Their work becomes the legacy they have to offer, literally part of their purpose in life. Since a sense of purpose is not about money but more about psychic payoff, perhaps this is why it is that so many millionaires continue to work.

In building a legacy, the focus is on living one's passion, defining the individual, "double-clicking" on what is personally most important and expressing it. Building and living legacies develops powerful role models who enable and empower everyone in the organization.

The Broad View

Legacy is not the sole province of senior or high-ranking members of the organization. Leadership is a way of acting, not a position or title. Leadership and legacy are for anyone who wants to make an impact beyond the execution of his or her assigned tasks.

In assessing your desire to build, live, and leave a legacy, a few key questions should be pondered: Are you setting direction or pace? Can you reflect on events and, perhaps with others, make sense out of what has happened, and does that help you tackle the next round? Are you interested in what you know? Are you grooming others around you to develop themselves in your way of thinking, the meanings you take away, or your particular style? Have you become a storyteller in your organization?

Legacy evolves from an individual's experience and perspective, even if the track record is not a brilliant one. Becoming aware of what you have to give away in terms of knowledge and learning to articulate it will make your legacy valuable. After all, learning from failure can have tremendous value. We know of a young entrepreneur who hired a technology officer for his Internet start-up company. The man he hired was a Romanian refugee whose experience was vast in the design and development of e-learning products on the Internet. There was no question that his new employer valued this man for his technology experience. However, his experience also included several failed companies of his own. When the technology officer wanted to draw on his experiences to offer advice to his new employer on how to market and position the business, his advice was refused.

Because the founder felt that the technology officer had had a poor track record as a businessman, his experience was discounted. We would argue that his failures amid volatile market conditions gave him valuable business knowledge, which his new employer might find useful. For example, when the new company proposed to give its product away free of charge, a typical strategy of Internet software companies, the technology officer suggested that the strategy was misguided. Though common, this strategy was ill-considered in this case because the company had no profit-making follow-on product or service to sell once it had given its product away. Unfortunately, this and other advice was not taken, and today the company no longer exists.

Recognizing That Continuing Learning Is Vital

Building legacy and sharing it with others requires constant learning by an individual and continual transfer of that learning to others. In fact, for a growing percentage of the workforce, many of whom may stay in any one organization for a couple of years at most before moving on or whose career is made up of a series of short-term contracts, legacy is on the short list of to-do items. Understanding what legacy is and bringing that knowledge to the organization may be an individual's most important value-added accomplishment.

Legacy is a valuable gift to the organization. Offering this gift is possible only when individuals are aware of the powerful learning they possess. Those in the field of knowledge management have pointed out that knowledge has an unusual property among assets: when you give it away, you don't diminish your own reserve. Arguably, an even more unusual characteristic distinguishes legacy in that giving it away actually increases the individual's supply.

Legacies are bequeathed regularly throughout an organization, though they may not be named or recognized as such. Whenever people take time to talk about their work, how it was accomplished, the learning that was gleaned, and then offer interpretation or words of wisdom about other alternatives, legacy is being built, lived, and passed along.

Betsy Jacobson, president and founder of Betsy Jacobson and Associates, is an international organizational change consultant with more than two decades of experience. She works with organizations in both the public and private sectors, providing a wide range of training, coaching, and consulting services. She has published numerous articles on leadership and career development. Her expertise lies in helping organizations and individuals increase their capacity to be more self-correcting and therefore more successfully competitive.

Beverly Kaye, coauthor of the international best seller *Love 'Em or Lose 'Em: Getting Good People to Stay* and author of the classic *Up Is Not the Only Way*, is one of the nation's leading authorities on career development, mentoring, retention, and engagement. She is founder and president of Career Systems International. As a sought-after speaker and consultant on talent management issues, she counts some of the nation's leading corporations as her clients. She is an active member of the American Society for Training and Development, and she has received their National Career Development Award and Best Practice Award for her work with some of her clients. Contact: http://www.careersystemsintl.com; http://www.keepem.com

Chapter Twenty

Developing New Ideas for Your Clients—and Convincing Them to Act

Andrew Sobel

"I've met several times with the CEO," I told my colleagues, "and his need is pretty clear: his company is faltering abroad, and he wants to develop a new international strategy to help jump-start growth outside the United States." At the time, I was a senior partner with a large international consulting firm. The occasion was an account development session to brainstorm new ideas to propose to a client of mine.

In the back of the room someone piped up: "This company doesn't just need an international strategy—it needs to completely transform its business."

"That may be," I replied, "but I think right now the international piece is what the CEO is focused on." A chorus of voices drowned me out, however, insisting that I had misread the situation and that what the client really needed was a wholesale overhaul of its organization, including its operations, marketing, and sales.

Even as I kept resisting, one of my colleagues told me that the "company is a prime candidate for our business transformation services."

"We need to take a fresh look at the U.S. market as well," said another.

Frustrated, I ended the session and thanked everyone for contributing. A few months later, I left the firm to start my own independent consulting practice.

This anecdote illustrates one of the major pitfalls of developing new ideas for clients: failing to distinguish between what your clients really need or want from what you think they must have. All too often, we look at our clients' situation through the lens of our own product or service offering—and our own desire for a sale—and fail to offer ideas that will really work for them.

Developing New Ideas

Let's first look at some of the fundamental strategies you can use to develop new ideas for clients and customers. Rather than talk about traditional research and development (R&D), with its focus on technology evolution and science, I'm going to suggest a variety of low-tech, less talked about, inexpensive but highly effective techniques you can use to create value-added ideas. Then I'm going to turn to an equally important subject: how to get those same clients to accept and act on these ideas.[1]

Create a Client Panel

Every year in March, ERM, a large environmental services consulting firm, brings its senior management and about thirty-five top clients to a summit meeting in Phoenix, Arizona. Many companies hold meetings like this, but they tend to be "schmoozefests" with lots of golf and alcohol and at best a few morning seminars where subject matter experts hold forth for an hour or two. ERM takes a very different approach: its senior executives conduct workshops to explore the most important and most problematic issues that its client executives face, as defined by the executives themselves. These executives share experiences in an open atmosphere, and ERM opens a valuable window onto the daily challenges facing its clients, who in turn benefit from these valuable peer-to-peer exchanges.

"But doesn't it seem like you're pumping them for their issues just to go back later and try to sell them on something?" I asked an ERM board member who participates in these sessions.

"It works precisely because we don't do that," he replied. "We don't go back a month later and try to sell them on a solution to an issue they raised. That by itself reinforces trust. Just by creating these forums, we're adding value in ways that our competitors can't and don't. The experience enhances our relationship with the executives, giving us insight into their issues; thus we're able to better evolve our own service offerings."

Some firms create a small client panel that has a fixed number of client executives (ten or fifteen) who meet once or twice a year to provide advice on overall strategy and service offering development. Others, such as ERM, invite a large group of clients, whose composition changes slightly from year to year, to an annual event. In the technology arena, many manufacturing firms create user groups, which provide this type of feedback on a regular basis.

Conduct Innovative Industry Research and Analysis

This is a time-honored but underutilized approach to uncovering potential client needs, and it can also garner valuable publicity. I recall vividly a study done some years ago at the strategy advisory boutique where I began my own consulting career. My firm had analyzed the financial performance of hundreds of publicly held banks and then had sorted them into a two-by-two matrix, with return on equity and cost of equity representing the x and y axes. Each of the four quadrants was given a fancy name. The "sharks," whose returns well exceeded their cost of equity, were poised to eat the "minnows," whose profitability was weak. The study attracted enormous media attention and stimulated dozens of meetings with potential clients to talk about their position in the industry and whether they were doing enough to bolster their financial returns. Sometimes simple frameworks synthesized from industry research—or just an in-depth knowledge of your client's operations—can become powerful tools to get clients to open up and discuss their issues, which leads to idea-generating opportunities. The Boston Consulting Group's work with Texas Instruments in the early 1970s, for example, led to the development of the "experience curve" concept, which says that cumulative manufacturing volume leads to predictable decreases in unit cost. This then led to the famous "Growth/Share" matrix, which BCG used to strategically position different businesses, depending on their competitive prospects and investment needs. A division that has a small market share of a slow-growing market, for example, is a "dog" and should be divested; a high-market-share business in a low-growth market is a "cash cow," which should be harvested for cash; and so on.

Despite the effectiveness of this type of broad-based strategic research, it's typically the preserve of a few high-end consulting or investment banking firms. Manufacturers often focus more specifically on technology research and development, and few services firms make these corporate-level investments in new ideas about industry evolution.

Make "Home Visits" and Observe

My father, Raymond Sobel, is a retired psychiatrist who chaired the department of child psychiatry at Dartmouth Medical School. A highly successful therapist, he used to have a packed schedule of patients nearly every day. He routinely did something very unusual, however, that set him apart from all of his peers: early in his relationship with each patient, he visited the patient in his or her home or family environment. He describes his unique approach this way:

> I almost got kicked out of the psychoanalytic society for doing home visits. They had this crazy notion that you had to be unseen and ambiguous, a nonperson, in your treatment of patients. I wanted to see what was going on in patients' homes, however. I learned a tremendous amount that helped me be a better therapist. When you walk into the house of a patient and you almost fall through a hole in the hallway floorboards that's been there for two years, what does it say? Or you get there and an enormous German shepherd is

lunging at the screen door and the patient tells you, "Oh, I forgot to tell you about the dog." What does it say about the patient's relationship with you? I would ask for a tour of the house, which might be a disaster area—or so compulsively clean you could eat off the floor. You'd see how kids kept their rooms, what they put on the walls. For five minutes they would act like they do in therapy, but after that they would revert to their real selves and lapse into their normal relationships. The children would be eating standing up, the husband and wife would stop talking to each other, and so on.

Not all therapists do this, because a home visit can take three or four hours. Therapists don't know how to bill for it or if they can bill for this kind of time. Furthermore, from a personal point of view, visiting a patient outside your office makes you vulnerable. What does it say if you drive up in a BMW or in an old wreck? What if you're a few minutes late? How will you react to an embarrassing situation?

The dynamics my father describes closely resemble those of client relationships in a business setting. The insights you gain from taking the time to make, metaphorically, a "home visit" to your client's world, the difficulty of charging for the time you spend, the personal vulnerability you feel—most of us have experienced these with our clients.

Years ago, when the advertising great David Ogilvy won the prestigious Rolls-Royce account, such a "home visit" resulted in an extraordinary idea for his client. At the time, most of Ogilvy's colleagues wanted to hole up in a conference room and brainstorm approaches for the advertising campaign they had been contracted to develop. Ogilvy, however, went out and spent weeks interviewing Rolls-Royce managers and engineers. He drove their cars. He absorbed dozens of engineering reports and technical manuals. Finally, in an obscure technical specifications sheet, he read that "the ticking of the dashboard clock is the loudest sound the driver can hear at 60 miles per hour." Ogilvy had found his idea: What to an engineer seemed like a mere statement of fact became for this creative advertiser the headline for an award-winning advertising campaign that dramatically increased the sales of Rolls-Royce cars. Since then, interior quietness has been a hallmark of a great deal of automotive advertising.

Talk to Your Clients' Customers

Some of the best ideas for clients will be discovered by talking to their customers. These discussions can yield invaluable insights into service requirements, new product opportunities, and competitive trends. I've seen firms do this in the proposal stage, subsequently embedding valuable perspectives about the client's strengths and weaknesses in the final sales proposal, as well as during the ongoing relationship. Some former colleagues of mine wrote an excellent article on this subject, "Spend a Day in the Life of Your Customer."[2] It's the concept of the "home visit" applied, so to speak, farther down the food chain.

Form Innovation Partnerships

During my research on long-term client relationships, I have occasionally observed "innovation partnerships," in which a supplier and a customer formally contract for a continuing set of new ideas. Mike Mulica, senior vice president of sales and customer operations for Openwave Systems, the leading supplier of mobile Internet software for cell phones, describes how powerful these partnerships can be:

> Early on in the development of this market, a number of other large players were entering with competing products. There was a limitation on the number of companies that could really create and manufacture software for the wireless Internet environment, however, and we decided to use this fact to develop some partnerships that would create advantages for both sides. I sat down with the VP of marketing at BT [formerly British Telecom], and we mapped out a partnering arrangement that went way beyond the typical product

purchasing agreement. Fundamentally, we offered BT, and they contracted for, a lock on our factory capacity for two years and a series of as-yet-unknown product innovations in five different product categories. In other words, they bought guaranteed industry capacity and future innovation from us, all in the context of a long-term partnership. This client became our biggest advocate in the industry and helped us springboard our sales to other major telecommunications companies.[3]

Use Comparative Benchmarks

The use of comparative and competitive benchmarks is an excellent way to stimulate your client's thinking and get him or her to talk about possible needs. It can be powerful to say to a client, "Your company spends 3 percent of revenue on research and development, whereas the industry average is 4 percent—and you bring out 20 percent fewer new products each year. What do you think accounts for these differences?" You might get a number of responses to this question, each with different implications for needs. Your client may have chosen this strategy on purpose, for example, or may in fact be disadvantaged due to weak internal practices or processes. Being able to benchmark your client presupposes that you've made a significant investment in understanding his or her business—goals, strategy, organization, and industry environment.

Talk to Company Observers

There are many sources of data and perspectives on a given company that you can tap as a way of identifying client needs. If the company is publicly held, some stock analysts can be a fertile source of information, and nowadays, many of their reports can be obtained at no cost from your broker or banker. Other "experts" can include suppliers, consultants who specialize in the industry, and trade association executives.

Ask

Often clients cannot properly articulate the ideas they seek, but you still have to ask. Most of the time, our interactions with clients are focused on either selling to them or talking at them. Several times a year, sit down and ask good, thought-provoking questions, such as "What's been keeping you up at night?" "What's the most intractable problem you face right now?" "If your market suddenly stopped growing, what would you do?"

Influencing Clients to Accept Your Ideas: Finding the Hidden Creases

Physical labor is often a fundamental part of Zen training. During his studies with a famous Zen archery master in Hawaii, Kenneth Kushner found himself engaged in the arduous task of moving large rocks to make way for a new footpath. A psychotherapist by training, Kushner found it nearly impossible to dislodge the heavy boulders, and he was quickly exhausted. In his book *One Arrow, One Life*, he writes about an important lesson he learned from his Zen teacher:

> Tanouye Roshi watched me with considerable amusement. He explained I was trying to impose my will on the rocks; I was trying to make them go where I wanted them to go. "You have to learn to push the rock where it wants to go," he explained to me. He explained further that if I could do that, I could coax the rocks to where I wanted them to go. He then showed me that because the rocks are unevenly shaped, there is usually one direction in which, if pushed, the rock is easier to unbalance and flip over. He told me that I must learn how to utilize the direction in which the rock "wanted" to go in order to move it where I wanted it to go. . . . He continued to demonstrate how by repeating the process of pushing the rock in its favored direction and occasionally spinning the rock so as to reorient the direction it "wanted" to go, it was quite easy to move it where I wanted it to go.[4]

DEVELOPING NEW IDEAS FOR YOUR CLIENTS 227

Influencing clients to accept your ideas, I believe, is very similar to moving boulders. All of your clients will have in mind a direction that they wish to take, and you will naturally try to persuade them to follow your direction. A client's favored direction could be thought of as a "hidden crease"—he or she will be predisposed to moving that way, just as a piece of paper will easily fold again where it has been previously creased. The Zen approach to life is to find the hidden creases in every activity—the "naturally correct" way of doing things, as Kushner says.

You don't have to become a Zen Buddhist to influence clients, but this principle is relevant to client relationships. The best strategy with clients, in other words, is not to bludgeon them into taking your advice and accepting your ideas but rather to understand where they want to go and then influence their trajectory 10 or 20 degrees at a time. As Ben Franklin said, "If you would persuade, you must appeal to interest rather than intellect."[5]

How do you put yourself into a position in which clients will listen to your ideas? First of all, they have to trust you. This is an obvious point, but the problem is that most professionals misunderstand the essential nature of trust. They mistake professional credibility—"These data and technical details are accurate and true"—for broad-based trust, which is very different.

There are five key elements to trust:

1. *Integrity*. In this post-Enron world, clients are especially concerned with the integrity of the professionals and firms with whom they have dealings. Integrity encompasses ethics and values, consistency, reliability, and discretion.

2. *Competence*. I might trust a babysitter to take of my children for an evening but not to take them on a three-day river-rafting trip in Utah. Your clients' trust in you will go up or down depending on their perception of what you're actually competent to do.

3. *Client- versus self-orientation*. Clients are always wondering, "Are you suggesting this because it's in your interest or my interest?"

4. *Familiarity*. Research has demonstrated repeatedly that familiarity builds trust. Many professionals forget that face time is crucial to building clients' understanding of your integrity, competence, and general character.

5. *Risk*. Clients' perception of the risk of trusting you will greatly influence the amount of trust they place in you. That's the main purpose of guarantees: they reduce the risk of purchase.

In influencing clients to accept your ideas, a final consideration is the fact that every new idea will have rational, political, and personal implications for your client. Initially, for example, the movie industry was completely unsupportive of the digital video disk (DVD) format. Although manufacturers could make a strong, rational case for the product, a host of political and personal issues made studio executives unresponsive. They feared that DVDs would upset the balance of power between studios, artists, and consumers, and certain individuals did not want to put themselves out on a limb to support a new technology that could ultimately hurt their careers if it went badly. Niccolò Machiavelli alluded to this phenomenon in *The Prince*, his great book on power and leadership written nearly five hundred years ago. Hinting at these political and personal dimensions, he tells us, "The innovator makes enemies of all those who prospered under the old order, and only lukewarm support is forthcoming from those who would prosper under the new."[6]

Human nature has changed little since Machiavelli's time. New ideas will always face resistance from many fronts. The first step is to create as fertile a ground as possible from which to develop these new ideas. Then you've got to think of clients as boulders, which will be nearly impossible to move unless you find their "hidden creases," the direction in which they are inclined to go. Broad-based personal trust then gives you a base from which to exert your influence. Finally, you have to carefully understand not just the rational business case for your idea but also the political and personal impact that it will have in your client's organization.

Andrew Sobel is the leading authority on client relationships and the skills and strategies required to earn enduring client and customer loyalty. A noted business strategist, he is the author of *Making Rain: The Secrets of Building Lifelong Client Loyalty* and the coauthor (with Jagdith Sheth) of the best-selling book *Clients for Life: Evolving from an Expert for Hire to an Extraordinary Advisor*. A sought-after speaker on building long-term business relationships, Sobel has been featured in the national media, including CNBC and ABC. He is president of Andrew Sobel Advisors, Inc., an international consulting and professional development firm. Contact: andrew@andrewsobel.com

Chapter Twenty-One

Making Knowledge Move

Jon L. Powell

My piano teacher once told me that one reason to play music for others is that music not performed doesn't really exist—if no one hears it, it just sits there, notes in a book. Knowledge is a lot like music. By its nature, knowledge is neutral—literally *point mort* ("dead point") in French. It just sits there, inert, waiting to be discovered and acted on.

There are an infinite number of ways to orchestrate knowledge management to get it performed and heard. However, to get knowledge acted on—to make it move—requires another ingredient: engagement. People who are *engaged,* defined as "in gear" or "committed," are seekers; they are more interested in questions than answers. They get turned on by discovery and turned off by being lectured to. They also get turned off by clumsy orchestrations and bad performances.

Early attempts to engage people through knowledge management were a lot like looking through the wrong end of the telescope—it's a misuse of the tool, and the objective looks really far away (if you can see it at all). The main problem was a focus on documents. Specifically, converting hard copy to electronic format and building electronic repositories of material. Similarly, most knowledge management initiatives focused heavily on technology in order to store and deliver these documents. And documents, as inert as they are, don't tend to foster engagement.

As Internet technologies (Web-based systems) became a more standard technology infrastructure, the knowledge management focus shifted from technology and digital content to people, human interactions, and learning. We became interested in how people acquire knowledge, why employees are reluctant to share what they know, and what kinds of knowledge people need. However, we still think too much in terms of changing people's behaviors and not enough in terms of tapping into the potential people have for doing better, doing more, and getting smarter.

By reviewing our knowledge management journey of the past ten years, this chapter highlights successes and failures along the way, provides "tips" (dos and don'ts), and suggests that we leverage the energy that people already exhibit when fully engaged.

First We Discovered Documents

Early knowledge management focused on "things," mostly documents, or in knowledge management terminology, *artifacts*. Part of the reason was that we didn't have any. Sure, there were libraries of procedures, manuals, methodologies, and the like, but these were not easily accessible and were often out of date.

Under the heading of "if we only knew what we know," companies conceived of digitizing and capturing documents, hoping that this would resolve their knowledge management challenges. Thus early knowledge management was extremely document-centric,[1] following the mantra "Capture it, and they will come."

At a global management consulting firm, we put in place a simple capture. Toward the end of a consulting engagement—actually when the project reached 80 percent of its budgeted hours—we reached out to the project manager for deliverables, tools, methodologies, and so on.

Tip: If you're in a project-based business and you want to capture a project's work products, don't wait until the project is completed. By the time the final report is being presented, the project team will already have been dispersed. Find a way to identify when the project is around 75 percent complete, and then reach out to the project team to solicit content. If you like to aim high, build in the capture steps as part of the project plan.

Then we posted the electronic versions of these documents in a database, organized loosely in subject areas that we hoped would make sense to the consultants. In knowledge management, we call these subject areas the *taxonomy* or *classification scheme*.

While we were worrying about how to restrict access to confidential client information, one of the global practice leaders distributed a computer disk worldwide of his practice's entire content. He was quickly elevated to hero status by his practice for circumventing network connection and bandwidth constraints in getting his people content they could use (especially outside the United States).

The epiphany that was associated with this "bootleg CD" caused us to create a more robust firmwide intranet so that people could find documents and then to acquire a document management system to manage our growing document inventory. This evolution from capturing documents to organizing documents to storing documents was fairly typical for management consulting firms.

One of the side roads we went down was figuring out how to "mine" the content of a PowerPoint document, since a single document could require minutes to download. Imagine searching for a problem-solving approach that worked in the past and trying to find it among twenty-five PowerPoint documents at slow connection speeds. So we split the content into "nuggets" of knowledge, naming them things like "techniques," "tools," "methodologies," and "plans," and we tried to put enough context around each nugget to make it meaningful and searchable by others. Although we could declare victory on "nuggetizing" the knowledge embedded in large PowerPoint documents, it was clear that the work

---

Tip: When creating these classification schemes, ask people who will be looking for the documents where they would expect to find them. Then go with their first choice. Overengineered taxonomies make it hard to find things and are terribly difficult to maintain.

needed to do this (we couldn't figure out how to automate it) far exceeded the potential returns.

> Point of Interest: Another global consulting firm didn't want to use "pictures" in its documents, considering them "cartoonish." As a result, all their documents were in Microsoft Word, which take about one-tenth the space of PowerPoint documents. A completely serendipitous by-product of this decision was that their consultants were much more capable of accessing and using their document repositories because the limitations of dial-up connection speeds didn't deter them from obtaining the right information.

It was the nuggetizing exercise that caused us to think that documents might not be the answer. Furthermore, looking at this from the perspective of how engaged people were with the knowledge, the answer was "not very." We were completely reliant on natural curiosity and people's desire to grow professionally as the behavioral drivers that would cause them to sift through the databases. This is a formula for medium to low levels of engagement.

Then We Rediscovered People

Following the corporate motto, "People are our most important asset," knowledge management evolved from a document-centric view toward a more person-centered view of knowledge sharing and transfer. There were four main reasons for knowledge management's shift toward people:

1. As we filled up our repositories with documents, we started to give more thought to how people would engage with the repositories to find material, as well as what we were hoping they might do once they did find the material.

2. Our growing body of experience showed us just how hard it is to represent knowledge on paper with enough context that other people can find and apply it to their specific situation.

3. We came to realize that documents were limited to "explicit" knowledge (what we know we know) and that the real payoff might be in finding ways to share "tacit" knowledge (what's in our unconscious, or what we don't know we know).

4. Workforce demographics showed an aging population of deeply knowledgeable people who were going to retire in a narrow time frame. This issue is especially acute in the government, for which specific programs have been developed to retain as much of this "institutional memory" as possible.[2]

Point of Interest: A cousin to early knowledge management efforts was benchmarking and best practices, which sprang up in the 1980s.[3] "Site visits" were conducted between companies to share best practices on such topics as how to reduce manufacturing setup times or how to bring products to market faster. Interestingly enough, these early site visits were very people-centric—the companies involved knew that the value came from collaboration and not so much from an exchange of manuals or operating procedures. Formal knowledge management needed a few years to recognize the importance of face-to-face meetings and trusted relationships.

This people focus gave rise to new techniques (and newly discovered old techniques) to describe the people-to-people interactions. I've selected three that exemplify this new focus: communities of practice or expertise, storytelling, and expertise location. However, there are others, including collaboration, social network analysis, and social capital, that offer additional insights into the central role people play in knowledge management.[4]

Communities of Practice or Expertise

Communities are one of the most powerful and intuitive knowledge-sharing mechanisms. People connect with others to whom they feel some kinship, and the levels of trust that exist within a community facilitate the exchange of information and knowledge.

> **Tip:** To support communities of practice or expertise in your orga-
> nization, identify the places where energy is already in abundance;
> make it easier for people to connect and engage with each another,
> share information, and grow their community. Also, don't change
> the goals of the community for the first year; let the community take
> shape before attempting any adjustments.

Thus communities transcend the typical organizational and geographical boundaries that can impede knowledge flow. Critically
important for any global company today, "success in global markets
depends on communities sharing knowledge across the globe."[5]

According to Wenger and his colleagues, "Communities of
practice are groups of people who share a concern, a set of problems, or a passion about a topic, and who deepen their knowledge
and expertise in this area by interacting on an ongoing basis."[6]

The critical element for effective communities is the same
aspect that makes communities hard to "legislate" or build from the
top down: people participate in communities because they want to.
Hence striking the right balance between top-down structure and
infrastructure support for communities with the bottom-up, grass-
roots nature of communities is more art than science.

Storytelling

In Stephen Denning's book *The Springboard*, he uses the word *springboard* because the impact of a story comes more through a "leap of
understanding" than the ability to transfer lots of information.

He begins the book by admitting that he stumbled on storytelling because "nothing else worked" and goes on to say,
"Storytelling enables the individuals in an organization to see
themselves and the organization in a different light, and accord-
ingly take decisions and change their behavior in accordance with
these new perceptions, insights, and identities."[7]

> **Tip:** Before documenting and publishing a slew of stories, identify the desired behavior changes you're seeking. According to Denning, the powerful impacts—the ones that can cause profound change—came from the *storytelling experience* and not necessarily the stories themselves.

Storytelling has made the knowledge management radar because it engages people in a way that almost no other method can, and through that engagement, the knowledge and learning come alive—no longer *points morts*.

Expertise Location

Finding expertise grew out of the notion that "if I could just talk to someone for a few minutes who knows all about this, I could get my questions answered in real time and keep my momentum." This is not a new concept—everyone has personal networks—it's just that to leverage the know-how of a large, global firm requires more than someone's personal network. Early and successful attempts at expertise locators were company "yellow pages," organized by topic area and listing the best people to call for information.

These hard-copy solutions aged quickly, and so companies posted these directories on their intranets for easier access and maintenance. However, whether in hard-copy or electronic form, these directories are notoriously difficult to keep up-to-date. Software vendors have responded to this challenge with an array of fascinating products that automatically profile everyone's expertise, based on electronically eavesdropping on what they read or write or on questions they respond to (and how well they respond).

I am particularly fascinated with these software solutions and piloted one several years ago. Data from the pilot suggested a return on investment in excess of 300 percent, but after careful observation of this topic for several years, success stories are few and far

> **Tip:** Don't get caught up worrying that your "experts" are going to be bogged down with questions. Focus more on stimulating the demand for questions by asking what work behavior would stimulate a question. In general, people seem more comfortable providing answers than they do risking appearing ignorant with their questions.

between. Perhaps the answer lies with social capital theory as espoused by Cohen and Prusak: knowledge is based on a trust economy, and therefore, digital connections simply cannot precede trusted relationships.[8] Or perhaps we just don't like the thought of a computer sifting through our e-mail.

Behavior Management Doesn't Necessarily Translate into Engagement

Along with the people-centric view have come attempts to balance more carefully the interdependence among people, process, and technology. As knowledge management projects became more encompassing of these three elements, the noise grew around motivating the right behaviors. For example, "How can I get my people to follow the new knowledge-sharing processes and procedures?"

Behavioral issues aren't exclusive to knowledge sharing. Sooner or later, everyone and anyone attempting to change employee behaviors will zero in on the performance management program because "if it's worth doing, it's worth putting in the performance plan." For this reason, most of us carry a multitude of performance objectives, measures, and intentions—some of which are in conflict with each other. However, "employees throughout a company make decisions about what to pay attention to based on the *perception* of what their leaders pay attention to,"[9] not necessarily what's in their performance plan.

Objective setting is a key element to aligning and moving an organization, and I don't mean to imply that it shouldn't have a central role in the management process. In fact, at my company, we

> **Tip:** When you find yourself saying, "We'll add this to the performance objectives," understand that this may be number 16 on the list of really critical things to do this year. Better to find ways to embed behaviors into existing processes and to use champions to help keep people engaged.

are raising the visibility of knowledge management using leadership's performance objectives. My recommendation is to make sure that you don't stop there. Davenport and Beck note that you cannot control what people focus on (except in the short term) and that ". . . ultimately, people direct their own attention. . . . Controlling one's own attention is the one freedom an individual will always possess."[10]

Conclusion

So orchestrating knowledge to make it move and, perhaps more important, to make it moving to the user requires more than a solely technical approach. If you've ever listened to a piece of music that was played with technical proficiency but without heart, you know why knowledge management has to be performed by engaged people who feel free to share and learn from each other.

Creating, sharing, and using knowledge is much like playing the piano for the love of music, the joy of entertaining others, and the inspiration that comes from performing the work of great composers. It has to be a blend of the technical basics that soon fade into making each performance personal and tied to the everyday motivation and practice of the performers. When we learn to manage knowledge as conductors orchestrate symphonies, bringing out the best in each performer yet inspiring each to blend it into the sound of the whole, we will make knowledge move, and the knowledge we produce will move us to great performance.

Jon L. Powell is the chief knowledge officer at Hewitt Associates, a global outsourcing and consulting firm that delivers a complete range of human capital management services to companies. He is responsible for the firm's global knowledge management strategy and execution. He has spent nearly twenty-five years in management consulting, most of that time with A. T. Kearney and KPMG Consulting (now BearingPoint). As a result of his consulting experience, Powell has developed a passion and an expertise around knowledge sharing in professional service firms. He is an adjunct professor at Northwestern University, where he teaches applied knowledge management in the Center for Learning and Organizational Change. Contact: Jon.Powell@hewitt.com

Chapter Twenty-Two

The Role of Change Management in Knowledge Management

Marc J. Rosenberg

We often spend so much time introducing what seems to us as a great idea that we fail to notice when people either don't care about it or don't want it. Knowledge management (KM) can fall into this trap. KM is more than an information technology (IT) project or the deployment of a new tool. It almost always represents a fundamental organizational transformation that requires careful attention to helping people accept and adopt a new way of working. Make no mistake: there will be resistance. The question is, how can we overcome that resistance before it engulfs us?

This chapter argues that change management is critical to implementing a successful and sustainable knowledge management initiative. It presents twelve change management factors that must be addressed to ensure that the KM system is not only launched successfully but accepted as well. Ignoring even one of these factors can put KM efforts in jeopardy. A knowledge management and change management checklist is provided to jump-start this process.

"If you build it, they will come." While this famous line may have proved prophetic for Kevin Costner in the movie *Field of Dreams*, they may not come so readily to the new and promising world of knowledge management. As we deploy better knowledge systems in our organizations, we hope that new tools, technologies, and approaches to improving the way people create, access, and share information will be welcomed with open arms. This is wishful thinking.

To create a knowledge management system, and an associated knowledge environment, that delivers on its promise, we must ensure that those who will use and are affected by KM willingly accept it and the changes it represents.

However, what if users reject the new knowledge management approach? What if they see the initiative as too disruptive or burdensome? What if they feel they are not adequately prepared or that they haven't been told enough about it? If this happens, they could treat it as just another gimmick and quite possibly reject it, making the next KM effort much tougher.

This can easily happen. Over time, workers build their own personal, comfortable, and possibly inefficient knowledge systems. They rely on their personal system whether it is accurate or not. When they need to know something, they ask their buddies or their boss. Over the years, they've built unique personal directories, e-mail files, or collections of information on scraps of paper, "just in case."

Change Management Strategy

Changing the way people work, especially if the change has the potential for disrupting personal comfort levels or an existing organizational culture, is tough work that is not to be taken lightly. When the change appears to add more structure or process to how people do their jobs or when it appears to conflict with individual work styles, even if these perceptions are incorrect, the challenge is even greater. Research in organizational dynamics, diffusion of innovation, and change suggest that failure to pay attention to prevailing attitudes, beliefs, and practices, even when the benefits of a new way of doing things are totally obvious to all, invites disappointment if not disaster.

To avoid the cynicism and disappointment (not to mention the business setback) that could come with a failed knowledge management initiative, a comprehensive change management strategy is critical. What does this mean? What should be done? Here are twelve "change management factors" to consider when building a change management plan:

1. Leadership and role models	7. Impossibility
2. Success stories	8. Priorities
3. Consequences and incentives	9. Fear of technology
4. Value proposition	10. Sink-in time
5. Level of participation	11. Training
6. Hassle	12. Ongoing support

Leadership and Role Models

Nothing is more important to the success of a knowledge management initiative than the support of leaders and the visibility of KM role models. Generally speaking, the higher up in the organization these role models are the better. When executives tout a KM system but refuse to use it themselves, they send two clear messages. The first is that they don't value the KM initiative, regardless of their rhetoric. This leads to perceptions that KM is just the "flavor of the month" and, given time, will go away. The second message is that KM is for "workers" and not for executives. This can be perceived as elitist and can result in widening the gap in the way work is done rather than closing it. When leaders have a separate knowledge network from that used by their organizations, they cannot possibly pay enough attention to the overall KM effort. It's far better for everyone to use the same approach, even if there must be different levels of use or access based on a person's level in the firm.

If you can't get your leaders on board, your KM initiative may be doomed before it gets started. On the other hand, when leaders at all levels (supervisors, managers, and executives) use the KM system, they encourage others to do the same. Here's a test. Look at any major change in any organization. See where the change has taken hold and where it has faltered. Now look at the level of leadership support in these groups, and there will undoubtedly be a positive correlation between leadership support and KM adoption.

Success Stories

Nothing succeeds like success, and the appeal of success is motivating to people who are trying something new. When they hear from others, like themselves, that KM has made work easier, improved performance, or helped serve customers better, for example, they are more likely to believe that they can benefit as well. It's simply not enough to tell people about the benefits of KM or even show them. You must find ways for potential users to see themselves in the future state.

Whether you present these stories in live meetings, in text, on video, online, or in any other format, the key to their effectiveness will be their authenticity. Refrain from hiring actors or trying to create hypothetical situations. Use real people who can relate their personal experiences, perhaps including early struggles and how they overcame them. Success stories, possibly drawn from pilot KM projects or from early adopter groups, will give the broader population a way to truly understand that "if they can do it, so can I."

Consequences and Incentives

People are much more likely to adopt KM when they believe that both they and the organization will benefit. On the other hand, if people believe that the new system brings with it more work, lots of hassle, and perhaps punishment of some kind (for example, a conflict with how the boss wants work done), they'll avoid it like the plague. So when introducing knowledge management, provide the right incentives so that people will do more than try it out: they'll stick with it. It is also important to remove any consequences of participation. Both are essential.

On the incentives side, consider how people will be encouraged to contribute to or use the KM system. There are many creative approaches that can be tried. Think about including monetary incentives for high-value contributions (perhaps based on user feedback), special perks for contributors, or just special recognition of individuals for their expertise (removing the Rodney Dangerfield "I get no respect" attitude). It's also important to recognize that participation can be seen as new work that takes time away from other work. When potential knowledge contributors complain that they have no time, they are surfacing consequences you must deal with, either by reevaluating workloads or by convincing participants that work levels will actually decrease as a result of the new KM system (maybe by using success stories or role models).

Value Proposition

To get real and sustainable acceptance, knowledge management systems must offer value to users and the business as a whole. Implementing KM because it's "cool" technology or because everyone else is doing it is hardly a reason for long-term, serious support. The value proposition for knowledge management must address at least two groups of people, and it may be different for each group. For executives who support and fund the initiative, knowledge management must bring benefits to the business. Increased productivity, enabling people to access more accurate information more quickly, is one form of value. However, good value propositions should be more specific. How might the KM system improve sales results? How might it enhance the customer care component of the business or improve the capabilities of the research and development department? The more clear and precise the value proposition is both quantitatively and qualitatively, the more likely it will be to gain long-term support.

The value proposition should also address users. Why should they accept and use KM? From a change management perspective, people respond positively to benefits. When developing a value proposition for KM users, focus on the system's benefits, not its features. Will the KM system make their work easier? Will it help improve their job performance and contribute positively to their appraisal? KM features, such as the functionality of the search engine or the ability to collaborate in an online community, are inadequate by themselves to generate support and commitment. Change management postmortems of disappointing KM deployments often discover that the failure to clearly communicate benefits is one of the major causes of nonadoption.

Level of Participation

Being a part of change is much more likely to lead to success than being the object of change. Those who will use the KM system should be part of its design. One of the best ways to do this is to form a steering committee, representing all stakeholders, from developers to users to managers, that will have, at the least, direct input into the design of the system and, at the most, some governance or decision-making power. If necessary, perhaps because executives and users might have different interests, several groups can be formed. It is crucial that the input of all groups, especially users, be incorporated into the project from the start.

These groups can also serve as a ready-made pilot population, "eyes and ears" in the field to report back on how the system is or is not being used and, if you do this well, a strong group of advocates during deployment that can make the difference between adoption and rejection.

The bottom line is that involving your stakeholders early on will lead them to accept the forthcoming KM system as being done *with* them and *for* them rather than *to* them.

Hassle

At the core of knowledge management is the assumption that it makes work and work life easier. Yet people may not accept this just because they are told it is so. Initially, they'll see more procedures, standards, and requirements to which to adhere. The key here is to identify how work is actually made easier by focusing on a lack of rework (as when the wrong information is provided), reduction of redundancy (eliminating multiple requests for the same information), and improved access (when knowledge can be found faster with less waiting for a response, like a call back or a return e-mail). One of the best ways to do this is through demonstration projects, testimonials, and success stories. When potential users see others using the new system with no problem, they are more likely to believe that the hassle factor will not be an issue for them.

Impossibility

"It can't be done." "It will never work." We hear this whenever something new is introduced. Negative attitudes, seeing failure before you even get started, can be disastrous to a knowledge management initiative. It's a mistake to think that these attitudes are entirely based on a desire to avoid something new and different. Often there is some truth in these feelings, likely the result of previous efforts that either were poorly conceived in the first place or were good ideas that were poorly introduced into the culture. While positive communications can significantly counter feelings that the project is going to fail, one of the best strategies is to select individuals and groups who are predisposed to a successful outcome. These "early adopters" tend to be more accepting of new ideas. They are first to try out new technologies, and they are the first to get on the bandwagon of new ways of doing things. However, early adopters can also be early rejecters. So in the early stages, care must be taken to avoid people and groups who focus on fads or who have short attention spans. Instead, try to select people and groups that have a history of trying out new things and, if proving useful, sticking with them. Look at how they reacted to the introduction of new systems in the past. Look at how well their managers promote new work processes and whether or not these new approaches have been incorporated into the work culture. Use them to pilot KM before full-scale implementation. Monitor their use and attitudes carefully, and provide as much support as needed. These will become your success stories that will boost acceptance of the system when you deploy it to the larger organization.

Priorities

One person's critical issue can be someone else's trivial concern. Assessing the priorities of users goes hand in hand with determining their view of the project's likelihood of success. People who think that knowledge management is critical (a high priority) but who also feel that it won't succeed are bound to be the most disappointed and discouraged if the KM initiative does fail. In addition, they may be more resistant the next time around. This is even worse if management attaches a high priority to KM but fails to instill it in those who will use the system. The result is lots of bewilderment and a feeling that KM is just another management fad. Again, the key is alignment—a high priority ("we need this") with a perception that the new KM system might actually work. This is a key criterion for early adopter selection.

Fear of Technology

In today's Internet-savvy world, it's easy to think that everyone is totally comfortable with technology. There are still lots of people who are new to computers. There are also lots of people who use computers every day who still have trouble upgrading to new operating systems, software packages, or applications. Clerks who have worked for years on mainframe, green-screen systems may have trouble moving to a Windows or mouse-based system. Managers who have stored critical documents on their C drive may be fearful of placing those same documents in a centralized knowledge repository. Always assume that any significant change in hard or soft technology, the way that technology is used, or how that technology alters work routines may instill some fear and trepidation.

Introduce new KM technology early, before people actually have to start using it. For end users, provide lots of demonstrations. Place prototypes around work areas for people to test-drive. Arrange for adequate training and human support. Identify more experienced technology buddies in each department to help out and serve as role models. For "techies" (who might lead the "it's impossible" charge), offer advanced technical briefings with the KM development team, and make sure the IT department is a full participant.

Sink-In Time

Almost all change initiatives meet resistance early on, but it's far worse when people feel that they're being rushed into something of which they're unsure. They want and need time to consider how the change will affect them. If a knowledge management system is being launched on January 1, for example, telling people about it on December 31 is too late to expect that they'll be ready and open to the new approach. A significant period of disruption will occur as people try to figure out what it all means and whether it's "for real." This can sometimes overwhelm the new initiative, and thus it won't catch on. Helping people understand, question, and ultimately accept KM before it is launched will dramatically reduce disruption time and will give the initiative a much greater likelihood of success. This calls for communication, success stories, role modeling, and demonstrations early on, even when the system is still under development (use prototypes).

Training

Knowledge management training is vital. It begins early, before deployment, and it may be classroom-based, online (as a part of the new KM system), or both. It should focus primarily on the user experience, be personalized to the user's skill and experience level, allow for lots of practice, and provide learners with realistic scenarios that depict how they will use the system and how it will benefit them (value proposition). It is not simply training on the new KM tools, features, and functionalities, which is often the only training that is offered. It is also training on how to manage knowledge: publishing, organizing, distributing, evaluating, expiring, and so on. We all know people who can't find key documents when they need them or who live with amazingly disorganized computer files. A KM system can help, but only if these people begin to learn and appreciate the value of organized knowledge and how to keep it that way. This area of training is as critical to the successful adoption of a new KM system as training on the system itself.

Another mistake trainers often make is focusing only on users and not on their managers. People in leadership and authority positions will be watched closely to see if they use the new KM system. Train them first, and make sure they understand their unique role not just in the KM initiative but in the change process as well. Finally, the use of good online help, developing managers as "knowledge coaches," and a liberal use of examples and models can extend the impact of the training back to the workplace.

Ongoing Support

Implementing knowledge management in small or large organizations often represents a change in the culture. Work is done differently, the expectation to share what you know is stronger, and employees are often appraised on their contributions to the knowledge base. Change management often begins and ends with the rollout. There is lots of communication, training, and hoopla around the new system, after which there is little follow-up. Initial enthusiasm can quickly be replaced with doubt and discouragement as problems arise without any means to resolve them. People become reluctant to contribute knowledge, reverting back to their C drive or e-mail as their primary knowledge store. Information in the system becomes stale and unreliable, collaboration falls off, and utilization falls with it.

This can be prevented, in part, through ongoing support. The best change management efforts extend well beyond initial deployment with continued training; help lines; newsletter; and other forms of communication (usually online), such as testimonials, success stories, and case studies. Even a local peer group that meets once a week to discuss how the transformation is proceeding and offer up suggestions for improvement can be valuable.

Conclusion

At the end of the day, no KM system can survive an organization that doesn't value it and won't accept it. If your investment in knowledge management does not include a corresponding investment in change management, you may be throwing more than your financial investment down a rat hole. You may be tossing a big piece of your credibility down there too. But paying attention to change management and the twelve change management factors presented in this chapter can make the difference between a successful KM implementation and starting over. Just following the checklist in Exhibit 22.1 is a good start.

Knowledge management goes beyond smart individuals to build a smarter enterprise, but you'll never get there if your KM system languishes because you failed to consider change management. If you build it and you prepare your people for it, they will come, use it, and support it.

Marc J. Rosenberg is an independent consultant and leading figure in the world of training, organizational learning, e-learning, knowledge management, and performance improvement. He is the author of the best-selling book *E-Learning: Strategies for Delivering Knowledge in the Digital Age*. Rosenberg is a past president of the International Society for Performance Improvement (ISPI). He has spoken at the White House, keynoted numerous professional and business conferences, and written more than thirty articles in the field. He is a frequently quoted expert in major business and trade publications. Contact: http://www.marcrosenberg.com

Exhibit 22.1 Knowledge Management and Change Management Checklist: How to Gauge the Potential Success of Your Knowledge Management Initiative

Change Management Factor	Good Signs	Bad Signs
1. Leadership and role models	Managers and leaders have stepped up as KM role models and are setting proper expectations about its use.	Managers and leaders are just giving lip service to KM; they are not employing it themselves and don't seem to require others to use it.
2. Success stories	Users can see how others have used knowledge management successfully.	Users do not see examples of the KM approach being successfully used, possibly leading to disbelief in its benefits.
3. Consequences and incentives	KM has positive incentives associated with it (such as recognition for contributing knowledge to the system or a higher performance rating due to greater efficiency of knowledge work).	KM has unintended consequences associated with it (such as a lower performance rating due to the inefficient ramp-up time that was necessary to master the system or a fear that the new system might eliminate jobs).
4. Value proposition	People understand and accept the reason for and benefits of KM, and they can discuss these with others.	People don't understand and can't describe what the benefits of the new KM approach are to themselves or to the organization.
5. Level of participation	Users believe KM is being implemented directly for their benefit; they feel included.	Users believe KM is being done *to* them rather than *for* them or *with* them.
6. Hassle	Users believe KM will make their work (and life) easier.	Users believe KM will create more work, not less.
7. Impossibility	Users believe they are adopting a winning approach.	Users believe, from the start, that KM can't be implemented; it will fail.

Exhibit 22.1 Knowledge Management and Change Management Checklist: How to Gauge the Potential Success of Your Knowledge Management Initiative, Cont'd.

Change Management Factor	Good Signs	Bad Signs
8. Priorities	Users see the importance of KM in the same way as others, especially organizational leaders, see it.	Users attach a different priority to KM than what was expected, or their priorities differ from those of their managers and leaders.
9. Fear of technology	Users see new technology as an easy "climb up" from what they are currently using.	Users are nervous about working with new technology that is fundamentally different from what they are used to.
10. Sink-in time	Users have had time to think about and absorb what will happen, before it happens.	Users believe they are being rushed into adopting the new KM approach.
11. Training	Users see themselves as appropriately skilled to handle the new KM system.	Users feel they are being asked to do something for which they believe they have not been adequately trained.
12. Ongoing support	Users and their managers feel supported in use of the KM system.	There is little or no support structure to help people adapt to the KM system.

Chapter Twenty-Three

Building Social Connections to Gain the Knowledge Advantage

Susan E. Jackson

Niclas L. Erhardt

Modern organizations face constantly changing competitive environments. Thriving and at times merely surviving in such environments requires developing capabilities that support innovation, change management, and continuous learning. Because effectively managing knowledge is essential to innovation and learning, it is an increasingly important source of competitive advantage.

During the past decade, many companies invested heavily in electronic knowledge management systems. Their hope was that electronic systems would increase their ability to store, sort, distribute, and perhaps analyze the vast array of knowledge residing, and often hidden, within the many nooks and crannies of organizational life. However, what experienced users of electronic knowledge management systems now realize is that electronic systems can be effective only when they are integrated into a total management approach for retaining ideas, creating new knowledge, and sustaining continuous learning.

When knowledge resources are recognized as essential to an organization, a wide array of management practices may be changed. Some new practices aim to create more opportunities for knowledge accumulation and thereby increase the organization's

Note: We thank Bristol-Myers Squibb Company, Deloitte Consulting, and Pfizer Inc. for their contributions to some of the ideas presented in this chapter.

knowledge stock. Other practices aim to speed the movement of knowledge through the organization, thereby improving knowledge flow. Besides electronic knowledge systems, work designed around multidisciplinary teams, communities of practice, and decentralized decision making are perhaps the most prevalent features of knowledge-intensive organizations. Some organizations also offer incentives and rewards to encourage employees to develop their personal knowledge and share what they know with others. A few organizations even create new measurement and accounting systems to track and assess the value of their knowledge assets.[1]

Formal policies and structures that create more opportunities for knowledge accumulation and movement are certainly a needed first step toward competing effectively in knowledge-intensive industries. Yet while formal systems have been transformed in recent years, managers have found that employee behavior is less malleable. Often subtle social barriers that are difficult to see interfere with the effectiveness of new management systems. In this chapter, we describe how social factors can impede or facilitate the development and flow of knowledge within and between organizations. Our presentation is organized around a few myths that seem to prevent some organizations from maximizing their knowledge management capabilities. For each myth, we propose an alternative reality and its implications for managing knowledge more effectively.

Myth 1 Versus Reality 1

Myth 1: The main objectives of knowledge management (KM) are archiving and distributing knowledge.

Reality 1: The most valuable knowledge management initiatives motivate people to create, consider, debate, and effectively use new knowledge.

It is probably no coincidence that many managers evaluate their organizations' knowledge management systems based on how well they store knowledge and make it easily accessible to others, for these are what electronic KM systems do best. Yet storing and distributing knowledge efficiently doesn't guarantee the success of organizations that compete on the basis of knowledge. As satisfying as it may be to corral what is already known, doing so may worsen a dangerous tendency of successful managers: relying too heavily on past experiences to navigate an uncertain future.

Scholarly investigations of the innovation process reveal that managers often rely too heavily on lessons learned from the past. They cling to approaches that have been successful before and often resist new ideas of all sorts. In fast-changing environments, these rigidities can be lethal. Ironically, when forward-thinking organizations begin to formally track and reward employees for archiving their knowledge and using the archived knowledge of others, they may exacerbate this problem.

To gain competitive advantage, new knowledge must be created and applied to develop new or unique perspectives, products, and value-adding processes. Creativity, in turn, is a fragile resource that can be nourished or destroyed by the social dynamics of the organization. To be sure, easy access to information supports creativity, but the emotional climate of an organization is perhaps even more important. Creativity blossoms in organizations that are characterized by open communication, cohesive relationships among coworkers, trusting and supportive managers who provide verbal encouragement and support for innovation, and a shared commitment to common goals.

Like creativity, learning also depends on more than mere access to information. As a first step, employees must feel motivated to learn: the value of learning must be apparent, and the costs of learning should be small. In many organizations, employees view "learning" as a remedy for a person's current deficiencies. The implicit assumption is that learning is a remedial activity that is needed when people's current knowledge is incomplete, old or even obsolete. These are conclusions that threaten self-esteem and thus they are likely to be resisted. This problem seemed to hobble the "lessons learned" sessions that one drug company established to improve its internal decisions concerning when to begin full clinical testing of new products. When the scientists involved in past decisions were reluctant to participate in discussion about past failures, some of the managers concluded that scientists just aren't interested in "that type of thing."

By focusing on the future instead of the past, learning-friendly organizations can transform learning into welcomed opportunities for future success. Siemens University provides employees with opportunities for action learning. Its in-house corporate training gives responsibility for solving real business problems to analysts and engineers from around the world, who work together in "student" teams. Instead of teaching students about what others already know, action learning at Siemens encourages teams to develop new knowledge that can be immediately applied. Management practices that encourage the transfer of best practices are another approach to creating new knowledge. At Colgate-Palmolive, best practices are spread and adapted to new situations by managers who routinely accept transfers to unfamiliar functions, divisions, and countries en route to higher-level positions. In both examples, learning is embedded in nonthreatening social relationships that are formed to find ways of improving the future. As ideas are tossed about and considered, participants feel comfortable sharing what they have learned, even if mistakes were made during the learning process.

Compare action learning to another common technique, asking teams to perform postmortems on failed projects or dissecting recent projects to identify what could have been done better. The objective of such learning techniques is the same: to improve future practice. Yet in the latter scenarios, it is much more difficult to eliminate finger pointing and defensive self-protection. As a result, few people will confess their mistakes and explain what they have learned from those mistakes.

The emotions experienced by people participating in these two different approaches to knowledge sharing and learning management are likely to be quite different. Action learning projects may be (and perhaps should be) stressful for the participants, but usually participants finish the projects feeling a sense of accomplishment and pride. They feel good about their learning, and they feel good about the people who have facilitated their learning. In addition to building knowledge, action learning helps build social capital. In contrast, postmortems surface more negative emotions. The learning experience and the people involved in it are associated with feelings of failure and embarrassment. Because the focus is on the past instead of the future, people attach less value to whatever learning does occur. Besides creating little new knowledge, such sessions may have the unintended consequence of destroying the social capital needed for further learning and knowledge sharing. Fortunately, challenges like these can be fixed. Often the cure is as easy as restructuring exercises in hindsight to activities aimed at achieving challenging and meaningful new goals.

Myth 2 Versus Reality 2

> **Myth 2:** For knowledge work, electronic communication is just as effective as meeting face to face.
>
> **Reality 2:** In a knowledge-based economy, personal relationships and face-to-face interactions are more essential than ever to understanding new knowledge and using it effectively.

For decades, science fiction writers have painted a future in which computers are as "intelligent" as humans. However, as scientists working in the field of artificial intelligence now know, the task of creating a computer that matches the abilities of humans— to learn, to see simple patterns embedded in a complex array of visual cues, to synthesize information and give it new meaning— has yet to be accomplished. Without question, computers are more effective than people when it comes to storing, manipulating, and distributing information. However, they can do so only to the extent that people articulate useful knowledge and enter it into the system. Even in the best companies, most knowledge never appears in documents or databases. The vice president of KM at Unisys recently estimated that only 2 percent of its knowledge is ever written down; 98 percent resides inside people's heads. Perhaps this is why, according to some estimates, knowledge management activities at Xerox, a widely recognized knowledge management leader, is 20 percent technology and 80 percent people.[2]

The problem companies face is not simply that people don't record everything they know; the problem is that people can't record everything they know because much of their knowledge is implicit or tacit.

Valuable tacit knowledge is often created and shared through social interactions with experts, with customers, and even with competitors. For this reason, learning organizations promote face-to-face encounters. Meetings around the water cooler are encouraged rather than discouraged. Social events, network builders, mentoring, classroom-based workshops, conferences, and community service are all seen as forums for developing and sharing tacit knowledge. Restructuring work places to include more shared community space also supports knowledge sharing and learning via informal conversations. These community spaces may include new forms of conference rooms without doors or walls specifically designed to invite, foster, and encourage informal conversations among employees. Looking for a new way to support face-to-face knowledge exchanges, one company considered moving its coffee shop from the in-house restaurant to the company library. Ultimately, the idea was never implemented due to building code restrictions. Nevertheless, this company was on the right track: it recognized that minor spatial arrangements can have major implications for the creation and sharing of knowledge.

Consider the tacit knowledge that is needed to function effectively in a new culture—for example, understanding how to close a deal with a major client in another country. One can read about the values and norms of that country, but the usefulness of written descriptions is limited. Understanding how a country's values and norms shape day-to-day business operations is virtually impossible without face-to-face conversations with experienced colleagues who have firsthand knowledge. The importance of cultural knowledge pervades business activities. In the pharmaceutical industry, for example, a company's ability to acquire tacit cultural knowledge about the Food and Drug Administration may result in superior drug applications, reduced time for review and approval, and an earlier product launch. Considering that a blockbuster drug may generate annual sales of billions of dollars, each day is critical in a highly competitive market.

Myth 3 Versus Reality 3

> **Myth 3:** Employees will freely seek out and share knowledge if they understand it is expected and if they are rewarded for it.
>
> **Reality 3:** Financial rewards and recognition may motivate some employees to seek out and share knowledge, but incentives do not eliminate the subtle (and not so subtle) social barriers that often frustrate innovation and the introduction of new ideas.

Whether tacit or explicit, knowledge creation and knowledge sharing almost always involve some direct communication and interaction between people who have expertise and people who wish to use the expertise. Thus knowledge-based activities must ultimately recognize and overcome a variety of social barriers. We have already alluded to one social barrier that blocks knowledge sharing: the finger-pointing blame game that often follows failure. Fear of losing power is another social barrier to knowledge sharing. Clearly, knowledge is power in today's knowledge economy; so sharing knowledge means sharing power or perhaps even losing power. In a turbulent and uncertain job market, tacit knowledge is a critical source of individual competitive advantage. The issue of power is woven into the fabric of a variety of social barriers related to knowledge sharing.

Another social barrier that restricts the free flow of knowledge stems from the judgments people make about each other's credibility and trustworthiness. Unfortunately, these judgments may be based on biases and stereotypes instead of the actual credibility and trustworthiness of the people involved. For many employees, it is difficult to trust a stranger. A user of Textron's knowledge management system put it this way: "We don't know the people responding [to electronic inquiries] in most cases, and there are no metrics for the quality of responses. [So] we'll make decisions based on people we know, not people we don't know. Credibility is the name of the game."[3]

In any large organization, people know only a subset of the members. Who do people tend to know? Management scholars have conducted numerous studies of the friendship and communication networks that develop in work organizations, and the findings are clear. People tend to know and more easily trust those who are similar: people of the same gender, approximately the same age, and of the same racial or ethnic background. How does this affect knowledge sharing? Studies of communication networks suggest that demographic differences between employees may interfere with knowledge sharing unless organizations take specific steps to override the natural tendency of people to communicate more easily with those who are similar and those who are familiar. A consulting firm did just that when it adopted the practice of setting aside the third Friday of each month as a day when everyone would get together. Typically, the consultants worked at their clients' offices, leaving the home office virtually deserted. Especially during the most active business periods, the consultants seldom had time for personal interaction with each other. To increase social contact and make it easier to keep up with internal developments, they agreed that each month, one of the offices would host a gathering on the third Friday. Over time, these gatherings provided the consultants with more opportunities to build personal relationships and establish greater trust among themselves.

Parties, social outings, face-to-face meetings, and other activities that encourage employees to get to know each other can help, but especially in large companies, they will never solve the problem completely. Recognizing that a more formal solution was needed, one company developed a network of "knowledge integrators." The knowledge integrators help bring together people in different areas of the company to share their knowledge. If a project manager needs to locate a subject matter expert for assistance with an acute problem, she contacts a knowledge integrator, who then locates the right person. Because the knowledge integrators have deep knowledge about the business as well as the people, they can locate relevant knowledge and filter through irrelevant information.

Myth 4 Versus Reality 4

Myth 4: If a team needs to engage in creative problem solving, the best way to staff the team is with as much technical and professional diversity as possible.

Reality 4: Having the wrong mix of participants or managing diversity poorly can interfere with productive debate and effective problem solving.

When the objectives of project teams or communities of practice include learning from others and developing creative solutions, most people agree that diverse perspectives are needed. Indeed, the growing use of teams reflects the faith that people have in the value of diversity. Beyond internal initiatives, many organizations develop alliances with suppliers, customers, and even competitors to gain new knowledge. International Sematech is an example of a multilateral alliance that supports learning through collaborative research. Through joint participation, thirteen semiconductor manufacturers from seven countries share knowledge and expertise in ways that ultimately influence the entire industry. Network structures like this are intended to maximize knowledge flows among organizations. Such links can improve the organization's understanding of problems that lie beyond its own boundaries as well as motivate other members in the network to share knowledge and expertise to find creative solutions.

Substantial research supports the view of diversity as a valuable resource. As anyone who works in a diverse team knows, however, creativity and learning do not always come easily for diverse teams. Interpersonal conflicts, slower decision making, and greater turnover of team members are among the costs of team diversity, and this is true regardless of the source of diversity (differences in functional expertise, industry experience, age, tenure, ethnicity, gender, and so on).[4]

When team members share too little common ground, the team may be unable to use its diversity effectively—not because the members lack basic competencies or because they are unmotivated but because effective communication is too difficult. Fortunately, communication problems, whether related to diversity or not, can be managed by using an agreed format and questions and by having clear roles depending on the meeting's level of importance. Having preestablished roles such as note taker, synthesizer, and knowledge integrator along with subject matter expert and facilitator may further reduce communication issues and foster knowledge sharing.

Conclusion

For many companies, knowledge management will be another fad that comes and goes. However, a few companies will understand that innovation and continuous learning are capabilities that are necessary for their success in the twenty-first century. These companies will continue to invest in finding new ways to synthesize, share, and leverage knowledge to support creativity and learning. They will experiment and continuously fine-tune myriad management practices. Gradually, they will overcome the many technical and social barriers that hobble their competitors, and learning-friendly cultures will evolve to support their knowledge-based strategies. At the heart of these learning-friendly cultures will be a wealth of tacit knowledge gained through trial-and-error experiences. Awaiting the firms that succeed will be a competitive advantage that others will envy but find impossible to copy.

Susan E. Jackson is professor of human resource management at the School of Management and Labor Relations at Rutgers University, where she also serves as graduate director for the doctoral program in industrial relations and human resources. Her primary area of expertise is the strategic management of human resources, and her special interests include managing for knowledge-based competition, improving team effectiveness, and workforce diversity. Among her publications on these topics are her recent books, including *Managing Knowledge for Sustained Competitive Advantage: Designing Strategies for Effective Human Resource Management* (with M. A. Hitt and A. S. De Nisi), *Managing Human Resources Through Strategic Partnership* (with R. S. Schuler), and *Diversity in the Workplace: Human Resource Initiatives.* Contact: sjacksox@rci.rutgers.edu; http://www.rci.rutgers.edu/~sjacksox

Niclas L. Erhardt is a doctoral student at the School of Management and Labor Relations at Rutgers University. He obtained his bachelor of science degree at Cornell University and his master of science degree at Iowa State University. His research interests are knowledge management, diversity, social networks, and their relationship with performance at multiple levels. Contact: nerhardt@rci.rutgers.edu

Part Five

Case Studies and Examples

Chapter Twenty-Four

Some Key Examples
of Knowledge Management

W. Warner Burke

At the time of this writing, the cause of NASA's shuttle *Columbia* tragedy, in which seven highly impressive astronauts died, was not known. We now know that the spacecraft was fatally damaged during the launch when a chunk of foam insulation that covered a strut attach point on the external tank peeled off and shattered a thermal protection panel on the left wing. The *Columbia* tragedy reminds us, of course, of the *Challenger* accident, a similar tragedy some seventeen years earlier. If you are like me, you know exactly where you were and what you were doing on that fateful day in 1986 when you heard the news. At that time, I was working with NASA as an external consultant. Previously, I had helped put into place agency-wide senior executive and manager development programs. These programs covered a range of topics from leadership, motivation, group dynamics, and managing change to interpersonal and intergroup conflict. Each program had at its core individual feedback based on multiple raters—self, direct reports, peers, and boss. The executive or manager practices on which individuals were rated consisted of behavioral statements especially tailored for NASA. There was a set of thirty-seven practices for mid- to upper-level managers (GS levels 13, 14, and 15) and a set of forty practices for the senior executive services (SES) level. The practices for the SES individuals covered six primary executive domains:

> Managing tasks—for example, "You are concerned about controlling project or operating costs."

Influencing others—for example, "You appropriately involve other executives and organizations in your planning process."

Managing the team—for example, "You face up to and attempt to resolve or work out conflicts constructively among your subordinates."

Working with subordinates—for example, "You communicate in a frank and open manner."

Ensuring openness—for example, "You admit a mistake when one is made."

Leading—for example, "You demonstrate by your behavior that you perceive yourself as a leader."

Among the forty practices on which the NASA senior executives were rated over a period of several years, the highest-rated by subordinates were such practices as "having technical knowledge required for your position" and "communicating with subordinates in a frank and open manner." The lowest-rated among the forty executive practices was "You present bad news in a constructive manner."

The *Challenger* accident, you may recall, was caused by faulty O-rings. The fact that these rings could break under extremely cold conditions was known. However, this fact was not communicated upward in the management hierarchy—at least not adequately or effectively. The messengers relating this fact were either ignored or told not to worry about it. Describing this issue as a communication problem, especially communicating upward, is no doubt an oversimplification; however, it reinforces the data that the lowest-rated of the forty executive practices was "presenting bad news in a constructive manner." This particular practice involved influencing others, primarily bosses—in other words, "managing up."

Thus a key example of knowledge management—and a simple lesson, if not a cliché, for executives—is "do not shoot the messenger."

Other key examples and perhaps lessons for leaders in the domain of knowledge management to be explored in this chapter are after-action review, tacit versus explicit knowledge, and organizational structure.

After-Action Review

After-action review (AAR) is a knowledge management activity that fosters organizational learning. It originated in the U.S. Army in the mid-1970s. As a consequence of the Vietnam War, U.S. Army officers spent considerable time in a reflective, introspective mode. What could be learned from that war? Being an all-volunteer fighting force, what could be done to ensure a more effective future? One critical step from this reflection was to exert a more concerted effort on training. The Army chief of staff, General Creighton Abrams, in 1973 created TRADOC—the Training and Doctrine Command. This command focused the Army's training, and new forms were established, such as the National Training Center in the Mojave Desert. General William Du Puy, the initial commander of TRADOC, was a great believer in leading and managing according to clear standards and, when an Army unit fell short of those standards, in learning why. What gradually evolved was a process of taking the time to review what happened after every training event. It is similar to, though not quite the same as, coaches and players reviewing the film of a football game the day after.

The purposes of an after-action review are simple: learning, improving, and doing better the next time. The participants sit down with a facilitator called an "observer-controller" who has been with them throughout the event, and they all discuss what happened. To do this effectively requires several things. First, there must be a fairly good basis for understanding what actually happened. In the training centers, electronic data collection enables high-fidelity recording and playback of events. This is very much like reviewing football films on Monday morning; you may think you know where you were at such-and-such a time, but in an environment where one hilltop can look pretty much like the next, you may or may not be correct. Thanks to unobtrusive sensors, the database can pinpoint exactly where you were and what you were doing. Soldiers call this "ground truth." Combined with ground truth, there must be a fairly unambiguous understanding of what should have happened, and that comes from having standards derived from doctrine.[1]

While the purposes are simple, the process is not. It is not a matter of sitting down and discussing what happened and how everyone may feel about it. An AAR is far more structural. The discussion is structured according to identifiable events and against measurable standards. AAR questions are (1) What happened? (2) Why did it happen? and (3) What should be done about it?[2] More specifically, the procedure is as follows:[3]

1. Review what the unit intended to accomplish (the overall mission and commander's intent)

2. Establish the "ground truth" of what actually happened by means of a moment-by-moment replay of critical battlefield events

3. Explore what might have caused the actual results, focusing on one or a few key issues

4. Give the unit the opportunity to reflect on what it should learn from this review, including what unit members did well that they want to sustain in future operations and what they think they need to improve

5. Preview the next day's mission and issues that might arise

The AAR is conducted at all levels of the Army, from platoon (about forty soldiers led by a lieutenant) to company (three to four platoons) to battalion (about five companies) to brigade (two or more battalions) to division (normally three brigades commanded by a major general). These different-level units conduct their own

AARs, and when integrated, the process is typically bottom-up, starting with reports from the platoons. The usual outcome to an AAR is that the unit stops doing things the same old way. Mistakes will be made in the future, but not the same ones; errors are rarely repeated.

Early civilian adopters of AARs in the 1990s were Shell Oil, Fidelity, IBM, and Harley-Davidson.[4] These adoptions were within certain business units, not usually across the entire corporation. Nevertheless, successes have been achieved in the corporate sector, and lessons have been learned. For example, some pitfalls to avoid include the following:[5]

- Not having sufficiently clear goals for an AAR
- Having too many people for the review, that is, not everyone having the real "ground truth" knowledge of the project
- Doing an AAR through individual interviews instead of bringing the whole group together
- Allowing a leader to misuse the review information by punishing someone who was involved

An AAR can concretize organizational learning and knowledge management at their best. However, to properly serve in this role, it must become an endemic part of an organization's culture, a fundamental way of doing things, and a normal everyday component of doing business.

Tacit Versus Explicit Knowledge

The late Herbert Simon, economist, cognitive science researcher, and Nobel Prize recipient, studied master chess players at one stage of his illustrious career. He was interested in their thought processes and also in whether or not he could "teach" a computer to play chess. He wanted to learn from the players so that he could then program the computer. He found that when he asked these master players how they did what they did on the chess board, how they managed to win, what their strategy was, and so on, they could not tell him. In other words, their knowledge of how they played the game was *tacit*—below the level of conscious awareness. Simon and his colleagues then proceeded to observe these players as they played the game. They eventually determined the strategy that each player used, which was unique to each player. This strategy was an *original pattern* of playing each game. When Simon would describe the pattern to a player, the master would then respond with something like, "Oh, yes; that's what I do when playing chess." What the player could not articulate before now became explicit, and the master could at last explain his or her strategy.[6]

Tacit knowledge is not limited to master chess players, of course. All of us know more than we can tell. As Joseph Horvath puts it, "Personal knowledge is so thoroughly grounded in experience that it cannot be expressed in its fullness. In the last 30 years, the term *tacit knowledge* has come to stand for this type of human knowledge—knowledge that is bound up in the activity and effort that produced it."[7] In other words, often it is difficult for us to express with clarity what we have learned from experience and what our intuition seems to "tell us."

Not all tacit knowledge is necessarily worthy of being made explicit. Although we may not be able to articulate it, the likelihood is that we have learned some things that are, after all, stupid. It may be best to let these lessons remain tacit. There is much, nevertheless, that is worth making explicit, especially for professionals.[8]

For the purposes of increasing organizational learning and managing knowledge more effectively, it is useful to tap into tacit knowledge and attempt to make it more explicit. The following four suggestions may be considered as ways to accomplish this tacit-to-explicit transition:

1. Like Herbert Simon and his colleagues, one way is to observe people with certain valued expertise at work—to look for patterns and strategies in how they achieve tasks, manage projects,

make decisions, and so on. Then, like Simon, feed these observations back to them so that verification can be made.

2. Have people who possess valued expertise tell stories about their work and give examples of projects they managed that went well and projects that did not go well. From these stories and examples, patterns of experience are likely to emerge that can be verified and then honed for organizational learning purposes.

3. Interview people who have valued expertise, asking such questions as these:

- Why did you approach the task or project the way you did instead of in some other way?
- Think of a metaphor or an analogy to express what you did or the approach you took. (This is especially useful if the person can't "find the right words" to answer the first question.)
- Using behavioral language, describe a project in which you were involved and explain what was done, when, and how. (Discussing actual behavior helps make tacit knowledge more explicit.)

4. Have people with valued expertise participate in activities that will lead to increased self-awareness, personality tests, and multirater feedback processes, for example. Increased awareness of self is likely to enhance the ability to access tacit knowledge and make it more explicit.

Organizational Structure

Most of us are familiar with Miller's law, "seven plus or minus two." George Miller himself called it "The Magical Number Seven."[9] In a series of studies, he found that human beings could, on average, keep track of or simultaneously deal with no more than seven categories. This is why telephone numbers are seven digits long. Of course, today we have to add area codes and perhaps other codes, but we have phones that can store our frequently used numbers, so we don't have to keep longer strings of numbers in our head. Some of us can keep in mind only five categories or, say, tasks on a to-do list at the same time. Some of us can keep track of nine categories simultaneously, but for most of us, seven is the benchmark, hence Miller's seven plus or minus two.

Until publication of Malcolm Gladwell's book *The Tipping Point*, most of us were probably not familiar with the "Rule of 150," although the documentation supporting the importance of this rule had been around for a long time.[10] Gladwell highlighted the rule as one of his many examples of "tipping points." The book's title is based on the phenomenon of how an activity can exist for quite some time without change or growth and then all of a sudden "take off." For example, a virus can for some period of time be limited to only a few organisms or human beings, and then suddenly a tipping point is reached and an epidemic occurs. A fashion trend can appear and for a while no one seems to notice or join in; then a tipping point of people joining in is reached and a raging fad ensues. Gladwell explains the significant and quick drop in the crime rate in New York City during the 1990s the same way.

The Rule of 150 is another example of a tipping point. When the number of people who interact with one another—at work, in a community, in a social club or society, or a commune—reaches 150, a tipping point occurs. Now let's look to the documentation and what the Rule of 150 means.

Gladwell points us to the work of British anthropologist Robin Dunbar, who has studied the relationship of brain size in primates and their social behavior.[11] He found that the larger the neocortex in the brain, the larger the average size of the groups the primates live with. One needs a sizable neocortex and overall brain to deal with the complexities of large social groups. For us humans, if we belong to a group of five people, we have to keep track of ten separate relationships—our own relationship with the four others in the group plus the six additional two-way relationships between the others. "That's what it means to know everyone in the circle,"[12]

Gladwell points out. He goes on to demonstrate that if you belong to a group of 20 people, you then have 190 two-way relationships—19 for yourself and 171 for the other relationships.[13] In other words, a small increase can make a huge "tracking" difference, and there is a limit—a tipping point—where our tracking capacity begins to break down, at about 150 people in a group.

Gladwell also refers to the Hutterites, a religious group that has existed for hundreds of years that has consistently structured its colonies to consist of no more than 150 people. Although Hutterites did not have the advantage of knowing about Dunbar's research, they found that when a colony became larger than 150 individuals, people tended to become strangers to one another. Another example Gladwell uses from the present is Gore Associates, a $1 billion, privately held company that produces high-tech fabric (Gore-Tex), coatings for computer cables, dental floss, filter bags, and other products. Gore Associates employs thousands of people, but no work unit, such as a manufacturing plant, has more than 150 people. Gore Associates has learned over the years that when a unit becomes larger than 150 people, inefficiencies regarding communication and decision making increase significantly.[14]

How can this phenomenon be explained? The research of psychologist Daniel Wegner helps us understand.[15] He points out that when people know each other well, a transactive memory system develops; that is, they join together in an implicit joint memory system and more or less determine who is best at what, who will remember what, who can be counted on to point out what, and so on. Take, for example, a group of faculty at a university. In my case, there are ten of us who compose the faculty for our graduate programs in social organizational psychology. I know each of my nine colleagues fairly well. When a subgroup of us serves together on a doctoral dissertation committee, I know who will take care of issues concerning research method (Caryn), who will focus on the statistics (Jim), who will raise the "so what?" question (Debra), and who will take care of issues concerning theory (me). So I do not have to concern myself too much with method, statistics, or application.

My colleagues will "be there" for those issues and concerns. Thus transactive memory is not that you simply know someone or that he or she is your best friend necessarily; the "system" that develops is more about knowing what the other individuals in one's group are good at, what they are capable of, what they know, where their skills lie, and which people you can count on for what. With the bonds of memory and expertise being transacted, as well as peer pressure (knowing that you are being counted on for a particular type of expertise), the social system can work effectively toward task accomplishments. Also, it is a matter of knowing people well enough so that what they think of you matters, but the tipping point is 150; beyond that our transactive memory begins to break down.

The relevance of the Rule of 150 to knowledge management and organizational learning should now be obvious. Keeping organizational structures and groupings to no more than 150 individuals facilitates knowledge exchange and "transactive memories."

Conclusion

Following NASA's *Challenger* accident in 1986, an independent presidential commission was appointed to determine what went wrong and why and to make recommendations for the future. The late Richard Feynman, a commission member, noted physicist, and Nobel Prize winner, was particularly skilled at demonstrating the consequences of extreme cold on an O-ring.

An independent group to study NASA's *Columbia* shuttle tragedy was also formed. These independent commissions can be very helpful in understanding more about technical problems, in particular, and in furthering NASA's organizational learning in general. However, independent study groups do not run NASA. It is therefore up to NASA executives, managers, scientists, engineers, and technicians to learn from these tragedies and take corrective action.

One form of corrective action can be improved knowledge management. NASA executives and managers may have now learned not to shoot the messenger. Let us hope so. With all due respect to NASA executives and managers, a modest suggestion for the future regarding knowledge management is to consider the following:

1. *Instituting after-action reviews.* This kind of activity for enhancing knowledge management and organizational learning now has a solid track record. It is also clear that its usefulness and applicability are not limited to the U.S. Army.

2. *Finding ways to tap into tacit knowledge.* NASA is loaded with expertise, so it behooves the agency to work even harder than usual on making tacit knowledge more explicit. This process can serve not only to enhance organizational learning but also to put into place more effectively management of knowledge as a *preventive* measure for dealing with projects involving high risk.

3. *Restructuring the organization so that no functional or operational unit has more than 150 individuals.* Transactive memory is critical to effective knowledge management, and an organization's structure should support and enhance this process, not hinder it. NASA would do well to take a hard, discerning look at its organizational design, especially with respect to unit size.

Although NASA has been the focal point at the beginning and now at the end of this chapter, let us not lose sight of the applicability of these key examples of knowledge management to all organizations.

W. Warner Burke is the Edward Lee Thorndike Professor of Psychology and Education and coordinator for the graduate programs in social organizational psychology in the Department of Organization and Leadership at Teachers College, Columbia University, in New York. He is also senior adviser to the organization and change strategy practice of IBM Global Business Services. Burke has consulted with organizations on business, industry, education, government, religious, and medical systems. A diplomat in industrial and organizational psychology and the American Board of Professional Psychology, he is also a Fellow of the Academy of Management, the American Psychological Society, and the Society of Industrial and Organizational Psychology. Past editor of both *Organizational Dynamics* and the *Academy of Management Executive*, he has also written more than 130 articles and book chapters in the fields of organizational psychology, organizational change, and leadership and authored, coauthored, or edited fourteen books. His most recent book is *Organization Change: Theory and Practice*. Burke has received numerous awards, including the Organization Development Professional Practice Area Award for Excellence, known as the Lippitt Memorial Award, from the American Society for Training and Development. Contact: wwb3@columbia.edu

Leadership and Access to Ideas

Allan R. Cohen

This chapter is based on three premises. First, spreading ideas is less about technology than about making who knows what clear to the people who want or need to know.[1] (I'd love to see a technology that is a good substitute for this relatively inefficient method but doubt it is in the offing.) No amount of technology can force people to share ideas, electronically or otherwise, if they don't want to share them.

Second, leadership creates the structure and climate that encourage or discourage the movement of ideas. Culture, which is partly a product of leadership, does the same. Individuals can and do subvert the leadership and culture, for good or ill, but organization is supposed to increase the odds for all, so we need to figure out what does that.

Third, as a consultant, I have never directly advised on "knowledge management" or "organizational learning," but they are always a close by-product of other interventions, such as strategic change, top team building, organizational restructuring, and leadership education. My best direct experience was when I was in a managerial role as VP for academic affairs at Babson College, so I will draw heavily from that. One case does not make for grand generalizations, but I believe there is learning to be gleaned from close and firsthand examination of a relatively small but complex organization (five hundred people) consisting of knowledge

The author thanks Tom Davenport for his helpful comments on an earlier version of this chapter.

workers. After all, that is the nature of how ideas move. The main problem of transferability is scalability to much larger organizations, and I will try to address that.

Think about what stops ideas from spreading in an organization:

- Fear of losing credit
- Dislike for the leadership or the goals of the organization
- Belief that sharing ideas will create jealousy or resentment
- Lack of knowledge that anyone knows what is desired
- Belief that only very special people (in one's inner circle) have a chance of possessing knowledge worth pursuing
- Lack of knowledge of how to find it if anyone does
- Stovepiped organization that discourages knowledge of or contact with others outside a specified area
- Few assignments that make it easy for people to contact one another
- The time it takes to share ideas, especially if there is no immediate need for them of which the giver is aware
- Fear of losing indispensability if unique talents are made available
- Inertia

Let me use an example from my consulting work at GE. Jack Welch tried for years to free up people and ideas throughout GE, with less success than he wanted and needed. In frustration, he and others developed WorkOut, which had two purposes: (1) to get rid of unnecessary work accumulated from the hundred-year history of the company and (2) to eliminate the fear of speaking up by putting the general manager of each business on the spot to respond to proposals from multilevel teams of employees. As the lead consultant of one of the most traditional businesses, I had the unpleasant opportunity to witness a senior manager screaming at his senior direct reports, "You are the stupidest people I have ever met! Doesn't a single one of you understand anything about managing?" As might be predicted, this group seldom moved positive ideas around and seldom volunteered anything that anyone thought might arouse his ire.

Yet the desire to hold back was not limited to those dealing with this one manager. Asked by the vice president of research in that business to help a small WorkOut team address a pressing job design problem, I worked with a knowledgeable group that at first resisted even addressing the problem. After considerable prodding, the group members finally dug in and eventually hit on a novel and far-reaching solution to the role of process engineers in the manufacturing operations. As the group was working through the ideas and preparing to present them to the VP, one old-timer suddenly exclaimed, "We can't present this! The VP might not like it, and you know that at GE you can't tell the truth to management!" All the air went out of the group. After I picked myself up off the floor, I managed to ask why he believed that. He told the story of a former middle manager who had years before stood up at a public meeting and tried to tell the general manager something controversial. "By the next week, he was gone!" When I checked, it turned out that the dissenter had been in a lot of trouble for poor performance and was already on the way out. However, the belief was deeply embedded, like an urban myth, and wasn't going away by countering with "the facts." That experience was the most vivid example of just how difficult it can be to create a culture that supports bringing ideas forward and overcoming the fear of making a career-limiting move.

Although the example is extreme, I believe it is emblematic of the deeply embedded assumptions in many organizations about being careful with what is said to more senior people. Of course, some of the situations calling for ideas on the move are more "expert-to-expert," but unless the fellow expert is someone known and trusted or the whole organization is used to the free flow of ideas and expertise, it isn't going to be easy.

Babson College

Through the 1980s and early 1990s, Babson College was a business school that reflected the effects of many cultural ills. Numerous attempts had been made at curriculum and other kinds of reform, but they all stalled in infighting, territorial disputes, and a decision-making system that punished initiators and rewarded upholders of the status quo. An attempt to do strategic planning had died in midstream for lack of consensus or willingness to make hard choices. As a result, people with ideas for improvement had retreated into individual pursuits. They took their pleasure from their students (when possible), their own research and consulting, and complaining about "the others" with their few sympathetic colleagues but didn't any longer think it was worth the effort to try to shape the organization to make it more innovative or more productive. Belief in the potential of collective action was very low.

In 1989, Bill Glavin, former vice chairman of Xerox, became Babson's president. Within a year, he had launched an elaborate strategic planning process that involved a large number of constituents, unleashing a great deal of early cynicism and eventually a few bold proposals for change. One of the most radical sets of ideas came from the graduate program task force, which broached the idea of a complete curriculum overhaul and building a new graduate school building—or closing down the full-time M.B.A. program. A year later, with the crucial job of VP for academic affairs unfilled and the developing ideas needing strong support from the top, I agreed to fill in for a year (and stayed seven). Many of the ideas floating around were similar to concepts I had been mouthing off about for a couple of decades or more, and I realized that I would not be able to rest easy if I didn't try to help them gain acceptance.

During the strategic planning process, several of the teams declared that they had good ideas for change but that with the current decision-making system, under which all faculty (about 110 at the time) made all curriculum decisions together, there was no point in advancing proposals. A new task force was therefore created to revise the governance system. It proposed a system that allowed a small elected decision-making body to make all curriculum decisions, with the fallback possibility of bringing disputed decisions to the faculty floor. However, the system put the burden of proof on dissenters, who first had to write a white paper explaining their disagreement, which would have to receive a majority vote just to be discussed. This was a major step in convincing people with good ideas that they might have a chance of succeeding. Many other steps were taken to reinforce this notion.

For example, funds were set aside to support activities that enabled the new curriculum to be developed. Participants were rewarded for playing, and they were given considerable attention and recognition. Performance appraisals were at least loosely tied to the college's new mission and vision. Decision-making bodies held open meetings where dissenters and proposers of ideas could find a forum for expression. Both the president and I worked hard to set a positive, excited tone so that innovators would feel encouraged.

In terms of changing the college's positioning and creating a positive climate, this all worked remarkably well.[2] We set a thousand flowers blooming and generated many innovations. Because the program reforms created a genuinely integrated curriculum, faculty were forced to collaborate in both course design and delivery. For many, this was painful, since by training and nature they knew much more about how to work alone than in teams, but it also created new opportunities for connections and information sharing. (Admittedly, during some of the pitched battles about "the right way to teach X," I doubt whether the participants thought of the discussions as "information sharing.") Many new relationships were made among people who had previously not known each other, and some new research areas and partnerships were formed.

A requirement that M.B.A.s gain international experience opened up another inadvertent opportunity for connection. In running courses in other parts of the world, we made it possible for faculty to go along for their own understanding of international issues. However, three weeks abroad with three to five almost random colleagues yielded intense collective experiences and new relationships that crossed traditional academic boundaries.

As the reforms spread to other programs, including undergraduate and executive education, we slowly realized a new problem: except when there was accidental personal knowledge, the faculty doing design and delivery were often reinventing the wheel, losing opportunities to leverage materials and ideas developed for other programs. All people involved were working harder than they ever had before: the designing process took much longer when colleagues had to agree on objectives, materials, sequence, and other things that had previously been mostly the province of the individual, and delivery was much more complex and demanding, since everything was new. This meant that not only did patience wear thin, but people didn't have time to seek help, or as used to be said at GE, they were too busy chopping wood to sharpen the ax.

Although I worried a lot about how to manage the knowledge or how to create a system to do that, it was apparent that it might be impossible to create one that would be used, for all the reasons others who have tried to do it have run into difficulties. In the meantime, without great planning, I was automatically starting to serve as a "switchboard" or "connector" for those with expertise ("mavens"),[3] linking them together when I knew of mutual interests or needs to solve problems. My position put me in touch with everyone, the performance appraisal process meant that I read a great deal about plans and accomplishments, and my "supervision" of the program deans meant that we were constantly discussing program issues so that I inadvertently became a repository for at least some of the kind of information that could be shared. After several years of doing this, I began to become more conscious about it and thought of my job as the "switchboard of Babson." Only then did I remember the old research on how faculty get the latest research findings: few read the journals, but most know the person who is an obsessive reader of current research and serves as a walking reference desk.

At the same time, a great deal of knowledge is shared at Babson by what I think of as carriers, people who teach in more than one program. They get an idea from doing, for example, a custom executive education program and then bring that into the M.B.A. program or the undergraduate program. Certain people are both by personality and position—the programs they teach in, the task forces they are on, the administrative assignments they take— likely to infect others with what they pick up. They do an amazing job of passing ideas around, bringing innovations along, and serving as the information lubricants of the organization. Organizations can make an effort to identify switchboards and carriers and put them in positions to acquire the relationships and knowledge that become a resource to others in the organization. This is where technology can be helpful, helping people find each other and letting them communicate once they have done so.

This may not appear to be as systematic as more formal systems, but I would argue that it is more likely to be effective. It seems logical to want to categorize and structure information in predetermined groupings so that as people need to know something, they can look it up. There are numerous problems with this orderly way of proceeding. As many have discovered, it is hard to induce busy people to enter their knowledge into such systems. It is inherently more difficult to determine in advance what knowledge will be needed, let alone to put it in clear categories. If you have people working on narrow, clearly defined problems, this wouldn't be so difficult, but in the knowledge business, things keep shifting, projects and ideas migrate rapidly from one area to another, and it is extremely difficult to know the exact categories in advance. Malcolm Gladwell makes this point in reference to piles of paper in the office.[4] He claims (and my own messy piles give validity to his argument) that knowledge workers are constantly finding unanticipated uses for information and cannot easily file it because that is too static a system, which hides the information out of sight. Piles make it possible to shift and recombine paper (information) and so are inherent in the work of such people.

For knowledge sharing, another model is needed. I like to think of serendipity, of ideas on the move, in a sort of Brownian motion. Get people colliding with one another, and unexpected information and relationships will emerge. The challenge is to get potentially valuable people into possible collision and to do it in a way that is appealing and not overly consuming of time.

I have made a few such attempts at "organized randomness," and they have yielded interesting results. For example, for several years, Babson ran executive education programs for managers at Digital Equipment. After more than three hundred managers had gone through our program, we wanted to have a "reunion" where people could meet others who had similar experiences. The question was how to let them know each other. We arranged an idea fair, where each person who attended could post on one flipchart sheet something interesting that he or she was working on as a result of the prior training. We posted these in a large room. Participants could stroll around, stopping where they saw something interesting to them, making a new connection. Indeed, people who do executive education know that no matter how good the teaching is, participants always say the best part of the program was meeting the others in it! This can be discouraging to faculty who do not understand the phenomenon, but it illustrates just how hungry organizational members are for chances to make new relationships and learn about other parts of their own or other organizations in ways that can turn out to be very valuable.

Xerox PARC, a pioneer in attempting to maximize the social nature of information sharing, had its researchers doing short postings outside their offices on current projects so that passersby could rapidly discern whether they might want to talk more with the occupant of the office.

One of the best applications of this idea I have heard of appeared in the *Harvard Business Review*.[5] The World Bank, notorious for its stodginess and for funding gigantic, often ineffective projects, developed an "innovation market" where new ideas could be posted for viewing by others with ideas or with funds for grants. This has blossomed in the past few years and is generating many good ideas with excellent payoffs. There is an initial vetting of ideas to choose those that seem to have potential, but then the "market" decides which are best. People can move around to see the posted ideas and proposals and act quickly.

Conclusion: Generating Initiative and Innovation

Of course, it is easier to see how to create opportunities for people to find each other when the organization, like Babson College, is relatively small and is in one physical location (though even different corridors, let alone separate buildings, can make for seldom-crossed oceans). Larger, multilocation organizations need to use more devices to create desired collisions.

Exhibit 25.1 lists some of the mechanisms that organizations use to generate initiative and innovation; many of these would increase opportunities and the willingness to share ideas.

Exhibit 25.1 Mechanisms Organizational Leaders Use to Stimulate Entrepreneurial Behavior by Others

1. Constantly reinforced, clear, entrepreneurial vision
2. Ample rewards and recognition, including stock options
3. Investment-oriented rewards, not just performance-oriented ones
4. Constant expectation of high, improving performance; no penalties for failure (unless repeated)
5. Reduced hierarchy, flatter organizations, reduced segmentation of units
6. Small units with cross-functional teams
7. Broad assignments and education encouraging initiative, experimentation
8. High levels of empowerment
9. Open access to information
10. Discretionary venture funds
11. Voice of the customer brought inside

Source: A. R. Cohen, "Mainstreaming Corporate Entrepreneurship: Leadership at Every Level of Organizations," *Babson Entrepreneurial Review*, Fall 2002, p. 8.

Not all of these mechanisms exactly fit the knowledge-sharing criteria, but most of them create new opportunities for contacts to be made and knowledge to be disseminated. By explicitly identifying and enabling carriers and natural switchboards (think of a talent-spotting portion of annual appraisals, for example) and by using such devices as cross-cutting task forces, broad assignments, and common educational experiences to gain access to people that will provide them with information to share, organizations can become much better at getting ideas on the move.

The Edward A. Madden Distinguished Professor of Global Leadership at Babson College, **Allan R. Cohen** recently completed seven years as chief academic officer, during which time he led major curriculum and organizational changes. He has since returned to the faculty to teach leadership, change, and negotiations. He is the coauthor of the best seller *Managing for Excellence and Influence Without Authority*. His latest book, *Power Up: Transforming Organizations Through Shared Leadership*, written with David Bradford, was selected as one of the best leadership books of 1998 by the Management General Web site. Among his many publications is the coauthored textbook *Effective Behavior in Organizations* and the award-winning *Alternative Work Schedules: Integrating Individual and Organizational Needs*, as well as the edited *Portable MBA in Management* compilation. Contact: cohen@babson.edu

Chapter Twenty-Six

Capturing Ideas, Creating Information, and Liberating Knowledge

Peter Drummond-Hay

Barbara G. Saidel

Some people think that the study and popularity of knowledge management was a fad. There has been decidedly less focus on it recently than there was in the late 1990s. Over the past decade, many companies identified chief knowledge officers (CKOs) and invested in portals, collaboration applications, or expertise locator systems. In some cases, these expensive enterprise systems were implemented along with the establishment of new staff roles: knowledge brokers to coach and encourage communities of practice and to encourage the flow of knowledge throughout the enterprise. In the past few years, with downsizing and cost reduction, much of this effort has been unwound. Many companies have reduced the scale or scope of their knowledge management initiatives. Either the firm has promoted or eliminated the CKO, or the learning budget has been dramatically reduced. Much of this effort has been chalked off as a luxury of the affluent 1990s and is now severely restricted.

This is not true for professional service firms. We believe that in professional services, knowledge sharing is the core of our business and is the core of what our clients value in our service. We need to care about this passionately and improve it all the time to deliver outstanding client service every day.

To outsiders, it may appear that executive search is a simple business. Surely, all that's needed is some judgment, a thick

Rolodex, and a telephone, right? Perhaps in a one-person firm that might be true, but in a global search firm, with multinational relationships, clients expect recruiters to identify and attract the best candidates in the world for every senior-level position. To accomplish that, we require sophisticated resources. We also require a healthy, open business culture that supports teamwork. In fact, with international client service teams, our business requires that we share knowledge about executives, industries, project progress, and our clients' companies across time and space. Our clients pay for knowledge.

With more than 25 percent of our assignments involving consultants in two or more offices, and all of our assignments including at least two associates and an assistant, collaboration is critical. That collaboration, supported by our culture and our technology, enables us to get searches done, share best practices, function as a team worldwide, mentor new associates, and always put the best team and the accumulated knowledge of the firm at the client's disposal. We cannot rely *only* on an individual recruiter's network of personal contacts or even on the contacts known to the recruiters in a particular office. We must bring the entire firm's knowledge to bear on each assignment so as best to serve the needs of our clients. Therefore, each assignment represents a test of our ability to identify, capture, and resynthesize the aggregate knowledge of the whole firm, both current and accrued, for the benefit of the client.

We believe that the challenges we encounter in identifying, capturing, and resynthesizing that knowledge are similar to those encountered in other professional service businesses. Thus we believe that our experiences may be instructive for others, even if their services differ from ours.

Trust and Knowledge Sharing

When organizations are small and their business cultures are healthy, they do not encounter knowledge-sharing issues. When everyone knows one another, trusts one another, and understands one another's work and skill, people know what to share and why. They are likely to know who needs to learn from them. They are open to requests, they are more likely to trust each other, and they are more likely to have social connections that enhance and reinforce their business connections. Smaller organizations that value sharing and reward teamwork are unlikely to have stagnant pockets of knowledge.

As organizations grow, however, the likelihood increases that cultural problems will undermine good intentions. In larger enterprises, people are less likely to work across the entire organization. They may work in different locations, different departments, or even in close proximity, but never work together. They may never meet each other, or they may know each other only peripherally and thus not accrue joint experiences that build trust. When people do not know each other well, they are less likely to trust each other. Collaboration will become less of a norm, and knowledge will get "stuck." In larger organizations, management must continually reinforce the values that encourage collaboration and trust, in order to ensure that the accumulated knowledge of the enterprise is brought to the benefit of each consulting client. This may be evident to any good manager, but many small bits of the management process and values of a firm combine to affect its ability to be successful at knowledge sharing.

Barriers to Knowledge Sharing

In our experience, there are many reasons why people do not share knowledge with their colleagues. Let's examine a few of them.

- *There is no recognition or reward for sharing knowledge.* People who live the values of the firm must be publicly acclaimed as heroes. Stories must be told about their values-driven behavior so that others will want to emulate them. The compensation system must also identify those who share, and reward them differentially. In our organization, we do not compensate recruiters on the basis of productivity alone. Rather, numerous partners participate in the subjective evaluation of each recruiter. Sharing knowledge with others for the benefit of clients is among the key criteria that are included. In addition, each client is surveyed by an outside consultant at the end of each assignment, and a key question on the survey concerns whether the recruiter brought new knowledge to the client.

• *People are competitive and believe that their knowledge increases their power.* In a recruiting firm, that would be indicated by the existence of candidates and sources not added to the corporate database. We require that every recruiter and researcher add every person relevant to a search to the global corporate database. Everyone must identify who these people are, how they are related to the search, and why they are or are not relevant to the assignment. In addition, the database is useful for both short-term project management and long-term knowledge sharing. If it is up-to-date, it can help recruiters manage their own work. In addition, if it is complete, others can learn from it and get ideas to more successfully execute future assignments.

• *There is no vehicle for storing and categorizing knowledge, or the existing vehicle is difficult to use.* We find that if the technology is even a little bit inconvenient, no one will use it. There is a very fine line that demarcates payoff and the willingness to enter information that may not seem to be immediately useful to the person. Technology has to be easy to use, and it has to be perceived as "good for me" to ensure that people will use it.

• *They don't know anyone would be interested in what they know.* In professional services, tacit knowledge is a major issue. If knowledge is not being shared, it may be merely because the first professional does not realize what he or she knows and is not aware that others might need to know that too. This is the hardest challenge for the manager. Such impediments can be overcome only in casual meetings among professionals, when there is time around the proverbial water cooler to exchange stories about getting the work done for clients. Only in these casual conversations will the sharing of tacit knowledge take place. The first person does not know what she knows or why someone else would be interested. The second person may not know what he needs to know or how to learn it. In these cases, only a chance meeting or a casual conversation has any chance of unlocking what the first person knows for the benefit of the second person. As Larry Prusak (former head of the IBM Institute for Knowledge Management and author of *Working Knowledge* and *In Good Company*) has told us repeatedly, we need to make time and space available for "water cooler conversations."

- *They don't share knowledge because they are not aware of what they know.* During the course of a search, recruiters call people and ask their advice. These people are called "sources." They may have some third-party relationship to the target position, such as bankers, if we are seeking a chief financial officer (CFO). The banker may have worked with many CFOs and may have opinions about which ones would have the skills being sought by our client. Or the source may have once worked with a person we are interested in learning about. During the forty or fifty or more phone calls made in the initial stages of a search, a recruiter will learn a great deal about the client company's image in the marketplace and its relative competitive position. The recruiter will also learn a great deal about various leaders in the industry. All this information is probably very interesting to the client. However, by interviewing clients, we discovered that recruiters sometimes forget to share this information with them. This oversight was caused by a misconception on the part of the recruiter that what he or she had learned was not special. The recruiter actually took it for granted that the client already knew what he or she had learned during the sourcing calls. We now encourage all recruiters to meet regularly with clients throughout the course of a search to relate as much as possible of what they have learned in the marketplace.

We also came to realize that we have skills and knowledge that could be put to work beyond the search process. We also now conduct executive assessment projects for our clients, evaluating the executives already on their team. This relatively new service has already made a major impact for some clients, who rely on our ability to benchmark their executives against our knowledge of the marketplace. Internally, the assessment practice has also been able to bring new thinking and new approaches to recruiting. Although recruiters were aware of alternative interview techniques and psychometric measures, they were unsure how these areas could practically contribute to recruiting. As our executive assessment practice has grown over the past few years, our recruiters have had the opportunity to learn about these from their colleagues in the executive assessment practice. The social framework, along with the opportunity to see competency-based behavioral interviewing and psychometrics in action, has fostered openness and creativity in the ways recruiters are interviewing and understanding their candidates. Members of the assessment team began to be invited to internal meetings to teach and train in these areas. Overall, there is a strong belief that Russell Reynolds Associates is providing an even greater service to its recruiting clients through new techniques for screening and qualification of candidates.

Our insistence on training recruiters to do executive assessment and linking them to mentors who are skilled organizational psychologists has also become a tool for us in ensuring that our recruiters are expert interviewers. Recruiters who have participated in executive assessment assignments have become more productive as search practitioners as well. We have in effect increased the skill levels of our recruiters by teaching them additional skills in executive assessment.

Fostering Knowledge Sharing Through Healthy Corporate Culture and Social Capital

Given the hypotheses we have cited as to why people don't share knowledge, it would seem that effective knowledge sharing begins with fostering a culture and an environment free of unhealthy politics, in which teamwork and sharing are recognized and rewarded. People who are open with each other and share knowledge should

be differentially rewarded over those who do not share. Furthermore, frequent social interaction and cross-team assignments will
further encourage the social connections that enhance trust and
engender sharing. This prescription for assertive corporate social
engineering presumes that cross-boundary connections are not left
to chance. Someone should consciously organize interactions
among individuals from different groups so as to promote such connections. Someone should take on the role of matchmaker or
connections sponsor. That person should introduce knowledge
sources to knowledge seekers. Malcolm Gladwell calls these types
of people "connectors."[1]

In our organization, we are committed to creating opportunities for our people to meet informally and formally to share best
practices. Since the inception of Russell Reynolds Associates in
1969, our recruiters and researchers have gathered together in each
office of the firm every Monday to share status and stories about
new projects, business development, and the outcome of each project. In addition, there are annual practice group meetings and
monthly conference calls in which we discuss client assignments
and potential work. We also have face-to-face training sessions for
new employees and advanced associates. In the strong economy of
the late 1990s, this was an important aspect of our growth and
development as a global firm. It enabled us to assimilate new
employees, fueling growth with people who were fired up with firm
culture and trained by our best and brightest managing directors.
We were able to assimilate new people and grow our business and
our staff in part because we were so committed to having frequent
meetings of various communities of practice.

In addition, we established what we call the Best Practices
Committee to identify and promulgate best practices in search execution, client communication, and business development. This
committee meets frequently, either in person or by phone, to
discuss exemplars of best practices and to identify ways to teach
others how to conduct searches and serve clients better. We have
made and released videos, published guidebooks and albums of best

work products, and created an e-mail campaign for sending peri-odic tip sheets to all practitioners worldwide.

In the past few years, we have found that even if we had the best technology in the world, technology by itself does not ensure that we share best practices and share knowledge. In fact, technol-ogy can be a subtle impediment to community building and infor-mal bonding. Frequent users of e-mail have had the experience that someone who relies heavily on brief electronic communiqués may misunderstand a message or attribute negative or wrong connota-tions to an e-mail they receive. In our opinion, the more heavily some people rely on e-mail, the less likely they are to build bonds with new people. They need to meet face to face, at least periodi-cally, to expand the scope of their trust network and social capital. They need the nuance of expression in face-to-face communica-tion to really get to know each other. E-mail alone cannot do that. People need opportunities to work together, to meet in person, and to build a history of shared experiences. Electronic interaction cannot replace the bond built with face-to-face shared experiences.

The shrinking economy of the past few years has increased the pressure to reduce the number of opportunities for face-to-face meetings due to cost considerations. We find ourselves spacing firmwide meetings at longer intervals, and inevitably, therefore, our associates see less of each other. At a time when business is chal-lenging, competition is intense, and our people are meeting less often, there is a real danger that the collegiality we so value will erode and that people will start acting selfishly and waste time competing with colleagues rather than focusing on how best to serve the client. Happily, this is where the wheel comes full circle. Technology, which as we have seen is not enough in itself to bind us together, now comes to our aid. Through conference calls, videoconferencing, remote online access, and Web conferencing, we interact with each other and are able to keep the ideas coming and moving and so preserve the social capital that is at the heart of our firm's success.

Peter Drummond-Hay is a managing director at Russell Reynolds Associates. He serves clients in professional services and conducts partner-level and firm leadership assignments for consulting firms and other professional service clients. He also leads senior management and board searches in other industries and oversees the firm's activities in Canada and Latin America and its executive assessment program. Prior to joining Russell Reynolds Associates in the early 1980s, Drummond-Hay was with the London-based merchant bank Arbuthnot Latham, where he served as director and senior vice president of Arbuthnot Export Services Inc. Previously, he spent five years in London and New York with Balfour Williamson & Company. Contact: pdrummondhay@russellreynolds.com

Barbara G. Saidel is a managing director at Russell Reynolds Associates, the international executive search and assessment firm, where she directs the global information systems, knowledge management, and research functions. Prior to joining the firm in 1994, Saidel was chief financial officer of the law firm Coudert Brothers in New York. Previously, she was with Simpson Thacher & Bartlett and earlier was vice president for operations and information services at First Boston Corporation. She also worked at Arthur Young & Company as a consultant and in retail operations management. She is a certified public accountant. She is coauthor, with Don Cohen, of *The Power of Social Capital*, and she frequently speaks on knowledge management issues in professional service firms. Contact: bsaidel@russellreynolds.com

Chapter Twenty-Seven

Learning at the Speed of Flight

Fred Harburg

Almost every executive has at one time or another felt overwhelmed at work and lamented the time starvation and relentless sense of confusion associated with it. E-mail was supposed to help, but it seems instead to have added to the problem. Most executives feel like they are flying blind and that the pace and turbulence are accelerating every day. What if executives had the same quality of systems and guidance that our best aviators have to help them get the right people to the right place at the right time with the right knowledge? What if executives had expert assistance from the most qualified advisers and used the best systems to integrate complicated information and help them achieve the mission with greater ease and effectiveness? What if they had expert help in identifying what they needed to learn and were then able to find the best source and method of learning at the touch of a button? This may sound like a fantasy, but it is becoming a reality for some executives. In today's demanding and confusing world, Motorola and other major corporations are beginning to provide interactive leadership support systems that help executives and their teams learn and perform with greater relevance, convenience, timeliness, and ease.

Simplifying the Complex

As a former Air Force pilot, I am intimately aware that the world of aviation represents a good example of the effective interplay between human beings and information processing technology in a complex environment.

The degree of complexity required to masterfully operate a supersonic aircraft in a hostile environment is very high. In fact, without technology and teamwork, it is overwhelmingly impossible. The variables involved in flight are almost endless: wind direction and intensity; barometric pressure; humidity; aircraft altitude; aircraft speed; ambient temperature; aircraft weight; distance from destination; amount of remaining fuel; required arrival time; changing visibility; engine efficiency; conflicting or hostile aircraft; restricted airspace; aviation regulations; information from electrical, fuel, hydraulic, navigation, and communication systems—and the list goes on. Add to this equation thousands of airplanes in airspace at any given moment, and you have world-class complexity.

Albert Einstein is said to have advised, "Make the solution as simple as possible, but no simpler." Aviation systems are designed with Einstein's advice in mind and work to distill the confusing universe of flight data into a few bits of vital, actionable information. These systems are designed to assist multiple pilots to consistently, safely, and successfully complete the objectives of their respective missions by simplifying the bewildering array of variables so that aviators can operate with relative ease in a large, complex environment.

The instrument landing system (ILS), the principal system that pilots use to extend human capability during low-visibility landings, is a good example. The ILS cockpit display looks like crosshairs imposed within a circle (see Figure 27.1). The horizontal bar represents the glide path to landing, while the vertical bar represents the course line. As long as the pilot centers the two bars and maintains correct airspeed, he or she will stay "on course, on glide path" and is guaranteed to arrive at the desired threshold for a perfect landing flare.

The genius of the ILS is that it integrates and simplifies all of the variables with which a pilot would otherwise have to contend during this critical phase of flight. Many phases of flight are forgiving of mistakes; the landing is not one of them.

Executives also face an extremely complicated set of variables when operating in the corporate environment. Customer demands,

Figure 27.1 Instrument Landing System

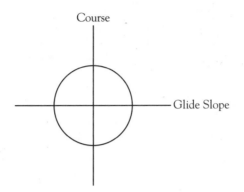

budget constraints, debt levels, liquidity rates, employee morale, cash flow requirements, milestones to product launch, scrape rates, return percentages, legal and environmental compliance, top-line sales, stock price, shareholder returns, inventory levels, market forecasts, yield rates, competitor moves, production schedules, personal performance feedback, and the continual bombardment of messages from a variety of different written, electronic, and telephonic sources all combine to make life exciting. Similar to the flight environment, this array of variables can be overwhelming.

The value of an effective leadership support system is its help in reducing an overwhelming set of variables into a simpler set on which a leader can act to stay "on course, on glide path." The key is to ensure that it is as simple as possible, but no simpler. Unless the system simplifies the inputs, it merely brings an overwhelming array of information to the executive more rapidly, and unless the system captures the richness of the executive's environment, it is a superficial distortion of the real environment.

Right Achievement, Right Behavior

Sustained success at goal attainment requires effectiveness in two dimensions. The first is task achievement, and the second is interpersonal behavior employed while in pursuit of goals (see Figure 27.2).

Figure 27.2 Goal Attainment

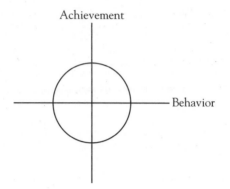

It is possible for an executive to focus exclusively on the achievement dimension of the executive challenge and to ignore the behavioral; however, in the long run, the environment becomes more and more hostile for executives and businesses that ignore the importance of both. The behavioral dimension encompasses the values and standards of conduct required for effective, sustaining, and engaging leadership. When the economy is robust, the most skilled employees have many options for employment. It is well documented that the primary reason that talented people leave a company is the behavior of their immediate manager. The cost of talent defection, the loss of productivity and opportunity associated with ineffective leadership behavior, will cripple the best businesses and can jeopardize their very existence—witness Enron and Arthur Andersen.

The corporate analogue to "on course, on glide path" is "right achievement, right behavior." To meet the critical threshold for sustained success, the effective executive must achieve critical objectives and do so with excellent leadership behaviors. In today's intensely challenging environment of global competition, leaders need the support of people and technology to integrate and simplify the overwhelming array of inputs. Then they can focus on the critical variables that will make the difference between success and failure.

Integrated Leadership Support System (ILSS)

After years of promises, we are now seeing the first real-time leadership support systems that extend human capability, enhance decision-making quality, and accelerate learning in relationship to goals. We are beginning to see the essential elements of an ILSS come together. We are gaining understanding about how to combine these elements to help executives and their teams perform at higher levels of excellence, learn more effectively, and enjoy better results. Our experience at Motorola and in other global companies is showing us how such systems can provide extremely powerful leverage for increasing leader effectiveness and development. Leadership support systems are transforming the leadership experience. We are digitizing performance and development systems while integrating them with the essential human touch.

The Motorola Leadership Supply System

In 1999, Motorola had a significant problem. When the senior leaders looked ahead, they could see clearly that the organization would not have the quality and quantity of leaders required to create a winning combination for the future. Planned retirements, the changing demands of the key leadership positions, and the growth of new sectors were creating an untenable gap between what would be needed for success and what the company had. The concept of leadership supply was created as a solution to avoid a midair collision with the future. The Leadership Supply System was built on three concepts from three different but related disciplines.

The first concept was the idea of efficient economic markets. When the pool of leaders for the company was viewed through a marketplace lens, it was obvious that the market for leaders at Motorola was inefficient. Demand far outstripped supply, and the right leaders were not showing up in the right jobs at the right time. Any efficient market depends on excellent forecasting, on channel strategies, and on sensitivity to price, supply, and demand variables. The second concept was portfolio theory, which led Motorola to view the pool of senior leadership talent as a diversified portfolio of talent for which there was no portfolio manager or investment strategy. The third concept was the idea of a leadership supply chain with a somewhat predictable life cycle. This perspective made it obvious that there was an insufficient line of sight to destination assignments, nor were there mechanisms in place to manage the flow of a leader from one stage of the life cycle to the next. The result of this analysis was the Motorola Leadership Supply System.

Personal Commitment: Goals at the Center of the System

The first building block of the system is the concept of personal commitment. Personal commitment is a documented understanding between a leader and a direct report concerning the goals and results for which the associate is responsible in the near term. In moving from being a company distinguished only for its engineering innovation to being a more consistently successful commercial enterprise, Motorola had to have a customer- and market-based scorecard for the company that drove a set of interlinked goals cascading from the CEO to the shop floor. Personal commitment became the mechanism for achieving that aim.

In my experience with a multitude of global corporations, this was the first time I had seen a viable implementation of this concept, and technology made it possible. The concept is similar to management by objectives, introduced decades ago, but the implementation is much more powerful. Once every quarter, all Motorola leaders sit down with each of their direct reports to review how they are progressing toward the achievement of the personal commitment objectives. The leaders also receive multirater feedback concerning how they are doing with respect to their behavior. This personal commitment process becomes quite cumbersome in a very large organization, and this is where the interplay between technology and good human practice comes into play.

Every Motorola associate has real-time access to the PC system that gives access to the scorecards and goals of the individuals above and below the associate in a line of responsibility. In addition, when a development dialogue takes place at each quarterly checkpoint, the results are entered and signed off by all managers and their respective direct reports. Each individual has continuous access to his or her current and past confidential multirater feedback reports, with a robust set of tools linked to development sources to help in understanding and addressing performance and behavior deficits. The system is fully integrated and fully secure. Associates can initiate an abbreviated multirater survey of four items on any behavior of their choosing and ask any number of others to help them assess progress at any time. Motorola has almost 100 percent participation in the system, since compensation is based on some of its dimensions. Although the system is far from perfect, it has been very well received, and most Motorola associates cannot imagine doing without it at this point.

Next Steps

As a leading technology company, Motorola is continually stretching the boundaries of its promise to provide intelligence everywhere—we have even trademarked the expression "intelligence everywhere." We are now experimenting with our own wireless devices and software to both update and provide access to vital information on a real-time basis to people wherever they might be. We are beginning to provide customized development packets to individuals on demand or on a push basis to help them stay "on course, on glide path" anytime, anywhere.

Just as in aviation, there is no substitute for human judgment, but in an increasingly complicated and demanding world, we have only just begun to realize technology's promise of making our lives safer, smarter, simpler, synchronized, and more fun.

Fred Harburg is the chief learning officer and president of Motorola University. He and his team are building the competencies, capabilities, and intellectual capital of Motorola associates through the provision of global business learning solutions and systems. Harburg served as a pilot and aircraft commander in the United States Air Force and was a faculty officer at the Air Force Academy, where he directed the industrial and organizational psychology and honors leadership curricula. Harburg has held leadership roles as a consultant and human capability architect for several of the world's premier Fortune 100 companies. He has played particularly fulfilling roles working with senior executives in major corporate change efforts. He is a frequent speaker, adviser, and facilitator in executive development efforts aimed at integrating spiritual, intellectual, emotional, financial, and physical capabilities for worthy aims. Contact: dharburg@hotmail.com

Chapter Twenty-Eight

The Audacity of Imagination

How Lilly Is Creating
"Research Without Walls"

Sharon Sullivan

Bryan Dunnivant

Laurie Sachtleben

"Every great advance in science has issued from a new audacity of imagination."[1] "None of us is as smart as all of us."[2]

Few enterprises are more complex, more costly, or more failure-prone than pharmaceutical research and development. From laboratory to launch, it takes between 10 and 15 years and up to $800 million to develop a single new medicine. The odds that an intriguing molecular compound will become the next blockbuster are, roughly, 1 in 5,000. By comparison, bringing a new automobile or computer chip to market is a snap.

Pharmaceutical companies also have a need for speed. The old expression, "The patient is waiting," has real and poignant meaning for the scientists searching for tomorrow's cures. Furthermore, pharmaceutical companies must keep their pipelines full to survive the inevitable loss of patent protection for top-selling products.

It is small wonder, then, that businesses like Eli Lilly and Company are reaching far beyond their own walls to turbo-charge their research and development (R&D) engines and mitigate the risk and cost of innovation.

The Challenge: Grow Organically

Based in Indianapolis, Lilly is a fully integrated, mid-sized pharmaceutical company with annual sales exceeding $11 billion. Lilly is independent and, in an industry in which mega-mergers are common, determined to stay that way. Its business strategy is simple: Outgrow the competition, even the giants of the pharmaceutical industry, by churning out a steady flow of superior new products. Doing so with current work processes requires even greater resources than the estimated $2 billion a year Lilly already spends on R&D or the more than 8,000 scientists and technicians it employs. For Lilly, organic growth requires new ways of thinking about knowledge, processes, and problem solving.

Historically, Lilly has relied on the creation of cross-functional, co-located teams and the use of advanced IT tools to improve flows of data. However, in an increasingly information-driven world, such measures are merely a first step.

"We're truly a knowledge business," says Sharon Sullivan, chief learning officer and vice president for human resources. "Every medicine we make is the result of an idea that has been probed, played with, tested, tweaked, iterated, reiterated, reviewed by regulatory agencies, and ultimately validated in the marketplace. Our challenge is to use knowledge tools both inside and outside the company to improve every step of this process."[3]

To meet this challenge, Lilly has taken actions that are untraditional, some might even say audacious. Chief among these was helping to create a wholly owned subsidiary called InnoCentive, Inc., based in Andover, Massachusetts.

A Bounty on Breakthrough Ideas

As the name implies, InnoCentive generates incentives for innovation by creating a Web-based community of "seekers," companies like Lilly with specific scientific challenges, and "solvers." A *solver* can be any scientist worldwide who registers online and enters the Web site's secure "project room," which contains data and product specifications related to the challenge. A science team at InnoCentive screens input from solvers and forwards potential solutions to the seeker company, who then issues a "bounty" of up to $100,000 for an answer that meets its needs.

As of mid-2003, more than 25,000 scientists from more than 125 countries had registered with InnoCentive, and more than 9,000 project rooms have been opened, mainly focusing on challenges in chemistry and biology, such as that of the following sample query: "The following N-Boc-7-azabicyclo [2.2.1] heptene is in need of an efficient synthetic strategy. This molecule has been reported in the literature, but the existing routes have several low-yielding steps. Devise and execute the best synthetic pathway."

The model has proved particularly attractive to solvers in countries like China and India, which have enormous scientific talent but relatively low pay scales. For example, in 2002, InnoCentive paid one of its largest awards to date, $75,000, to a scientist in India, where the average annual salary for a chemist is less than $25,000.

Users have described InnoCentive as an effort to tear down the walls of traditional R&D laboratories. "It's a vehicle for exposing important unsolved problems to, almost literally, the entire global scientific community," says Alph Bingham, chairman of InnoCentive and a vice president with Lilly.[4]

Bingham adds that InnoCentive is a classic example of a decentralized network approach to problem solving. "Its value increases exponentially with the number of participants. The more problems we post, the more attractive our site is to solvers. And as new solvers register, the collective IQ of the network increases, in turn encouraging seekers to post new and more sophisticated challenges. This virtuous circle serves to keep building and enhancing a true community."

Like Lilly, InnoCentive will have to grow in order to succeed. To date the enterprise has signed three more seeker companies, and already it is adding new features to its Web site, including pharmaceutical problems that extend beyond discovery research. Bingham believes scientists will continue to be attracted to InnoCentive—and not just for the money.

"Some scientists see InnoCentive as a chance to be a free agent. Others use it to bring recognition and reward to their own organizations, but every solver who logs in does it at least in part, I think, for the sheer joy of trying to solve a difficult problem," he says.

Clinical Trials: Ripe for Collaboration

Clinical trials, during which physicians administer a potential new drug to human volunteers in clinics and hospitals, are the costliest and most time-intensive phase in the development of any new medicine. Furthermore, as pharmaceutical companies pursue solutions to increasingly complex diseases, more procedures and more patients per trial are required.

To improve both the speed and the effectiveness of its global clinical trials, Lilly has gone online again, this time using a licensed "Web discussion tool" called CompanyWay. The tool has been used several times to create a global community among the several hundred clinical research physicians (CRPs) Lilly employs to oversee clinical studies of investigational products.

CompanyWay builds on the "swarm theory," in which populations of individuals self-organize, solve problems, and achieve new levels of collective intelligence with minimal hierarchy or central organization. It enables CRPs to collaborate on trial protocols and to share their methodologies and findings quickly and fluidly. Furthermore, CRPs can provide each other with peer evaluations by "voting" an assigned value or merit to specific ideas posted on the site.

"In the past, the difficulty of getting CRPs together meant that most trial protocols were dictated by headquarters in Indianapolis," notes Dr. Allan Weinstein, vice president for clinical research and regulatory affairs in most of Lilly's non-U.S. operations. A U.S. bias is undesirable, he says, because definitions of diseases, symptoms in patients, and the requirements of regulatory authorities vary widely from country to country.[5]

Take, for example, depression. Among U.S. patients, this condition manifests itself mainly with feelings of sadness or lethargy; while in Japan a depressed person's chief complaint is more likely to be a stomachache.

"Without experienced physicians from many countries weighing in on how the trial should be structured, what we should measure, and so on, we're forced to take a cookie-cutter approach," says Dr. Mike McDonald, vice president for global clinical research and medical affairs. "This tool provides a way to become truly global and more patient-centered in the way we handle clinical trials."[6]

Capitalist Tool

A third collaborative approach, while still in an experimental mode, may ultimately encourage better and more creative decision making at Lilly. Specifically, the company has conducted a simulation using a tool that applies the dynamics of the ultimate free-market symbol, the stock market, to the complex process of portfolio management.

Lilly has more promising drug candidates than resources to develop them. The fact that this problem makes Lilly the envy of most competitors does little to make the portfolio management process easier. Vast quantities of data, from toxicological studies to market projections to financial analyses of competing products, are weighed in order to make a "go" or "no go" decision and allocate resources to the candidate's further development. It is, of necessity, an excruciating process. It also requires speed, since the resources that are freed up when less productive projects are terminated can be redeployed in more promising directions.

Lilly's pilot used a tool from Incentive Markets, Inc., to portray drugs in its pipeline as securities or stocks. Supplied with information on their properties and market forces, company decision makers then bought and sold the securities on a simulated stock exchange. The traders quickly "voted" with their dollars, and clear lines were drawn between the prices of winning and losing molecules. In fact, the prices distilled the collective knowledge of the traders, providing rapid shorthand insight into the likely success of each potential drug.

Gwen Krivi, vice president for project management at Lilly Research Laboratories, notes that although the tool was used only for simulated portfolio decision making, participants were excited and energized by the approach. The company plans to run additional pilots in the near future. Borrowing a slogan used by Incentive Markets, Krivi says, "Market forces are the financial equivalent of natural selection, and history is written by the survivors."[7]

More Breakthroughs to Come?

Lilly leaders concede that initiatives and experiments like these are just a beginning. The 127-year-old company is still a long way from replacing its traditionally rigid structure with colonies of knowledge-based communities. Nevertheless, the motivation to change is high.

"Ours is an industry of breakthroughs, not just in the form of scientific discoveries, but also in the ways we work," says CLO Sullivan. "We need to challenge notions of how ideas develop, who does what work, and how we leverage knowledge. That's where our next big breakthroughs may lie."

Sullivan adds that Lilly's knowledge management and e-business teams share a mission of helping the company stay on a constant course of experimentation and growth. Team members remind themselves that the patient is indeed waiting. "Our ability to help this company become more powerful in its use of knowledge could mean the difference between a lifesaving drug becoming available one year from now or five. That's all we need to know to keep going."

Sharon Sullivan is vice president, human resources–global compensation and benefits, learning, and effectiveness for Eli Lilly and Company. She is responsible for organizational effectiveness, Lilly University, global security, global human resource process and data integration, global compensation and benefits, human resource services, corporate health services, and executive compensation.

Bryan Dunnivant joined Eli Lilly and Company in 1982. He worked in Lilly's engineering component, doing design work for manufacturing facilities before moving to Lilly's financial division in 1986. Since then, Dunnivant has shouldered a wide variety of financial responsibilities, including managerial assignments in Europe. He moved into his current job as manager of operations for e.Lilly in September 2001. Contact: bpd@Lilly.com

Laurie Sachtleben is a senior writer and editor in Eli Lilly and Company's corporate communications group. She has nearly two dozen years of experience in journalism, public relations, crisis communications, speechwriting, and related functions. She joined Lilly in 1996. Contact: lrsa@lilly.com

Chapter Twenty-Nine

Developing a Learning Culture on Wall Street

One Firm's Experience

Steffen Landauer
Steve Kerr

Among the most basic tenets of organizational theory is that to be successful, organizations must be able to both differentiate and integrate. Usually omitted from this proposition is that the two endeavors are not equally difficult. Differentiation often comes easily, sometimes with no effort whatsoever, whereas integration almost never does. Most organizations spend a great deal of time, with no assurance of success, trying to get their different functions, regions, and hierarchical levels to be civil to one another, let alone to welcome and adopt anyone else's good ideas and best practices. A number of forces share responsibility for this state of affairs, from the difficulty many people experience in "telling truth to power" to the psychological barriers to knowledge transmission that have come to be known as the NIH ("not invented here") syndrome.

In addition to the universal impediments to the free trade of ideas within firms, and between firms and their external constituencies, several characteristics common to financial service firms further inhibit the exchange and assimilation of new information. First, many financial service firms have been successful without exchanging best practices from within or admitting new ideas from outside. Traditionally, firms in the industry have succeeded through (1) recruiting outstanding talent, partly by offering these talented individuals wealth creation opportunities superior to those of other industries; (2) having them learn key technical skills on the job from experienced master practitioners; and (3) engaging the entrepreneurial energy of business unit leaders by allowing them considerable autonomy to manage their businesses and relate to other parts of their firms.

The obstacles financial services firms face can be divided into two related but distinct categories: those relating to the nature of the organizations and those relating to the type of professionals who tend to work in them. On the organizational level, firms tend to define success predominantly in quantitative terms. Sales functions are focused on their annual sales numbers; trading desks tally their profit and loss at the end of each day; clients analyze the returns in their portfolio or the price at which their companies will be sold; and financial service CEOs scrutinize their earnings per share. In an industry obsessed with numbers, initiatives relating to the exchange of knowledge and ideas, where benefits are often realized over the long term and are difficult to quantify even then, tend to be underappreciated.

Furthermore, many investment banks are under regulatory obligation to set up formal barriers between securities underwriting and advisory units. These barriers tend to create silos within firms and inhibit communication. Much of the recent publicity about investment banks relates to these barriers and the extent to which they have or have not functioned effectively in recent years. (As we write this chapter, it is unclear what effect this increased public scrutiny will have on financial service firms' receptivity to outside ideas and internal information sharing.)

Another feature of these firms that can inhibit the free flow of ideas pertains to their decision-making processes. There is an interesting paradox in the process through which decisions are made in financial service firms. Because of the nature of the business, quick decisions are often needed. On a trading desk, decisions are made to commit hundreds of millions of dollars of capital in a matter of minutes. On merger deals, elaborate financial analyses and definitive recommendations need to be supplied to clients overnight. Successful financial service firms have sophisticated models for assessing risks, and they have processes in place to take enormous financial risks in very short order. Lines of accountability are drawn clearly for these types of decisions.

For internal organizational decisions, however, the process and outcome are often quite different. Many of these firms have a highly collaborative culture that demands broad consensus, sometimes approaching unanimity, on organizational matters. Decisions as simple as hiring relatively junior staff, changing responsibilities of key people, or writing a memo announcing a new hire can take many weeks and involve dozens of people. This laborious decision-making process militates against the swift adoption of best practices or new ideas. Particularly in organizations in which authority is relatively decentralized and overall financial results have generally been healthy, the momentum of the status quo can be difficult to break.

In addition to these organizational factors, individuals working in these firms are not always inclined toward the swift exchange of new ideas. For one thing, many of these talented professionals do in fact possess highly differentiated technical abilities. The skills of the mergers specialist are quite distinct from those of the government bond salesperson and the financial engineer who structures new derivative products. Even professionals who have acquired broad management responsibilities often continue to identify themselves with their professional skills and their client relationships rather than their management roles. These firms often describe their cultures as "producer-leader" or "player-coach," in which revenue production and client services are the primary bases for reward and recognition. The leaders of these businesses tend to retain highly specific technical roles and expertise, and they often look skeptically on ideas from anyone who is unfamiliar with the details of their businesses. An outside observer might suppose that a few thousand finance major M.B.A.s have a lot in common, but the individuals themselves tend to be keenly aware of differences between bankers, traders, and salespeople—even among those who perform identical functions for different products.

Largely because of the nature of these professionals and the work they do, the apprenticeship system evolved as the primary vehicle for knowledge exchange in financial service firms. People historically achieved technical excellence through the guidance and mentorship of master practitioners who worked alongside them on deals, with clients, or at trading desks. These mentors were highly respected for their knowledge and experience, and the strongest financial service firms developed a strong apprenticeship culture, which became a competitive advantage in the marketplace for top talent. The apprenticeship system had the further advantage of not requiring professionals to take time away from their desks. It was especially well suited to the temperament of financial service professionals, who tend to be highly practical people with a bias toward action. They are quick to dismiss as "too theoretical" any ideas without apparent and immediate application. (One of the most derogatory epithets from this highly educated group of professionals is "academic.")

Laying the Groundwork for Leadership Development at Goldman Sachs

All the foregoing notwithstanding, at least one financial service organization has decided that leadership development and knowledge transfer are important priorities. At Goldman Sachs, senior management asserted that the firm's traditionally strong apprenticeship culture needed to be supplemented with more structured means of knowledge transfer and leadership development. There was no desire to diminish the coaching and mentoring roles of more senior leaders; on the contrary, this was an aspect of the culture they wanted to strengthen. But they also felt, particularly in light of the firm's rapid growth and increasing globalization, that the apprenticeship model needed to be augmented with more formal approaches. The need for leadership development had simply outstripped the supply of experienced mentors.

As a result, in 1999 (also the year in which Goldman Sachs became a publicly traded corporation), a small task force composed primarily of business leaders was formed to benchmark other firms and decide how the firm should address the issue. After four months of study, the group came back with a set of recommendations, which led to the creation of a small group called Pine Street, named after the historic Wall Street–area headquarters of the firm. In its benchmarking visits, Goldman Sachs was attracted to the leadership development approach at General Electric. It subsequently hired the head of GE's leadership development center at Crotonville (Steve Kerr, coauthor of this chapter), to lead a group of eight professionals who reported directly to the firm's executive officer. The group's mission centered on leadership development—"to make the development of outstanding leaders a core competency of Goldman Sachs," as joint chief operating officer John Thornton put it[1]—and on the goal of disseminating internal and external best practices.

One of the early tasks that Pine Street set for itself was to agree on a set of internal "running rules" that outlined how the eight professionals in the group would work with each other and with their partners and clients within the firm. The basic premise was simple: the way the group works should reflect the concepts it seeks to teach. These running rules sought to model core strengths of Goldman Sachs in areas like client service and professional expertise while also putting in place some ideas that were less ingrained in the culture, such as boundarylessness and a "volunteer" staffing system. These rules (see Exhibit 29.1) have been a useful tool in maximizing the productivity and job satisfaction of the group.

Exhibit 29.1 How Pine Street Works

1. We work very hard to practice what we teach. In particular, we seek to operate smoothly across boundaries (divisional, regional, business unit, firm, client) and in a nonhierarchical manner.

2. We never slow a project down. If our client wants to do something tomorrow, that's when we do it. We regularly seek input from one another to improve the quality of our work, but we make every effort to avoid excessive meetings, postings, and consensus building. (We keep in mind that sometimes reaching consensus means disagree and commit.)

3. We always say yes to requests for our help. If we can't do something ourselves, we help identify someone who can do the job.

4. Since we are a small team, our preference regarding important projects outside Pine Street's core activities is that someone else in the firm does them but does them well. Our third choice is that they are done poorly or aren't done at all. Our second choice is that we do them. (Some portion of our workload derives from the fact that we hate to settle for our third choice.)

5. We search for opportunities to work with individuals from other parts of the firm. Sometimes this takes the form of a formal partnership, but we also benefit from "resources in place," people whose primary responsibilities are outside Pine Street but care enough about some Pine Street project to work with us on it. We also welcome opportunities to run pilot sessions of our programs within one division before rolling them out firmwide.

6. Each of us spends nearly all his or her time working on projects and programs. None of us is a "manager." We have a very flat organization and strongly believe in empowering people—giving them considerable operating freedom and expecting them to ask for help when they need it. All of our team members lead projects. Senior people regularly work for, and report to, more junior team members.

Exhibit 29.1 How Pine Street Works, Cont'd.

7. Any member of the team can speak for Pine Street and can commit Pine Street to a project or a completion date, and that commitment will always be honored.

8. Our first decision rule in staffing any project is to ask who has time and wants to do it. We don't stereotype people. We believe that most people have the good sense to sign up for things they are capable of doing and to ask for help when needed.

9. We support and encourage all team members, regardless of their level or years of service, to develop a particular area of expertise.

10. We work to develop each other, and we share credit. When someone leaves a voice mail about a completed piece of work, it is usually to boast about something another team member has done. We also see to it that whoever does the work gets formal recognition for that work (and gets to make the presentation, no matter to whom).

The First Pine Street Program: Executive Coaching

The first formal initiative Pine Street put in place was a one-on-one executive coaching program. Although informal mentoring had been a critically important aspect of the firm's culture, formal coaching had rarely been used at Goldman Sachs. The few coaches deployed in the firm were often given remedial assignments with individuals facing various interpersonal issues. From the outset, the Pine Street coaching program was structured as a very different undertaking:

- Coaching was offered not to remedial cases but rather to fast-track leaders for whom the firm had bigger plans.
- Participation was entirely voluntary at the invitation of senior business leaders, who sponsored selected leaders from within their businesses.

- Pine Street mandated that written developmental business-related objectives be established with the participation of the coachee's manager.
- The coaches selected were neither Goldman Sachs employees nor employees of the major coaching firms that have sprung up in recent years but rather were sole practitioners who had broad experience in management consulting or teaching.

Participants describe the program as a highly individualized, time-efficient approach to development, and it has become a core offering of Pine Street and a sought-after reward for fast-track leaders. A formal objective of many of these coaching assignments is to strengthen the coaching skills of the coaching "client," thereby further strengthening the apprenticeship culture of the firm. An interesting unanticipated benefit of the program has been that the core Pine Street coaches have become virtual members of the Pine Street team. Over time, they have acquired an intimate knowledge of Goldman Sachs's businesses and culture. Combining this knowledge with their broad experiences in many different firms, they have brought to Pine Street a number of ideas from outside organizations that have been adapted to fit the culture of Goldman Sachs. The group of coaches convenes periodically to exchange coaching best practices with one another and with Pine Street and to bring their perspectives and observations to the firm's leadership. Recently, for example, the coaches met with the team responsible for the firm's performance review process to discuss possible improvements. Pine Street also holds parallel best-practice exchange sessions for the coachees, which is focused on how Goldman Sachs professionals can get the most out of coaching relationships.

Partnering with Line Leaders

The fundamental structure of Pine Street is one of partnership with the line leaders of the firm. Other than the coaches and a few consultants and academics who teach an occasional course, all Pine

Street sessions consist of Goldman Sachs leaders teaching other leaders. This approach is consistent with the firm's apprenticeship culture and has the added benefit of being a powerful developmental experience for those who teach. Within the financial service industry, as in many other places, ideas move most efficiently and most credibly through the voices of respected line leaders. Even outstanding leaders, however, vary in their teaching skills. Pine Street tries to ensure high-quality instruction by (1) partnering with these leaders in developing course content, whether based on internal best practices (cross-marketing skills, leadership communications, delegation, and so on) or translation of ideas from outside the firm (such as cross-cultural skills and decision-making models), and (2) offering professional presentation coaching through an "educate the educators" initiative.

Pine Street's partnership with line leaders extends well beyond their teaching roles. They are also advisers and partners in executing its key initiatives. The Pine Street board of directors is chaired by joint chief operating officers John Thain and John Thornton, and it includes senior leaders from all the key businesses. Pine Street undertakes no major initiatives without the approval and active participation of board members and other line leaders, who are generous with their reminders that Pine Street's offerings must be linked with business priorities and be relevant to the challenges faced by line leaders.

Finally, of course, leaders participate as students. The courses they attend are primarily directed toward career transitions. Pine Street seeks to provide just-in-time learning for relatively homogeneous populations. For example, when people first assume managerial responsibilities, they are presented with models of vertical influence and are taught how to delegate, give feedback, and make effective use of financial rewards. As people progress in their careers and take on firmwide or global responsibilities, the emphasis becomes less on management and more on such leadership concepts as strategy, cross-cultural skills, and key business drivers across the range of the firm's businesses.

The Goldman Sachs Leadership Principles

One early challenge in developing content for the Pine Street leadership programs was the lack of definition of outstanding leadership or even a shared language to discuss elements of leadership. Due to its reliance on the apprenticeship system, the firm had held few formal leadership programs, and although Goldman Sachs had a set of business principles that were a cornerstone of its culture, these principles lacked actionable guidelines for what leaders should actually do. Due to the consensus-oriented culture of Goldman Sachs, the methodology for developing the Goldman Sachs Leadership Principles was a highly participative one. More than 90 percent of the firm's managing directors participated in discussions, led by senior leaders of the firm, of successive drafts of the principles. The process took more than a year but produced a document that reflected the input of virtually all of the firm's leaders (see Exhibit 29.2).

A decision was made quite early that consistent with the idea that every university has a research capability, so should Pine Street. The goal was not to produce research for scholarly journals but rather to generate useful, immediately applicable data that could be brought to bear on important organizational issues. The first effort in this regard was to seek to identify the experiences that were most important in preparing Goldman Sachs professionals for high-level leadership positions. The model for this effort was the "Session C" approach of GE, which systematically moves its promising executives through a series of managerial positions that serve to both assess and prepare them for positions of increasing responsibility. Among the frequent "career stops" within GE are the following:

- Leading both a short- and a long-cycle business
- Working in a consumer business and also in a defense industry
- Managing a start-up business and one that's well established
- Taking on a leadership role outside one's home country

Exhibit 29.2 Goldman Sachs Leadership Principles

1. *Act with a Profound Sense of Integrity and Fairness.* The daily stewardship and embodiment of these values—as highlighted in our Business Principles—is the primary responsibility of all leaders at Goldman Sachs. Integrity and fairness lie at the core of our firm's heritage, our service to our clients, and our cultural strength. Leaders at all levels of the firm must uphold these values in their daily decisions and actions and instill them in their people as well.

2. *Deliver Business Results Through Commercial Excellence and People Development.* Commercial excellence is the lifeblood of the firm and a key source of leadership credibility. Outstanding leaders create profitability not only through business development and client service but also through recruiting, coaching, developing, and retaining the best people. Leaders develop leaders, and leadership demands consistent and purposeful investment of time with our people.

3. *Build Strong Client and Other External Relationships.* The success of our firm depends on the quality of our relationships with a broad group of influential clients and leaders around the world. Our best leaders successfully develop long-term relationships across multiple cultures. They succeed through outstanding client service as well as playing leadership roles in external business and community groups.

4. *Drive Teamwork Within and Between Businesses.* Teamwork and dedication to the firm's greatest good are competitive advantages. Leaders maintain a strong network of relationships across the firm. They cross-market the firm's products and services and actively share ideas and talent across divisional, departmental, regional, and hierarchical boundaries.

5. *Foster Learning, Innovation, and Change.* Leaders welcome and drive change. They constantly extract the learning from their own failures and successes as well as those of others—both

Exhibit 29.2 Goldman Sachs Leadership Principles, Cont'd.

internal and external to GS. They build on our past success but also take the entrepreneurial risks necessary to innovate and grow our businesses.

6. *Debate Freely, Decide Swiftly, and Commit.* Leaders challenge the status quo and have the courage to express and allow disagreement. However, they drive issues toward decisions, and they embrace decisions once they have been made.

7. *Promote Meritocracy by Welcoming and Leveraging Differences.* Our clients and employees comprise a heterogeneous group of successful, influential men and women from all cultures, races, and ethnicities. Leaders create meritocracies that recognize and reward the diverse people and talents the firm requires to succeed around the world. They ensure that all employees have opportunities, free from artificial barriers, to rapidly advance to the utmost of their abilities.

8. *Develop Strategy and Execute.* Leaders develop and articulate a clear vision and strategy for their business and set concrete goals toward realizing their strategy. They move quickly, make tough decisions, and show excellent judgment. Finally, they are relentless in prioritizing actions and executing to the highest standards.

9. *Create Trust and Credibility Through Honest Communication.* Our best leaders communicate fully, directly, and candidly, and they follow with action. They are also good listeners. Above all, they recognize that the power of their personal example is greater than the power of their words.

Among the lessons from the research conducted within Goldman Sachs was that an assignment outside one's home country is as important in financial services as at a firm like GE. Cycle times, by contrast, are so compressed within financial service firms that this factor is nowhere near as important as at GE. Since this original study, Pine Street has completed or is working on studies investigating the pitfalls and best practices pertaining to expatriation and repatriation, keys to successfully hiring senior people from other firms, and the circumstances leading to the success or failure of divisional heads serving individually or jointly.

Pine Street Services for Goldman Sachs Clients

The fastest-growing aspect of Pine Street's activities is the array of programs and services offered directly to the firm's major clients. These activities serve to leverage Pine Street's expertise in leadership development and strengthen the firm's client relationships. In the first two years, Pine Street has reached more than two hundred of the firm's key clients, with services ranging from individual discussions with senior leaders to training sessions for these leaders to joint Goldman Sachs–client leadership programs. The latter programs, which entail clients learning side-by-side with GS counterparts, facilitate the free exchange of ideas and often lead to broader and more interesting discussions than are possible with participants from a single firm. The programs are led by senior GS leaders, external consultants, and faculty from the client organizations.

These client service programs in many ways exemplify the broader methodology through which Pine Street, in what is still its early days, tries to create and spread applied intellectual capital:

- The programs seek to diminish boundaries among the businesses of the firm and between Goldman Sachs and its clients.
- The Pine Street faculty, which frequently includes the chairman and the operating heads, consists largely of leaders teaching leaders, plus a few longtime consultants and clients.
- Initiatives are focused on commercially productive activities.
- The effort builds on Goldman Sachs's historic strengths (in particular, powerful client relationships and an exceedingly strong client service ethic), while seeking to introduce and spread new ideas and new ways of operating throughout the firm.

Challenges

A number of challenges remain. These include the following:

- Keeping the focus and interest of line leaders through an extraordinarily difficult market environment
- Applying the Pine Street "running rules" to an expanded mandate and an organization, which has grown to more than seventy people
- More fully integrating Pine Street's developmental offerings with measurement and reward systems within the firm
- Broadening our partnership with line leaders beyond those who have been so helpful to date

It is still too early to judge how successfully these and other challenges will be met. Nevertheless, some initial successes indicate that financial service professionals, for all their proclivities toward short-term focus and quantifiable results, can respond to and benefit from an active and efficient marketplace of ideas that add value to their business.

Steffen Landauer is vice president and chief operating officer of Goldman Sachs's Pine Street Group, a small team that focuses on leadership development and organizational effectiveness for the firm and its clients. Steffen's current responsibilities include overall leadership of Pine Street's various initiatives for Goldman Sachs clients, including the Goldman Sachs Emerging Leader program for select Goldman Sachs leaders and key clients of the firm; an executive coaching program for the firm's leaders, which he founded two years ago; and various other leadership initiatives focused on key career transitions. Since the inception of Pine Street several years ago, he has been involved in building Pine Street and developing many of its key programs. He has worked with Goldman Sachs since 1987 in various roles involving design and delivery of learning and development initiatives. Contact: steffen.landauer@gs.com

Steve Kerr is chief learning officer and a managing director of Goldman Sachs. From 1994 to 2001, he was vice president of leadership development and chief learning officer for General Electric, which included having responsibility for GE's renowned leadership education center at Crotonville. He was formerly on the faculties of Ohio State University, the University of Southern California, and the University of Michigan, and he was dean of the faculty of the USC business school from 1985 to 1989. Kerr is a past president of the Academy of Management. His writings on leadership and "on the folly of rewarding A while hoping for B" are among the most cited and reprinted in the management sciences. Contact: Steve.Kerr@gs.com

Notes

Chapter Two, "Five Dilemmas of Knowledge Management"

1. I. Nonaka and H. Takeuchi, *The Knowledge-Creating Company: How Japanese Companies Create the Dynamics of Innovation* (New York: St. Martin's Press, 1995).

Chapter Three, "Effectively Influencing Up"

1. P. F. Drucker, *The Essential Drucker* (New York: HarperBusiness, 2001), p. 207.
2. Drucker, *The Essential Drucker*, p. 212.
3. Interview of Marshall Goldsmith, *Harvard Business Review*, Oct. 1, 2002, pp. 22–23.

Chapter Four, "Where 'Managing Knowledge' Goes Wrong and What to Do Instead"

1. Conceived by Alan Turing, a British mathematician who invented much of the mathematics that provides the foundation for computer science, the Turing Test is a test for machine intelligence. Essentially, the idea is that if a human being were at a terminal, communicating with two entities, one computer and one human, over the equivalent of a network connection and could not tell which one was the computer and which one was the person, we could say that the computer was intelligent. No computer comes anywhere near passing the

Turing Test. It is simply too difficult to teach a computer to make good small talk. When we refer to the Turing Test in the text, we are using the term by analogy. For example, if a trained judge like Daniel Denison can look at two interpretations of the meaning of 360-degree feedback scores, one created by our program and one written by a trained human coach, and evaluates the program's interpretation as at least as good as the coach's, we would say the program passes the test.

Chapter Five, "Knowledge Management Involves Neither Knowledge nor Management"

1. R. E. Silverman, "Growth at McKinsey Hindered Use of Data," *Wall Street Journal*, May 20, 2002, p. B6.
2. N. W. Foote, E. Matson, and N. Rudd, "Managing the Knowledge Manager," *McKinsey Quarterly*, 2001, no. 3, pp. 120–129; S. Hauschild, T. Licht, and W. Stein, "Creating a Knowledge Culture," *McKinsey Quarterly*, 2001, no. 1, pp. 74–81.
3. *Merriam-Webster's Collegiate Dictionary* 10th ed., (Springfield, Mass.: Merriam-Webster, 1993), p. 647.
4. A. Banco, "The Twenty-First Century Corporation: The New Leadership," *Business Week*, Aug. 28, 2000, p. 100.
5. J. Fitz-Enz, "Blueberries from Chile," *Workforce*, Apr. 1, 2000 [http://www.workforce.com/archive/article/22/01/64.php.]
6. T. A. Stewart, "Software Preserves Knowledge, People Pass It On," *Fortune*, Sept. 4, 2000, p. 392.
7. I. Greenberg, "Knowledge-Management Rivals Go to Asia," *Wall Street Journal*, June 21, 2001.
8. T. A. Stewart, "Mapping Corporate Brainpower," *Fortune*, Oct. 30, 1995, p. 209.
9. D. Pringle, "Learning Gurus Adapt to Escape Corporate Axes," *Wall Street Journal*, Jan. 7, 2003, p. B1.
10. Ibid.
11. S. Koudsi, "Actually, It Is Like Brain Surgery," *Fortune*, Mar. 20, 2000, p. 233.

12. T. A. Stewart, "Knowledge Worth $1.25 Billion," *Fortune*, Nov. 27, 2000, p. 302.

13. Ibid.

14. M. Schrage, "Sixteen Tons of Information Overload," *Fortune*, Aug. 2, 1999, p. 244.

15. "Top Companies for Leaders 2002," Hewitt Associates, 2002.

Chapter Six, "The Real Work of Knowledge Management"

1. "Beyond the Precipice—amid Waves of Change: Strategic Scouts Explore the Future," ASAF Institute for National Security Studies and the Air University, 2000.

2. For additional information, see I. Nonaka and H. Takeuchi, *The Knowledge-Creating Company: How Japanese Companies Create the Dynamics of Innovation* (New York: St. Martin's Press, 1995); T. Davenport and L. Prusak, *Working Knowledge* (Boston: Harvard Business School Press, 2000); and T. Petzinger, *The New Pioneers: The Men and Women Who are Transforming the Workplace and the Marketplace* (New York: Simon & Schuster, 1999).

Chapter Seven, "Tangling with Learning Intangibles"

1. Many of the ideas presented here on organization learning capability come from work synthesized in A. Yeung, D. Ulrich, S. Nason, and M. A. Von Glinow, *Organization Learning Capability: Generating and Generalizing Ideas with Impact* (New York: Oxford University Press, 1999).

Chapter Eight, "When Transferring Trapped Corporate Knowledge to Suppliers Is a Winning Strategy"

1. For monthly news updates on supplier and alliance methodologies, subscribe at http://www.lsegil.com or call (310) 556-1778 for white papers and further information.

Chapter Nine, "Informal Learning"

1. M. A. Loewenstein and J. R. Spletzer, "Formal and Informal Training: Evidence from the NLSY," *Research in Labor Economics*, 1999, *18*, 402–438. This Bureau of Labor Statistics research was also used in the Center for Workforce Development's landmark study on informal learning, "The Teaching Firm: Where Productive Work and Learning Converge" available from the Education Development Center, http://www.edc.org

2. See "A World of Magnificent Maniacs: Learning at WD-40" at http://www.thelearningmoment.net/cgi-bin/page.cgi?articles2/articles/articles.

3. See, for example, E. Wenger and W. Snyder, "Learning in Communities," *Learning in the New Economy*, Summer 2000, at http://www.linezine.com/7.2/index.htm

4. For a wellspring of information, see "The Encyclopedia of Informal Education" at http://www.infed.org

5. See, for example, D. Grebow, "At the Water Cooler of Learning," *Transforming Culture: An Executive Briefing on the Power of Learning*, June 2002, at http:// www.darden.edu/batten/clc/primer_articles.htm; and A. Rossett and K. Sheldon, *Beyond the Podium: Delivering Training and Performance to a Digital World* (San Francisco: Jossey-Bass/Pfeffer, 2001), pp. 210–227.

6. See, for example, R. Cross, N. Nohria, and A. Parker, "Six Myths About Informal Networks—and How to Overcome Them," *MIT-Sloan Management Review*, Spring 2002, pp. 67–75.

7. For an extensive list of resources, learning styles assessments, and tools to help you create an environment where informal learning thrives, go to http://www.agelesslearner.com

Chapter Ten, "The Company as a Marketplace for Ideas: Simple but Not Easy"

1. Transactions cost economists, such as Oliver Williamson and David Teece, have written for many years about the choice between efficient "external markets" and building "internal

hierarchies" and markets to achieve superior economic performance. See also P. H. Rubin, *Managing Business Transactions: Controlling the Cost of Coordinating, Communicating, and Decision Making* (New York: Free Press, 1990).

2. See G. Szulanski, *Sticky Knowledge: Barriers to Knowing in a Firm* (Thousand Oaks, California: Sage, 2003).

3. Francis Fujiyama's book *Trust: Human Nature and the Reconstitution of Social Order* (New York: Free Press, 1995) spends considerable time developing this thesis.

4. M. Gladwell, *The Tipping Point: How Little Things Can Make a Big Difference* (New York: Little, Brown, 2000).

Chapter Eleven, "Knowledge Mapping"

1. K. E. Sveiby, *The New Organizational Wealth: Managing and Measuring Knowledge-Based Assets* (San Francisco: Berrett-Koehler, 1997), p. 8.

2. Examples from T. Stewart, *Intellectual Capital: The New Wealth of Organizations* (New York: Bantam Books, 1998), pp. 12–15.

3. Ibid., pp. 12–15.

4. For more information on this subject, see M. Beer, B. Spector, P. Lawrence, D. Q. Mills, and R. Walton, *Managing Human Assets* (New York: Free Press, 1994); and P. Senge, *The Fifth Discipline* (New York: Doubleday, 1990).

Chapter Twelve, "Just-in-Time Guidance"

1. J. Pfeffer and R. I. Sutton, *The Knowing-Doing Gap: How Smart Companies Turn Knowledge into Action* (Boston: Harvard Business School Press, 2000), pp. 2–4.

2. M. Goldsmith, H. J. Morgan, and M. Effron, "Changing Leadership Behavior: Impact of Coworkers and Coaches," in D. Ulrich and others (eds.), *The Charge Champions' Field Guide* (New York: Best Practice Publications, 2002), pp. 11–19.

3. D. Goleman, "Leadership That Gets Results," *Harvard Business Review*, Mar.-Apr. 2000, p. 89.

4. C. W. Wick, R.V.H. Pollock, and J. F. Bolt, "Increasing the Return on Investment of Leadership Development Programs," Fort Hill Company/Executive Development Associates, 2001.
5. M. W. Lombardo and R. W. Eichinger, *FYI: For Your Improvement*, 3rd ed. (Minneapolis: Lominger, 2000); S. H. Gebelein and others (eds.), *Successful Manager's Handbook: Development Suggestions for Today's Managers*, 6th ed. (Minneapolis: Personnel Decisions International, 2000); R. Heller and T. Hindle, *Essential Manager's Manual* (New York: DK, 1998).
6. P. F. Drucker, *Management: Task, Responsibilities, Practices* (New York: HarperCollins, 1973), p. 119.
7. For more information about this concept, see M. Goldsmith, "Try Feedforward Instead of Feedback," *Leader to Leader*, Summer 2002.
8. Ninth House, Instant Advice, http://www.ninthhouse.com.
9. Global Meridal, GlobalSmart, http://www.globesmart.com.

Chapter Fourteen, "Rethinking Our Leadership Thinking"

1. McGregor's two primary works are *The Human Side of Enterprise* (New York: McGraw-Hill, 1985) and *The Professional Manager* (New York: McGraw-Hill, 1967). The latter is now out of print but available in libraries.
2. A. Maslow, G. Heil, and D. Stevens, *Maslow on Management* (New York: Wiley, 1998), p. 3.
3. L. Knobel, "Lead Time," *WorldLink*, Jan.-Feb. 1999; http://backissues.worldlink.co.uk/articles/19021999195259/13.htm.
4. T. Stewart, "America's Most Admired Companies," *Fortune*, Mar. 2, 1998; http://www.fortune.com/fortune/articles/0,15114,376823,00.html.
5. Maslow, Heil, and Stevens, *Maslow on Management*, p. 16.
6. J. Carlzon, *Moments of Truth* (New York: HarperCollins, 1985), foreword (unnumbered page).

Chapter Fifteen, "Learning at the Top"

1. The following participants were interviewed as part of our survey of how CEOs learn. All of them have worked closely with CEOs in their careers. The practices reported in this chapter are derived from their firsthand observations on this topic.

James F. Bolt, chairman and founder, Executive Development Associates, Crested Butte, Colorado

Yury Boshyk, founding director, Global Executive Learning Network, Opio, France

Susan Burnett, vice president for workforce development and organization effectiveness, Hewlett-Packard Company, Palo Alto, California

Christine Gagnon, consultant and former president and chief executive officer, International Institute of Telecommunications, Montreal, Quebec

Marshall Goldsmith, founder and director, Alliance for Strategic Leadership, Rancho Santa Fe, California

Helen Hayward, principal, Johnston Smith International, Toronto, Ontario

Gary Jusela, vice president and chief learning officer, Home Depot Corporation, Atlanta, Georgia

Karen Kendrick, vice president and chief learning officer, Allianz Dresdner Asset Management, Newport Beach, California

Carlos Marin, senior consultant, Executive Development Associates, San Diego, California

Donna B. McNamara, vice president for global education and training, Colgate-Palmolive Company, New York, New York

Jim Moore, senior consultant, Executive Development Associates, Palo Alto, California; previously, director for workforce planning and development and head of Sun University at Sun Microsystems and chief learning officer at Nortel and Bell South

Alexander J. Ogg, head of human resources, Unilever BestFoods, and formerly senior vice president and director, Office of Leadership, Learning, and Performance, Motorola, Inc., Schaumberg, Illinois

Jeffrey S. Peris, chief learning officer, American Home Products Corporation, Madison, New Jersey

Don Sherritt, vice president, Western Management Consultants, Vancouver, British Columbia

Sharon Sullivan, chief learning officer and vice president of human resources, Eli Lilly & Company, Indianapolis, Indiana

Ray Vigil, vice president and chief learning officer, Humana, Louisville, Kentucky; previously, vice president and chief operating officer for learning at Lucent Technologies

Bill Wiggenhorn, chief learning officer, Cigna, San Francisco, California; previously, executive vice president and chief human resource officer, Providian Financial Corporation, and president, Motorola University

Mark Woodhouse, director of learning and development, Rolls-Royce, Derby, United Kingdom

Chapter Sixteen, "Unleash the Learning Epidemic"

1. *Economist*, Mar. 15, 1997, p. 12.

Chapter Seventeen, "Leading"

1. P. Vail, *Learning as a Way of Being* (San Francisco: Jossey-Bass, 1996).

2. J. Pfeffer, *The Knowing-Doing Gap* (Boston: Harvard Business School Press, 2000).

3. P. Senge, *The Fifth Discipline* (New York: Doubleday, 1990).

4. A. Gregerman, *Lessons from the Sandbox* (New York: McGraw-Hill, 2000).

5. Ibid., p. 139.

6. Vail, *Learning as a Way of Being*, pp. 53–54.

7. E. Langer, *Mindfulness* (Reading, Mass.: Perseus Books, 1989).

8. Vail, *Learning as a Way of Being*, p. 75.

Chapter Eighteen, "What's the Big Idea?"

1. J. M. Kouzes and B. Z. Posner, *The Leadership Challenge*, 3rd ed. (San Francisco: Jossey-Bass, 2002), p. 20. This material is used by permission of John Wiley & Sons, Inc.

2. R. Gandossy and M. Effron, "The 20 Best Companies for Leaders," *Chief Executive*, June 2002, pp. 26–30; M. Effron and R. P. Gandossy, *Leading the Way: Three Truths from the Top Companies for Leaders* (New York: Wiley, 2004).

3. R. Slater, *Saving Big Blue: Leadership Lessons and Turnaround Tactics of IBM's Lou Gerstner* (New York: McGraw-Hill, 1999), p. 269.

4. All anonymous quotes in this chapter are from interviews conducted by Marc Effron, Bob Gandossy, and Lauren Cantlon in January, February, and March 2003.

5. From the poem "Risks," author unknown; http://www.exrx.net/Psychology/Risks.html

6. http://www.brainyquote.com/quotes/quotes/s/sirwinston131192.html

7. http://www.quotationspage.com/quotes/Evenius

Chapter Twenty, "Developing New Ideas for Your Clients—and Convincing Them to Act"

1. In this chapter, I use the word *client* not just in its traditional sense of a purchaser of consulting, financial, and other professional

services but also to describe large, sophisticated corporate accounts that purchase complex products and services.

2. F. J. Gouillart and F. D. Sturdivant, "Spend a Day in the Life of Your Customer," *Harvard Business Review*, Jan. 1, 1994, pp. 116–121.

3. Interview with Mike Mulica, May 2002.

4. K. Kushner, *One Arrow, One Life* (Boston: Tuttle, 2000), p. 62.

5. http://www.quotedb.com/quotes/459.

6. N. Machiavelli, *The Prince* (New York: Bantam Books, 1984), p. 19.

Chapter Twenty-One, "Making Knowledge Move"

1. D. Sullivan, "Converging Technologies: Data Warehousing and Knowledge Management," *e-Business Advisor*, Nov. 1998, p. 20.

2. When NASA discovered that 60 percent of aerospace workers were slated to reach retirement age in the next few years, it needed to find a way to capture knowledge from exiting workers and make it available to remaining and future workers. See T. George, "E-Learning Helps Companies Capture the Knowledge of Retiring Employees and Gain Competitive Edge," *InformationWeek*, Mar. 2003, p. 930.

3. B. P. Sunoo, "How HR Supports Knowledge Sharing," *Workforce*, Mar. 1999, pp. 30–34.

4. See, for example, Y. Harari, "Manage the 'Other Half' of Your Knowledge," *KMWorld*, Oct. 2002 (special supplement), pp. 10, 11; S. Wasserman and K. Faust, *Social Network Analysis: Methods and Applications* (Cambridge: Cambridge University Press, 1994); and D. Cohen and L. Prusak, *In Good Company* (Boston: Harvard Business School Press, 2001).

5. E. Wenger, R. McDermott, and W. M. Snyder, *Cultivating Communities of Practice* (Boston: Harvard Business School Press, 2002), p. 7.

6. Ibid., p. 4.

7. S. Denning, *The Springboard: How Storytelling Ignites Action in Knowledge-Era Organizations* (Boston: Butterworth-Heinemann, 2001), p. xv.
8. Cohen and Prusak, *In Good Company.*
9. T. H. Davenport and J. C. Beck, *Attention Economy* (Boston: Harvard Business School Press, 2001), p. 137.
10. Ibid., p. 141.

Chapter Twenty-Three, "Building Social Connections to Gain the Knowledge Advantage"

1. For an extended discussion, see S. E. Jackson, M. A. Hitt, and A. S. DeNisi (eds.), *Managing Knowledge for Sustained Competitive Advantage: Designing Strategies for Effective Human Resource Management* (San Francisco: Jossey-Bass, 2003).
2. K. Husted and S. Michailova, "Diagnosing and Fighting Knowledge Sharing Hostility," *Organizational Dynamics*, 2002, *31*(1), 60–73.
3. N. Foote, E. Matson, L. Weiss, and E. Wenger, "Leveraging Group Knowledge for High-Performance Decision Making," *Organizational Dynamics*, 2002, *31*(3), 288.
4. See S. E. Jackson, K. A. May, and K. Whitney, "Understanding the Dynamics of Diversity in Decision Making Teams," in R. A. Guzzo and E. Salas (eds.), *Team Decision Making Effectiveness in Organizations* (San Francisco: Jossey-Bass, 1995); T. Kochan and Associates, "The Effects of Diversity on Business Performance: Report of the Diversity Research Networks," *Human Resource Management Journal*, 2003, *42*, 3–21.

Chapter Twenty-Four, "Some Key Examples of Knowledge Management"

1. G. R. Sullivan and M. V. Harper, *HOPE Is Not a Method: What Business Leaders Can Learn from America's Army* (New York: Times Business/Random House, 1996), pp. 191–192.

2. Ibid., p. 195.
3. M. J. Darling, and C. S. Parry, *From Post-Mortem to Living Practice: An In-Depth Study of the Evolution of the After Action Review* (Boston: Signet Consulting Group, 2000), p. 8.
4. Ibid., pp. 15–21.
5. Ibid., p. 21.
6. W. G. Chase and H. A. Simon, "Perception in Chess," *Cognitive Psychology*, 1973, *4*, 55–81.
7. J. A. Horvath, "Tacit Knowledge in the Professions," in R. J. Sternberg and J. A. Horvath (eds.), *Tacit Knowledge in Professional Practice* (Mahwah, N.J.: Erlbaum, 1999), p. ix.
8. Sternberg and Horvath, *Tacit Knowledge*.
9. G. A. Miller, "The Magical Number Seven," *Psychological Review*, 1956, *63*(2), 81–97.
10. M. Gladwell, *The Tipping Point: How Little Things Can Make a Big Difference* (New York: Little, Brown, 2000).
11. R.I.M. Dunbar, "Neocortex Size as a Constraint on Group Size in Primates," *Journal of Human Evolution*, 1992, *20*, 469–493; R.I.M. Dunbar, *Grooming, Gossip, and the Evolution of Language* (Cambridge, Mass.: Harvard University Press, 1996).
12. Gladwell, *Tipping Point*, p. 179.
13. Ibid.
14. Ibid., pp. 183–187.
15. D. Wegner, "Transactive Memory in Close Relationships," *Journal of Personality and Social Psychology*, 1991, *61*, 923–929; D. Wegner, "Transactive Memory: A Contemporary Analysis of the Group Mind," in B. Mullen and G. Goethals (eds.), *Theories of Group Behavior*)New York: Springer-Verlag, 1987), pp. 200–201.

Chapter Twenty-Five, "Leadership and Access to Ideas"

1. See D. Cohen and L. Prusak, *In Good Company: How Social Capital Makes Organizations Work* (Boston: Harvard Business

School Press, 2001), and T. A. Davenport and L. Prusak, *Working Knowledge* (Boston: Harvard Business School Press, 2000).

2. For a more complete accounting of the changes and how they were accomplished, see A. R. Cohen, "Transformational Change at Babson: Notes from the Firing Line," *Academy of Management Learning and Education Journal*, 2003, 2(2), 155–180.

3. The terminology of "connectors" and "mavens" comes from M. Gladwell, *The Tipping Point: How Little Things Can Make a Big Difference* (New York: Little, Brown, 2000).

4. M. Gladwell, "The Social Life of Paper," *New Yorker*, Mar. 25, 2002, pp. 92–96.

5. R. C. Wood and G. Hamel, "The World Bank's Innovation Market," *Harvard Business Review*, 2002, 80(11), 104–111.

Chapter Twenty-Six, "Capturing Ideas, Creating Information, and Liberating Knowledge"

1. M. Gladwell, *The Tipping Point: How Little Things Can Make a Big Difference* (New York: Little, Brown, 2000).

Chapter Twenty-Eight, "The Audacity of Imagination"

1. John Dewey (1859–1952), American psychologist, philosopher, and educator. From J. A. Boydston, *The Quest for Certainty* (Carbondale: Southern Illinois University Press, 1984).

2. Phil Condit, chairman and CEO, the Boeing Company; also Ziggy, cartoon character by Tom Wilson.

3. Interview with Sharon Sullivan in *LLYNEWS*, Fall 2002.

4. Personal communication, Jan. 2003.

5. Personal communication, Jan. 2003.

6. Personal communication, Jan. 2003.

7. Personal communication, Jan. 2003.

Chapter Twenty-Nine, "Developing a Learning Culture on Wall Street"

1. Presentation by John Thornton, Pine Street Leadership Program, Sept. 25, 2002.

Index